RAHEL M. FELIX   PETER FELIX

HAUS MARKE

WEGE DES IMMOBILIENMARKETINGS

BRANDING PROPERTY

APPROACHES TO REAL ESTATE MARKETING

BRAUN

INHALT
CONTENTS

ANHANG
APPENDIX

VORWORT
PREFACE

Peter Felix und Rahel M. Felix, Geschäftsinhaber/-führer
Unternehmensgruppe Felix Partner
Peter Felix and Rahel M. Felix, proprietors/managing directors
Felix Partner Group of Companies

HEUTE IST DIE ZUKUNFT VON GESTERN UND WIR BEWEGEN UNS HEUTE IM MORGEN

Wer früher Visionen hatte, war damit seiner Zeit meist Jahre voraus und galt als weitsichtige Persönlichkeit. Wenn wir heute unsere Visionen anschauen, sind diese schon fast auf morgen und nicht mehr auf in zehn Jahren ausgelegt. Denn seit wir vor 20 Jahren angefangen haben, in Marken und Immobilien zu denken – der Vorläufer unseres aktuellen Immobilienmarketings – ist alles extrem viel schneller geworden. Visionen und die damit einhergehenden Ideen müssen im Jetzt laufend angepasst werden, damit sie sich nicht selbst überholen. Ganz nach dem Motto: Stillstand ist Rückschritt. Was sich jedoch nicht verändert hat in unserer Arbeit ist der Mensch: Er steht im Zentrum bei allem, was wir tun.

Sprechen wir von Immobilienmarketing, denken wir an weit mehr als nur die Vermarktung eines Wohn- oder Geschäftshauses. Schaut man sich den Prozess einer Immobilie an, so reicht dieser von der Standortfrage über die architektonische

TODAY IS YESTERDAY'S TOMORROW AND WE ARE SHAPING TOMORROW TODAY

In earlier decades, people with foresight were usually years ahead of their time and considered far-sighted visionaries. Today, in contrast, our sight is often set at tomorrow rather than at ten years from now. This is due to the incredibly faster pace of life compared to the time when we first started thinking in terms of brands and real estate 20 years ago – the predecessor of our current real estate marketing approach. Nowadays, our visions and the ideas that accompany them have to be constantly adjusted to the here and now to stay ahead of things. All actions are based on the underlying motto that you have to keep moving not to lose ground. However, one thing has not changed in our work – our central focus on people in everything we do.

Our approach to real estate marketing encompasses much more than the mere marketing of a residential or business building. The development process of a real estate property ranges from the question of location via architectural planning and

Planung und den Bau bis hin zur Fertigstellung und Bezugsbereitschaft. In dieser Gesamtheit kann das Immobilienmarketing schon in der Projektentwicklung seinen Einfluss geltend machen. Mit einer sorgfältigen Analyse der künftigen Bewohner nach Eigenheiten, Gewohnheiten, Bedürfnissen und Wünschen zum Beispiel. Oder mit Farbkonzepten, Material- und Innenraumgestaltungen. So beeinflusst das Immobilienmarketing bereits früh die Architektur, den Angebotsmix und auch das Preisniveau des künftigen Angebots. Das Herzstück jedoch bildet die zu erschaffende Marke. Diese orientiert sich an äußeren Faktoren wie Lage, Architektur und Lifestyle sowie am Menschen. Er ist es ja, der zum Schluss in einer Immobilie lebt und arbeitet und der sich wohlfühlen soll. In diesem Buch wird eine Auswahl an verschieden gearteten Immobilienmarketingprojekten präsentiert, die wir in den letzten Jahren entwickelt haben und die beispielhaft aufzeigen, wie Marken mit Leben gefüllt und Menschen ins Zentrum gesetzt werden.

«Das Immobilienmarketing beeinflusst bereits früh die Architektur, den Angebotsmix und das Preisniveau des künftigen Angebots.»

Spannend in diesem Kontext sind auch die Ausführungen unserer vier erfahrenen Gastautoren. Ergänzend zu unseren Inhalten schafft jeder für sich mit zeitgenössischen und gleichzeitig visionären Essays nochmals einen anderen und neuen Blickwinkel auf das Gesamtthema und eröffnet so eine zusätzliche Dimension rund um unser Schaffen. Dass die Meinungen dabei auseinandergehen und jeder seine Linie vertritt, gefällt uns außerordentlich. Wir freuen und daher ganz besonders, die Zukunftsforscherin Oona Horx-Strathern mit ihrem Ausblick in das Wohnen der Zukunft für dieses Buch begeistert zu haben. Ebenso wie Martin A. Meier, der uns in die technologische Welt des Cyberspace entführt; Sven Ruoss, dessen Abhandlungen über digitale Transformationen bereits legendär sind und last but not least Prof. Dr. Cary Steinmann, der gekonnt den Bogen zur Marke und zum Marketing spannt.

building up to its completion and readiness for occupation. Real estate marketing can already play a decisive role in all stages of this comprehensive process. For example, by carefully analyzing the future occupant's characteristics, habits, needs, and wishes. Or through color concepts, material and interior design. This way, real estate marketing already influences the architecture, the mix of offers, and even the price level of the future offer. However, the core element is the creation of a brand that incorporates external factors such as location, architecture, and lifestyle, while focusing on people. After all, it is people who will, in the end, live and work in the real estate property and should be comfortable doing so. This book presents a selection of widely varied real estate marketing projects, which we developed in the past few years that are telling examples of how brands can be filled with life and centered on people.

"Real estate marketing already influences the architecture, the mix of offers, and the price level of the future offer."

Within this context, the essays of our four experienced guest authors are also very enlightening. Each one of them complements our contents with contemporary and at the same time visionary essays to present a different and new viewpoint on the general topic, evoking a new dimension related to our work. We are happy to note that they have different opinions and follow their own line of thought. Therefore, we are particularly pleased to have been able to gain trend researcher Oona Horx-Strathern with her outlook for living in the future for this book. The same goes for Martin A. Meier who takes us into the technological world of cyberspace; Sven Ruoss whose treatises on digital transformation have already become legendary, and last but not least, Prof. Cary Steinmann who cleverly creates a bridge to brands and marketing.

EXKURSE
ESSAYS

LEBEN UND WOHNEN IN DER ZUKUNFT
LIVING IN THE FUTURE

OONA HORX-STRATHERN

Oona Horx-Strathern, Autorin und Trendberaterin
Oona Horx-Strathern, author and trend consultant

LEBEN UND WOHNEN IN DER ZUKUNFT

Wie grundlegend verändert sich das Leben im 21. Jahrhundert? Wenn wir den Herausforderungen einer neuen Ära begegnen wollen, müssen wir die großen Veränderungen verstehen, die nicht nur eine alternde Gesellschaft umfassen, sondern eine zunehmend individualisierte, miteinander verbundene und urbanisierte. Es wird geschätzt, dass von den 75 % der Weltbevölkerung, die bis 2050 in den Städten leben wird, 50 % Singles und 30 % über 60 Jahre alt sein werden. Das Verständnis der wichtigsten Megatrends wird uns helfen, für die Lebensräume der Zukunft zu planen. Denn nicht nur unser Leben und unsere Städte verändern sich, sondern auch die Definition dessen, was für uns ein Zuhause ausmacht, und wie wir in ihm leben werden.

LIVING IN THE FUTURE

How is the way we live fundamentally changing as we move further into the 21st century? As we face the challenges of a new era, we need to understand the big changes that embrace not just an ageing society, but an increasingly individualized, connected and urbanized one. It is estimated that of the 75 % of the world's population who will live in cities by 2050, 50 % will be singles, and 30 % over 60 years old. Understanding key megatrends will help us plan for the living spaces of the future. For not only are our lives and cities changing, but our definition of what constitutes a home, and how we will live in it.

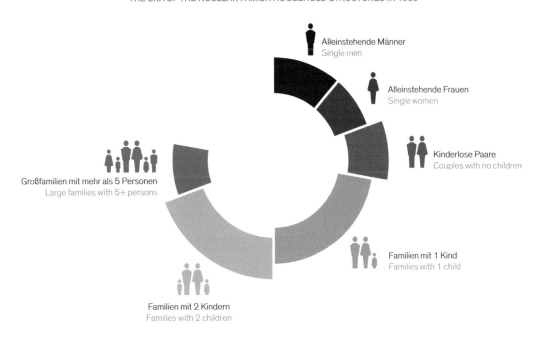

DIE ÄRA DER KERNFAMILIE: HAUSHALTSSTRUKTUREN 1960
THE ERA OF THE NUCLEAR FAMILY: HOUSEHOLD STRUCTURES IN 1960

Alleinstehende Männer
Single men

Alleinstehende Frauen
Single women

Kinderlose Paare
Couples with no children

Familien mit 1 Kind
Families with 1 child

Familien mit 2 Kindern
Families with 2 children

Großfamilien mit mehr als 5 Personen
Large families with 5+ persons

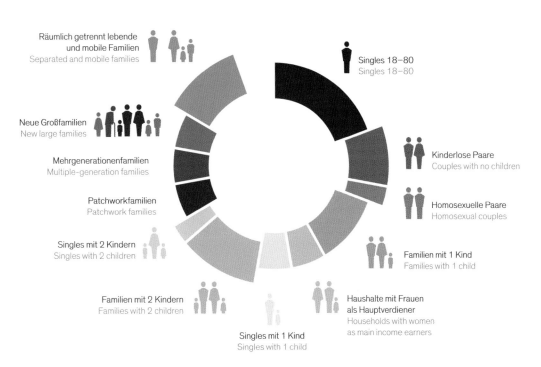

DAS MODELL EINER MULTI-MODULAREN BIOGRAFIE IM HAUSHALT VON 2020
THE MODEL OF A MULTI-MODULAR BIOGRAPHY IN THE HOUSEHOLD OF 2020

Räumlich getrennt lebende
und mobile Familien
Separated and mobile families

Neue Großfamilien
New large families

Mehrgenerationenfamilien
Multiple-generation families

Patchworkfamilien
Patchwork families

Singles mit 2 Kindern
Singles with 2 children

Familien mit 2 Kindern
Families with 2 children

Singles mit 1 Kind
Singles with 1 child

Haushalte mit Frauen
als Hauptverdiener
Households with women
as main income earners

Familien mit 1 Kind
Families with 1 child

Homosexuelle Paare
Homosexual couples

Kinderlose Paare
Couples with no children

Singles 18–80
Singles 18–80

OONA HORX-STRATHERN

Erinnern Sie sich an die Zeit, als avocadogrüne Badezimmer und aprikosengelbe Küchen der angesagte Trend in der Innenarchitektur waren? Und der Flur der einzige Ort war, um einen Anruf zu tätigen? Oder daran, dass wenn Sie als Kind ungezogen waren, zur Strafe in Ihr Zimmer geschickt wurden? Das alles ist nicht so lange her, wie wir manchmal denken. Doch in den letzten 30 Jahren haben sich Design, Technik und Lebensstil nicht nur auf den ersten Blick unglaublich verändert. Bäder sind zu Tempeln des Minimalismus geworden, Küchen zu Hightechumgebungen. Die Handy-Technologie hat uns von der Öffentlichkeit des Flurs befreit und unsere Kinder wären froh, wenn wir sie zur Strafe in ihr Zimmer schicken würden: Spielkonsolen, Wi-Fi und vieles mehr lassen grüßen.

«Ist Ihr Zuhause Ihr Schloss oder Ihr ‹Kokon›?»

Hinter diesen scheinbar oberflächlichen Veränderungen stehen Megatrends: die großen Verschiebungen in unserer Gesellschaft. Sie sind dafür verantwortlich, wie wir jetzt und in naher Zukunft leben. Mit dem Wissen über diese treibenden Kräfte können wir grundlegende Fragen stellen: Inwieweit brauchen wir noch unsere Häuser, um die Grundfunktion des Schutzes und der Privatsphäre vor der Außenwelt zu gewährleisten? Und ist Ihr Zuhause, wie die Briten sagen, noch Ihr Schloss oder, wie von Faith Popcorn in den 1990er-Jahren gepriesen, Ihr «Kokon»? Der Philosoph und Schriftsteller Alain de Botton wies darauf hin, dass sich unser Leben in nur wenigen Generationen so stark verändert hat, dass unsere Häuser, oder besser unser Zuhause, weder ständig bewohnt sein noch unsere Kleidung verstauen muss, um als solches bezeichnet zu werden. So kann ein Daheim ein Flughafen oder eine Bibliothek, ein Garten oder eine Autobahn-Raststätte sein. Für welches «Zuhause» wir auch immer uns entscheiden, es wird in Zukunft nicht weniger als eine multifunktionale, flexible Basis für ein mobiles Leben sein.

Do you remember the time when avocado colored bathrooms and apricot colored kitchens were the hot look in interior design? When the hallway was the only place to make or take a phone call? Or when if you were naughty as a child you were sent to your bedroom as a punishment? It wasn't as long ago as we like to think. Changes over the last 30 years in design, technology, and lifestyle mean homes have, at first glance, changed immeasurably. Bathrooms have become temples of minimalism and kitchens high-tech environments. Mobile phone technology has freed us from the public nature of the hallway, and our children are gladly sent to their rooms, thanks to widespread availability of game consoles and Wi-Fi.

"Is your home your castle, or your 'cocoon'?"

Behind the facade of these seemingly superficial changes are megatrends – the big shifts in our society. They shape how we live now and in the near future. With the knowledge of these driving forces, we can ask such basic questions as to what extent do we still need our homes to provide the basic function of shelter and privacy from the outside world? Is your home, as the British say, still your castle, or your "cocoon" as extolled by Faith Popcorn in the 1990s? The philosopher and writer Alain de Botton pointed out that our lives have changed so much in just a few generations that "our homes do not have to offer us permanent occupancy or store our clothes to merit the name. Home can be an airport or a library, a garden or a motorway diner." Wherever we decide to call "home" in the future, it will be nothing less than a multi-functional flexible base for complex mobile multi-biographical lives.

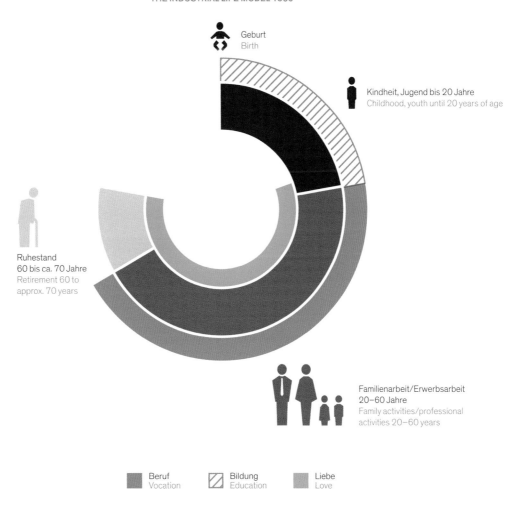

DAS INDUSTRIELLE LEBENSMODELL 1960
THE INDUSTRIAL LIFE MODEL 1960

Geburt
Birth

Kindheit, Jugend bis 20 Jahre
Childhood, youth until 20 years of age

Ruhestand
60 bis ca. 70 Jahre
Retirement 60 to
approx. 70 years

Familienarbeit/Erwerbsarbeit
20–60 Jahre
Family activities/professional
activities 20–60 years

Beruf
Vocation

Bildung
Education

Liebe
Love

Doch was hat zu dieser Revolution geführt, wie wir sie heute erleben? In den 1960er-Jahren konnten Herr oder Frau Durchschnitt eine einfache, dreiphasige Lebensplanung erwarten. Eine kurze Kindheit, eine geradlinige Karriere und privates Glück mit meist einem Ehepartner und ein paar Kindern. Und wenn sie Glück hatten, durften sie sich auf ein paar Jahre im Ruhestand freuen, bevor sie dann im Alter von 65 Jahren oder etwas mehr starben. Heute haben wir eine Lebenserwartung von über 80 Jahren und diese «Extra-Zeit» bedeutet, dass wir jetzt länger und facettenreicher leben können. Es ist das, was wir eine mehrphasige Biografie nennen. Wir haben mehr Zeit

What has led to this revolution in how we live? In the 1960s, Mr. or Mrs. Average could expect to have a simple three-phase life biography. A short childhood, a single career, a marriage usually for life, and a couple of children. If they were lucky, they could also look forward to a few years of retirement before dying at the average age of 65. Today, we can expect to live to at least 80 years old, and this "extra time" means we can now have a much longer and multi-faceted life. This is what we call a multi-modular biography. We simply have more time for differentiated life phases. We can, if we like, fit in several different careers, live out periods of self-discovery, and have multiple

für differenzierte Lebensphasen. Wir können, wenn es uns gefällt, verschiedene Karrieren verfolgen, Selbstfindungsphasen ausleben und mehrere Beziehungen oder Ehen führen. Wir haben Zeit für unsere Identitätsentwicklung, für neues Lernen, das Ausleben von Leidenschaften und das Einlassen auf Berufungen und Neigungen. Seit den 1970er-Jahren – in nur 40 Jahren also – hat sich das Durchschnittsalter der Heiratenden von 20 auf 29 verschoben. Das Ergebnis davon ist für viele eine Periode des sogenannten verschobenen Erwachsenwerdens in ihren Zwanzigern bis frühen Dreißigern. Die Familiengründung wird nach hinten geschoben, man bildet sich, reist, lernt das Leben kennen. Spannend dabei ist, dass dann in der Zeit ab 30 oft eine Phase des Aufholens stattfindet, die sogenannte Rush Hour. Diese Phase tritt ein, wenn Menschen, vor allem Frauen, im Eiltempo herauszufinden versuchen, was wir ein wenig ironisch «Life Balance» nennen. Das bedeutet zu lernen, die Karriere, einen Partner und mögliche Kinder unter einen Hut zu bringen.

«Heute sind wir allein, morgen Teil einer Patchworkfamilie und übermorgen leben wir mit drei Generationen unter einem Dach.»

Aufgrund unserer komplexen Lebensläufe brauchen wir Lebensräume, die sich flexibel an Veränderungen anpassen. Heute sind wir allein, morgen schon Teil einer Patchworkfamilie und übermorgen versuchen wir, drei Generationen unter einem Dach zu vereinen. Und später sind wir vielleicht zu zweit. Eine interessante Lösung für das Wohnen im Zeitalter sich wandelnder Lebensformen hat der österreichische Architekt Klaus Kada entwickelt. Für eine Neubausiedlung im Sonnwendviertel in Wien hat er eine räumlich flexible Wohnung kreiert, die sich an jede Lifestyle-Änderung anpasst. Die Räume sind, anstelle von Wänden, mit großen, vom Boden bis zur Decke beweglichen Schränken bestückt, was die Schaffung eines einzigartigen flexiblen Grundrisses ermöglicht. Spannend dabei: Das klassische Wohnzimmer als Begegnungsort ist ausgelagert.

relationships or marriages. We have time not just for developing our identity but also for new learning, passions, callings, and repositioning. Since the 1970s – in just 40 years – the average age of marriage has shifted from 20 to 29. The result of this is, for many, a period of so-called suspended adulthood in their 20s to early 30s. The classic responsibilities of founding a family are postponed in favor of travel and experiencing life. It is interesting to note that this phase is often followed from around 30 years of age by a period of catching up – the so-called rush hour. This phase happens when people – particularly women – start "rushing about" trying to find what we now a little ironically call "life balance." This means learning to juggle a career path, a partner, and how on earth to fit in having children before it is too late.

"Today we live alone, tomorrow maybe in a patchwork family and after tomorrow we live with three generations under a single roof."

As a result of our complex lives, we need our living spaces to be flexible in order to adapt to these changes. Today we live alone, tomorrow maybe in a patchwork family and after tomorrow we live with three generations under a single roof. After that, we may again live as a couple. An interesting solution to the stresses that shifting lifestyles put upon our living spaces has been proposed by the Austrian architect Klaus Kada. For a new housing development in the Sonnwendviertel in Vienna, he developed a spatially adaptable apartment that adjusts to any lifestyle change. The rooms are divided with large floor to ceiling movable cupboards rather than fixed walls, creating a unique flexible floor plan. The interesting part is that the classical living room as a meeting place has shifted. The communal spaces of the apartment block include wide hallways with places to hang out and socialize, sport facilities, a cinema, a supermarket, and an extra long communal table and benches in the garden where people gather to gossip, cook together and meet their friends and neighbors.

DAS MODELL EINER MEHRPHASIGEN BIOGRAFIE
THE MODEL OF A MULTI-MODULAR BIOGRAPHY

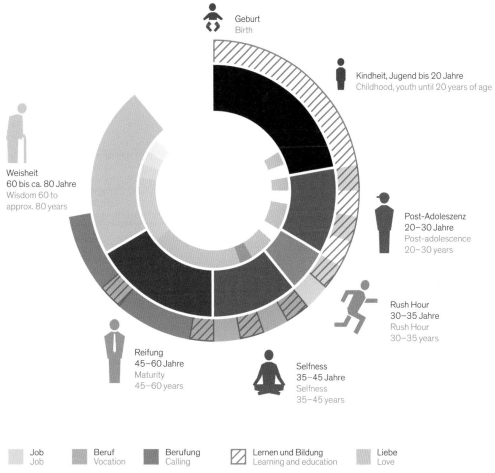

Geburt
Birth

Kindheit, Jugend bis 20 Jahre
Childhood, youth until 20 years of age

Post-Adoleszenz
20–30 Jahre
Post-adolescence
20–30 years

Rush Hour
30–35 Jahre
Rush Hour
30–35 years

Selfness
35–45 Jahre
Selfness
35–45 years

Reifung
45–60 Jahre
Maturity
45–60 years

Weisheit
60 bis ca. 80 Jahre
Wisdom 60 to
approx. 80 years

| Job / Job | Beruf / Vocation | Berufung / Calling | Lernen und Bildung / Learning and education | Liebe / Love |

Die gemeinschaftlichen Räume des Wohnblocks umfassen breite Flure mit Plätzen zum Entspannen und Kontakte knüpfen, Sportanlagen, ein Kino, einen Supermarkt und einen extra langen gemeinschaftlichen Tisch mit Bänken im Garten, wo die Leute zusammenkommen können, um zu plaudern, zusammen zu kochen und um ihre Nachbarn und Freunde zu treffen.

Unser Zuhause muss zukünftig aber nicht nur auf verschiedene Lebensphasen ausgerichtet sein, es wird sich auch mehr an die länger gewordene Lebenszeit anpassen. Die Tatsache, dass wir alle länger leben, bedeutet auch, dass es mehr ältere Menschen

As well as catering to different life phases, homes will also have to be more adaptable to longer life spans in the future. The fact that we all live longer means there will be more older people to house, to care for and to plan for – all part and parcel of the challenges of the so-called megatrend Silver Society. The expectation of a generation that is retired and sitting knitting by the fireplace is definitely no longer up to date. This generation is in part still working, and is still active and attractive and needed by society. As such we won't be focused on building for the aged in the old sense of the word anymore – but for the so-called pro-agers, an older generation with an unprecedented life span and vitality.

geben wird, die untergebracht, gepflegt und versorgt werden müssen – alles Teil der Herausforderungen eines weiteren Megatrends, der sogenannten Silver Society. Die Vorstellung einer Generation, die im Ruhestand ist und sich am Kamin sitzend mit Stricken beschäftigt, ist aber definitiv nicht mehr zeitgemäß. Diese Generation arbeitet zum Teil noch und ist sowohl aktiv als auch attraktiv und wird von der Gesellschaft gebraucht. Wir werden uns also nicht mehr auf die Alten im alten Sinne des Wortes konzentrieren, sondern auf sogenannte Pro-Agers, eine ältere Generation mit einer noch nie dagewesenen Lebenserwartung und Lebensfreude.

Diese neue Generation von Oldies, die länger gesund ist als früher, wird sich als Free-Agers definieren, die so lange wie möglich das Beste aus ihrer gestiegenen Lebenserwartung machen. Angetrieben von einer positiven Lebenskraft statt mürrischer Schicksalsergebenheit, werden sie in allen sozialen Schichten eine aktive Rolle spielen und erwarten, dass ihr Zuhause, ihre Lebensumstände und ihre Umgebung dies widerspiegeln. Was nichts anderes heißt, als dass die traditionellen Wohnungslösungen der Alten- und Pflegeheime wie ein schlecht sitzender Anzug zur aktiven, relativ wohlsituierten und sehr designbewussten Babyboomer-Generation passen.

Wie gestalten wir nun aber attraktive Wohnungen und passenden Wohnraum für sie? Der gefeierte US-Soziologe Richard Sennett sagte in einem Interview mit dem *Süddeutschen Magazin*: «Für ältere Menschen können Co-Living-Systeme große Vorteile bieten. Es gibt Programme mit großem Potenzial wie ein Experiment, in dem ältere Menschen mit Studenten und Behinderten zusammenleben. Diese neuen Lebensformen interessieren mich. Ich möchte mit jungen Leuten leben, die mir Zigaretten holen können und all das, was man in einem normalen Altenheim nicht zulässt.»

Das zunehmende Interesse und der Trend zum generationenübergreifenden Miteinanderwohnen ist das direkte Ergebnis eines weiteren Megatrends, nämlich der Individualisierung der Gesellschaft. Dieser Megatrend hat große Auswirkungen

This new generation of oldies with a longer health-span will define themselves as so-called free-agers making the most of their increased life span as long as possible. Driven by a positive vitality as opposed to grumpy resignation, they will play an active part in all walks of society and expect their home, how they live, and their surroundings to reflect this. This means that the traditional residential solutions such as old people's homes for the retirement age are already proving to be an ill fitting suit for the active, relatively well off and very design-conscious baby boomer generation.

So how do we design attractive homes, apartment and living space for them? The acclaimed US sociologist Richard Sennett said in an interview with *Süddeutsche Magazin*: "For older people co-living schemes can provide great advantages. There are schemes with great potential such as an experiment where older people live together with students and the disabled. These new forms of living interest me. I would like to live with young people who can get me cigarettes, and all those things you aren't allowed in a normal old people's home."

The increased interest in, and trend towards co-living across the generations is the direct result of another key megatrend, that of the individualization of society. This megatrend has huge repercussions for how we will build for the future. The challenge will be how to satisfy all these individual needs and desires with increased housing demands. Also how to solve the increasing sense of isolation and loneliness associated with big city living.

"Once upon a time we were born
into communities and had to
find our individuality. Today we
are born as individuals and
have to find our communities."

Individualization or co-isolation has indeed brought about the need and desire for a new co-culture, for new forms of cooperation. As traditional family structures becomes less attractive

darauf, wie wir für die Zukunft bauen werden. Die Herausforderung besteht darin, all die individuellen Bedürfnisse und Wünsche nach erhöhtem Wohnraumbedarf zu befriedigen. Und darin, wie man, speziell in Großstädten, der Isolation und Vereinsamung von Menschen entgegenwirkt.

«Es war einmal, dass wir in Gemeinschaften geboren wurden und unsere Individualität finden mussten. Heute sind wir als Individuen geboren und müssen unsere Gemeinschaften finden.»

Individualisierung oder Co-Isolation hat in der Tat die Notwendigkeit und den Wunsch nach einer neuen Co-Kultur, nach neuen Formen der Zusammenarbeit und des Zusammenlebens hervorgebracht. Da traditionelle Familienstrukturen immer weniger attraktiv und verbindlich sind, werden andere Verbindungen und Systeme stärker. Je individueller wir werden, desto wichtiger ist paradoxerweise die Notwendigkeit der Unterstützung durch andere Menschen. Daher sehen wir die Entstehung neuer Gemeinschaften, die durch zeitliche und gemeinsame Interessen und nicht durch DNA miteinander verbunden sind. Wie die amerikanische Agentur K-Hole ausführt: «Es war einmal, dass wir in Gemeinschaften geboren wurden und unsere Individualität finden mussten. Heute sind wir als Individuen geboren und müssen unsere Gemeinschaften finden.» Die Forderung nach Co-Wohnbau, gemeinschaftlichem Wohnen und vielfältigem Generationenleben ist also zum Teil das Ergebnis einer zunehmend individualisierten Gesellschaft, verbunden mit den Möglichkeiten, welche die genannten neuen und längeren Lebensphasen mit sich bringen.

Bei jüngeren Menschen und Singles geht der Trend in eine ähnliche Richtung. Populäre Programme wie das Wohnprojekt «The Collective» in London spiegeln diese Nachfrage wider. Es soll das weltweit größte Co-Living-Programm sein und wurde als eine neue Art zu leben angekündigt. Es basiert auf dem Prinzip, dass zukünftig die Menge an privaten, persönlichen

and binding, other connections and systems become stronger. Paradoxically, the more individualistic we become, the more important becomes the need for support from other people. Hence we are seeing the emergence of new communities connected by temporal and common interests rather than DNA. As the American agency K-Hole points out, "Once upon a time we were born into communities and had to find our individuality. Today we are born as individuals and have to find our communities." The demand for co-housing, collaborative living and multi-generational living is in part the result of an increasingly individualized society combined with the possibilities that the aforementioned new and longer life phases bring.

The trend among younger people and singles points in the same direction. Popular schemes such as "The Collective," a housing project in London, are reflecting this demand. Claimed to be the world's largest co-living scheme and heralded as a "new way to live in London," it is based on the principle that in the future the amount of square meters we have for ourselves, for our private exclusive use, will be less important than the quality of the shared spaces. In "The Collective" up to 550 people can rent a so-called "Twodio," a serviced flat of around only ten square meters with just room for a bed, a small bathroom with a toilet and shower and a tiny two-hob kitchen. In return residents have access to communal spaces including a full range of services that are needed for modern life — from co-working spaces, to a spa, laundry, a large kitchen for communal cooking, gym, terrace, library and a games room. There are also affordable in-house restaurants and the option of an all inclusive rate (including Internet, gas, electricity, as well as linen and cleaning every two weeks). The entrepreneur behind this scheme, James Scott, believes that the housing needs of the Millennial Generation (born from the mid-1990s to the early 2000s) is headed for a future "where everyone is homeless" (in the sense of real estate). To him this is because members of Generation Y (also known as Generation "Why"), are more socially liberated, preferring convenience over commitment. Which also means preferring to rent instead of buying. This generation was once famously described by the *New Yorker* as "the most indulged

Das Co-Living-Projekt «The Collective» in London bietet eine Vielzahl an Gemeinschaftsräumen

The co-living project "The Collective" in London offers a variety of communal spaces

Quadratmetern als weniger wichtig eingestuft werden wird als die Qualität der gemeinsamen Räume. In «The Collective» können bis zu 550 Personen ein sogenanntes «Twodio» mieten, eine Service-Wohnung von nur etwa zehn Quadratmetern mit Platz für ein Bett, einem kleinen Bad mit WC und Dusche und einer kleinen Küche mit zwei Kochfeldern. Dafür haben die Bewohner Zugang zu Gemeinschaftsräumen, inklusive einer Palette an Dienstleistungen, die für das moderne Leben benötigt werden: eine große Küche für das gemeinsame Kochen, ein Spa, die Wäscherei, ein Spielzimmer, eine Bibliothek, Co-Working-Räumlichkeiten, ein Gym sowie eine Terrasse. Dazu noch Restaurants mit erschwinglichen Preisen sowie die Möglichkeit, das alles in einem All-Inclusive-Tarif zu mieten (mit Internet, Gas, Strom sowie Bettwäsche und Reinigung alle zwei Wochen). Der Unternehmer hinter diesem Programm, James Scott, glaubt, dass der Wohnungsbedarf der Millennial Generation (geboren ab den frühen 1990er- bis Anfang der 2000er-Jahre) zu einer Zukunft führt, in der jeder obdachlos (im Sinne des Wohneigentums) ist. Begründet sieht er dies in der Generation Y (auch bekannt als Generation «Why»), die sozial mehr befreit ist und Bequemlichkeit über Engagement stellt. Was auch lieber mieten statt kaufen bedeutet. Diese Generation wurde durch einen Artikel im *New Yorker* berühmt als «die am meisten verwöhnten jungen Menschen in der Geschichte der Welt». Allerdings sind viele dieser zum Teil noch jungen Erwachsenen von einer Kombination aus Schulden, Arbeitslosigkeit und steigenden Immobilienpreisen gebeutelt und es ist das erste Mal in der industrialisierten Geschichte, dass die Einkommen einer neuen Generation nicht am steigen, sondern am fallen sind.

Was heißt das nun für die Art wie und wo sie leben? Angel Gurría, Generalsekretär der Organisation für wirtschaftliche Zusammenarbeit und Entwicklung (OECD), sagt, dass die Situation für junge Menschen schwierig ist: «Reduziertes Einkommen bedeutet, dass selbstständiges Wohnen und Aufsteigen auf der Grundstücksleiter langsamer und härter sein wird.» Der Trend zu innovativen, flexiblen Mietwohnungssystemen sowie geteilten und kleineren Lebensräumen ist daher nur der Anfang und ein Teil der Lösung.

young people in the history of the world." However, many of these young adults are facing a combination of debt, joblessness and rising house prices and it is the first time in industrialized history that the incomes of a new generation are dropping instead of increasing.

So what are the implications for how and where they will live? Angel Gurría, secretary general of the Organization for Economic Cooperation and Development (OECD), says the situation is tough for young people, "Reduced income means that independent living and getting onto the property ladder will be slower and harder." The trend to innovative flexible rental co-housing schemes, shared and smaller living spaces, is just the start and part of the solution.

Another of the megatrends that is a key factor in how we will live in the future, is increasing urbanization. One of the solutions to architectural challenges based on this will be a trend towards increased modularization, pre-fabricated homes or apartment blocks that can be pre-formed and put up on site quickly, quietly and efficiently.

An underestimated issue in cities alongside space limitations and logistical challenges for building sites in dense urban areas, are the issues of environmental and noise pollution. Today, due to the dual pressure of time and cost it is often underestimated how long-lasting noise and emissions of building sites can negatively affect local residents.

"Today, it is often underestimated how long-lasting noise of building sites can negatively affect local residents."

The more people and city planners concern themselves with the wider reach of environmental issues and the well-being of a neighborhood, the more we will turn to pre-fabricated modular building, which can be assembled on site cheaply and quickly in a matter of weeks or even days. Pre-fabs have,

Ein weiterer Megatrend, der beim Thema «Wie wir künftig leben werden» eine Schlüsselrolle spielt, ist die zunehmende Urbanisierung. Eine der Lösungen für die daraus resultierenden architektonischen Herausforderungen wird die Entwicklung hin zu mehr Modularisierung, Prefab-Häusern oder -Apartmentblöcken sein, die vorgeformt und vor Ort nur noch schnell, leise und effizient zusammengesetzt werden.

Ein unterschätztes Problem in den Städten, nebst Raumbeschränkungen und logistischen Herausforderungen für Baustellen in dichten Stadtgebieten, sind Aspekte der Umwelt- und Lärmbelästigung. Heute wird aufgrund von Termin- und Kostendruck viel zu wenig darüber nachgedacht, was länger andauernder Baustellenlärm und die mit den Baustellen verbundenen weiteren Immissionen für Auswirkungen auf die Anwohner haben.

«Heute wird viel zu wenig darüber nachgedacht, was länger andauernder Baustellenlärm für Auswirkungen auf die Anwohner hat.»

Je mehr Menschen und Stadtplaner sich mit der größeren Reichweite von Umweltfragen und dem Wohlergehen einer Nachbarschaft beschäftigen, desto mehr werden wir auf die vorgefertigten, modularen Gebäude setzen, die in wenigen Wochen oder sogar Tagen kostengünstig und schnell montiert werden können. Vorgefertigte Bauten hatten jedoch lange einen schlechten Ruf. Man assoziiert sie noch immer mit den Nachkriegs- und Plattenbauten oder den Fertighäusern aus den 1970er- und 1980er-Jahren. Dank neuer Materialien, fortgeschrittenen Techniken und Computer-Modellierung kommen heute nun aber verschiedenste, maßgeschneiderte und ansprechende Designs auf den Markt und in unsere Städte. So beauftragte beispielsweise die Firma Revolution Precrafted, die Ende 2015 gegründet wurde, Stararchitekten wie etwa Zaha Hadid und Ron Arad, vordefinierte Pavillons und Häuser in einer Preisspanne von $ 50 000 bis $ 500 000 zu entwer-

however, long had a negative image. They are associated with poorer temporary post-war buildings or prefabricated houses of the 1970s and 1980s. Today, new technologies, computer modeling and new materials are bringing varied, custom-made, sexier designs onto the marketplace and into our cities. Revolution Precrafted, a new design platform launched at the end of 2015, commissioned star architects such as Zaha Hadid and Ron Arad to design limited edition pre-fabricated pavilions and homes at prices ranging from $50,000 to $500,000. The company founder Robbie Antonio plans to unveil a new prefabricated design every few months.

"Can technology alone make our homes better and smarter?"

Another of the big challenges to building and living in the future is how to deal with technology and the repercussions of the megatrend Connectivity. While mobile technology enables these fundamental societal shifts to a more nomadic flexible lifestyle, we are also being seduced by the notion of so-called smart homes and smart cities. But can technology alone make our homes better and smarter? Or is it a distraction from the real issues of living and interacting? The so-called Internet of Things that will contact us to our devices, to each other, and devices to devices, is the buzz word in the tech and home building industry. But will we really want to have such things as a smart mattress with a lover detection app or an intelligent fridge with web cams and sensors to determine the level of ketchup left in the bottle, or expiration of yoghurt? And that maybe even automatically places an order with the nearest supermarket?

In the cliché image of the smart home of the future we like to envisage a pasha-like life of ease, where we can control our homes with an app, voice control, a glance, or just a thought. Is that what we really want though? Should not rather we be smart, wise and intelligent rather than be condemned to a life of couch potatoes? Of course, there are also useful technological solutions. For example, technology companies worldwide

fen. Der Firmengründer Robbie Antonio plant dabei, alle paar Monate ein neues vorgefertigtes Design zu präsentieren.

«Kann Technologie allein unser Wohnen besser und intelligenter machen?»

Eine weitere, ebenfalls große Herausforderung für das Bauen und das Leben in der Zukunft, ist der Umgang mit der Technik und den Auswirkungen des Megatrends Connectivity. Während die mobile Technologie die fundamentalen gesellschaftlichen Verschiebungen zu einem nomadischeren, flexiblen Lebensstil ermöglicht, werden wir von der Idee der Smart Houses und Smart Citys auch verführt. Aber kann Technologie allein unser Wohnen besser und intelligenter machen? Oder ist es eine Ablenkung von den realen Fragen des Seins und des Tuns? Das sogenannte Internet der Dinge, das uns mit unseren Geräten und unsere Geräte mit anderen Geräten in Verbindung bringt, ist das geflügelte Wort in der Tech- und der Hausbau-Branche. Doch wollen wir wirklich Dinge wie kluge Matratzen mit Liebhabererkennungs-App oder intelligente Kühlschränke mit Webcams und Sensoren, die uns sagen, wann die Ketchupflasche leer ist oder die Joghurts abgelaufen sind? Und vielleicht noch eine automatische Bestellung beim nächsten Supermarkt aufgeben?

Im Klischee des intelligenten Zuhauses der Zukunft stellen wir uns ein Pascha-artiges, bequemes Leben vor, in welchem wir mit einer App, durch Sprachsteuerung, einen Blick oder eines Tages auch nur durch einen Gedanken unsere Häuser und Wohnräume kontrollieren können. Ist es das, was wir wollen? Oder sollten nicht wir anstelle der Dinge smart, klug und intelligent sein und uns nicht zum Leben als Couch-Potatos verdammen lassen? Natürlich gibt es auch hilfreiche Technologielösungen. So wird weltweit an der intelligenten Gesundheitsversorgung älterer Menschen geforscht. Fußböden mit Aufprallsensoren, die bei einem Sturz Alarm auslösen, Roboter mit termingesteuertem Medikamenten-Service oder Maschinen, die ihnen das Abendessen kochen.

are researching smart healthcare for the elderly. Floors plastered with sensors that initiate an alarm when someone falls, robots with medication reminders service, or butlers that can cook for you.

"Many studies have shown that the more independence is given to people of all generations, the happier they are."

The main question to ask when we look at smart technology and the megatrend Connectivity, is not if these promises can live up to the hype – because in terms of technology they can or will – but if technology can make us happier and, above all, if it is able to solve all our current and future social problems and challenges.

Many studies have shown that the more independence is given to people of all generations in how they live, the happier they are, the better they function, and the longer they live. This is what scientists call "mindfulness," and it will be the key to better thinking about building in the future.

So how do we find more mindful solutions for living in the future? Thinking socially is an increasingly important aspect in the building industry and one in which real estate developers and building companies can gain great image advantages with creative and sometimes relatively small effort and input. It is perhaps no coincidence, therefore, that the recent recipients of the 2015 Turner Art prize in the UK were the architects of Assemble for their urban regeneration project in Toxteth, Liverpool.

Real estate developers and service providers will in the future increasingly position themselves as service providers and curators of mindful lifestyle communities. Living in the apartment buildings of the future will be like living in a club for mindful living. One in which everyone will want to be a member in the future.

«Viele Studien haben gezeigt, dass
mehr Unabhängigkeit die Menschen aller
Generationen glücklicher macht.»

Die zentrale Frage jedoch, die wir bei der Betrachtung der intelligenten Technologien und des Megatrends Connectivity stellen müssen, ist nicht, ob diese Versprechen dem Hype gerecht werden können, – denn technisch gesehen sind oder werden sie dazu in der Lage sein – sondern ob uns die Technologie glücklich macht und vor allem unsere aktuellen und zukünftigen gesellschaftlichen Probleme und Herausforderungen lösen kann.

Viele Studien haben gezeigt, dass mehr Unabhängigkeit die Menschen aller Generationen glücklicher macht und sie besser funktionieren und länger leben lässt. Das ist es, was Wissenschaftler «Achtsamkeit» nennen, und es wird der Schlüssel zum besseren Bauen in der Zukunft sein.

Wie finden wir nun mehr bewusste Lösungen für das Leben in der Zukunft? Soziales Denken ist dabei ein zunehmend wichtiger Aspekt in der Bauindustrie und einer, mit dem Immobilienentwickler und Bauunternehmen mit kreativen Ideen und manchmal relativ geringem Aufwand große Imagevorteile gewinnen können. Vielleicht ist es daher kein Zufall, dass die Architekten von Assemble mit ihrem grundlegenden Konzept für die Regeneration, Stadtplanung und Entwicklung in Toxteth, Liverpool, 2015 den Turner Kunstpreis in Großbritannien gewonnen haben.

Immobilienentwickler und -dienstleister werden sich in Zukunft also zunehmend als Dienstleister und Kuratoren von Achtsamkeitsgemeinschaften positionieren. Das Leben in den Wohngebäuden der Zukunft wird wie das Leben in einem Club für bewusstes Leben sein. Ein Club, in dem jeder Mitglied sein möchte.

Was bedeuten all diese Trends für das Vermarkten von Immobilien in der Zukunft?

Das «Wohnen für die Ewigkeit» gehört der Vergangenheit an. In einer Welt, in der lebenslange statische Einkommen selten werden, ändern sich die Zeithorizonte. Sie verkürzen sich innerhalb des eigenen Lebens, verlängern sich aber über die Generationen hinweg. Die kommenden Generationen werden an den Übergängen der Lebensphasen, zwischen Aufbruch, Festigung, neuem Aufbruch und langem Finish (zwischen 70 und 90) neue Wohnsituationen suchen. Sie brauchen maßgeschneiderte Konzepte für ihre Lebensphasen, mit Exit-Strategien und Leasing-ähnlichen Konditionen. Immobilien-Verkäufer werden dann immer mehr zu Life-Coaches, die womöglich einen Kunden über Jahrzehnte begleiten. Vermögens-, Lebens- und Immobilienberatung werden verschwimmen, ineinander übergehen und sich vermischen.

ZENTRALE FAKTOREN FÜR DAS IMMOBILIENMARKETING DER ZUKUNFT

Time Shift: Die steigende Mobilität und die Flexibilisierung von Lebensphasen führen zu einer langfristigen Abkehr vom «Ein-Haus-Ein-Leben-Prinzip». Häuser, Apartments, Wohnungen, Lofts werden nicht mehr wie bisher nur einmal im Leben gekauft und dabei alles Vermögen investiert.

Soft Gentrification: Neue Baugenossenschaften machen Schule. Mieter und Käufer wollen in den großen Städten immer mehr an ungewöhnlichen Objekten mitbauen. Die Transformation alter Fabriken oder die Entwicklung neuer urbaner Gemeinden erzeugen einen neuen Stil in der Immobilien-Entwicklung: Objekte werden vor Ort mit Interessenten entwickelt. So hat etwa die Entwicklung eines der größten Projekte, der Industrial City in Brooklyn, Jahre gedauert und wurde mit Partys an den Wochenenden vorangetrieben. So wurden Immobilienmakler zu Entwicklern, die direktes soziales Networking betrieben. Exklusivität und Hip-Faktor inklusive.

What are the implications of all these trends for the marketing of real estate in the future?

The concept of "dwelling for eternity" is a thing of the past. In a world in which lifelong static incomes are becoming rare, the time frames are changing. They become shorter within one's own life but longer across generations. The future generations will seek new living situations in the transitions between life phases, between departure, stabilization, new departure and long finish (between 70 and 90). They need tailor-made concepts for their life phases, with exit strategies and leasing-like conditions. Real estate agents will increasingly turn into life coaches who possibly accompany customers for decades. Investment, life, and real estate counseling will become blurred, merge and mix.

CENTRAL FACTORS FOR REAL ESTATE MARKETING IN THE FUTURE

Time shift: Increased mobility and more flexible life phases result in the long-term abandonment of the "One house one life" principle. As opposed to before, houses, apartments, suites and lofts are not bought once in a lifetime with an investment of all assets.

Soft gentrification: New building cooperatives form a precedent. Tenants and buyers want to increasingly participate in the construction of exceptional objects in major cities. The transformation of old factories or the development of new urban communities create a new style of real estate development: building projects are developed on site together with interested parties. For example, the development of one of the largest such projects, the Industrial City in Brooklyn, took several years and was promoted by parties on the weekends. This way, real estate agents became developers who practiced direct social networking. Including exclusivity and hip factor.

Neighborhood Map vom Financial District und The Embargadero in San Francisco
Neighborhood map of the financial district and The Embargadero in San Francisco

Urban Experts: Eine zentrale Aufgabe wird es werden, Trends in den Städten frühzeitig zu erkennen. Denn wer absehen kann, welche Stadtteile im nächsten Immobilienzyklus angesagt sind, kann enorme Marktvorteile erzielen. Inzwischen gibt es praktikable Prognosetools zur Immobilienbewertung, wie etwa die von den Architekten von GRAFT entwickelte «dynamische Methode». Lage ist längst nicht mehr alles. Die dynamische Methode erfasst eine Immobilie nicht statisch, sondern ganzheitlich durch die Verknüpfung unterschiedlicher Datensätze, die für diese entscheidend sind. Verschiedene Faktoren wie zum Beispiel Marktmiete, Fluktuationsrate oder Demografie können verbunden oder wieder entkoppelt werden.

Big Data: Viele Makler und Immobilien-Marketer werden sich in Zukunft vermehrt in das Reich der Daten begeben. Dabei geht es um Informationsvorteile, die den langfristigen Wert einer Immobilie verbessern und Verkaufsargumente schaffen können. Zum Beispiel das Thema der Street Walkability: Wie organisch ist ein Objekt in seine Umgebung eingepasst? Mit Neighborhood Maps zeigt sich, wie welche sozialen Probleme oder auch Bauchancen in einem bestimmten Stadtviertel auftauchen.

Natürlich spielen im Wandel des Immobilienmarketings auch die digitalen Medien eine Rolle. Elektronische Versteigerungen werden sich im Massengeschäft durchsetzen. Aber mehr denn je ist eine Immobilie als Gegentrend zur Digitalisierung und Virtualisierung der Welt zu sehen. Denn wenn wir morgen virtuell dank Cyberbrille und Ganzkörper-Sensitive-Anzug auf dem Mars wohnen, fühlen und uns bewegen, steigt die Sehnsucht weg von der Illusion hin zu einem realen Lebensraum mit dicken Holzdielen und echten Messinggeländern.

Urban experts: It will become a central task to detect trends in cities at an early stage. Because those who know which city quarters will be popular in the next real estate cycle can gain great market advantages. Nowadays there are practical prospect tools for real estate evaluation, such as the "dynamic method" developed by the architects of GRAFT. It's no longer all about location. The dynamic method evaluates a property not statically but holistically by linking various databases that are important to it. Different factors, such as market rent, fluctuation rate, or demographics can be connected and disconnected at will.

Big Data: In the future, many realtors and real estate marketers will increasingly venture into the world of data. They are seeking information advantages that improve the long-term value of a property and can create sales arguments. For example, the topic of street walkability: How organically is a building project integrated into its environment? Neighborhood maps show which social problems or construction opportunities are present in a specific city quarter.

Of course, digital media also play a role in the changing nature of real estate marketing. Electronic auctions will gain ground in the mass market. Yet more than ever, a property can be regarded as a counter trend to the digitalization and virtualization of the world. Because if in the world of tomorrow thanks to cyber goggles and full body suits we will live, feel and move about on Mars, our longing is longer for the illusion, but for a real living environment with thick timber floor boards and genuine brass railings.

DIE GANZE WELT WIRD 3D – DIE BEDEUTUNG DER DIGITALISIERUNG FÜR DIE IMMOBILIENBRANCHE

THE WHOLE WORLD IN 3D – THE SIGNIFICANCE OF DIGITALIZATION FOR THE REAL ESTATE SECTOR

MARTIN A. MEIER

Martin A. Meier, 3D-Spezialist, Firmengründer und CEO
Martin A. Meier, 3D specialist, company founder and CEO

DIE GANZE WELT WIRD 3D – DIE BEDEUTUNG DER DIGITALISIERUNG FÜR DIE IMMOBILIENBRANCHE

Das architektonische Denken ist ein vieldimensionaler Prozess aus Raumabfolgen, Raumnutzungen, konstruktiven, zeitlichen und baulichen Abhängigkeiten und vielem mehr. Wieso beruht also der architektonische Entwurf auch heute noch oft auf 2D-Darstellungen von Grundriss, Fassade und Schnitt?

30 Jahre nach meinen ersten 3D-Versuchen arbeiten noch immer viele der Architekturbüros fast ausschließlich mit 2D-Plänen. Die Computerspieleindustrie ist hier bereits viel weiter, denn unsere Kinder bewegen sich völlig selbstverständlich in komplexen virtuellen 3D-Welten. Moderne Grafikchips machen dies in einer immer besseren Qualität möglich. Doch

THE WHOLE WORLD IN 3D – THE SIGNIFICANCE OF DIGITALIZATION FOR THE REAL ESTATE SECTOR

Architectural thinking is a multi-dimensional process of spatial sequences, room uses, structural, temporal and constructional interrelationships, and much more. Why is it then that architectural designs even today often continue to rely on two-dimensional presentations of layouts, facades and sectional views?

30 years after my first 3D experiments many architectural offices still work almost exclusively with two-dimensional plans. The computer game industry is already much more advanced, as can be seen by our children, who move around totally naturally in complex virtual 3D worlds. Modern graphic chips allow this in improved excellent quality. Yet the influence of increasingly

Vom 3D-Modell zur Visualisierung, Limmat Tower, Dietikon, Zürich
From the 3D model to visualization, Limmat Tower, Dietikon, Zurich

VR-Brille Oculus Rift im Einsatz
VR goggles Oculus Rift in use

der Einfluss von schneller werdenden Computerchipsätzen ist schwierig zu verstehen, da dies alles auf einer abstrakten Ebene stattfindet. Die große Veränderung erfolgt aktuell über unsere Augen und unsere sämtlichen Sinne. Bereits in den 1960er-Jahren beschäftigte sich der Computergrafik-Pionier Ivan Sutherland mit Virtual Reality. In den 1990er-Jahren war die NASA ein Haupttreiber dieser Technologien, denn es gab diverse Simulationen, die im realen Falle nicht geübt werden konnten beziehungsweise viel zu kostspielig gewesen wären.

Im Vergleich zu heute waren all diese Simulationen vergleichsweise unbeholfen und stark technologiegeprägt. Doch das änderte sich rasant. Zuerst hat sich die Prozessorleistung (CPU) unglaublich stark entwickelt und zur Zeit ist es die Leistung der Grafikkarten (GPU), die um ein vielfaches schneller wird. Dies schafft völlig neue Möglichkeiten im Bereich von virtuellen Erlebniswelten, da sehr große Datenmengen in beinahe Echtzeit verarbeitet werden können. Daraus haben sich zwei dominierende Trends gebildet: Virtual Reality und Augmented Reality.

Bei Virtual Reality geht es um das Kreieren und Erleben einer Scheinwelt, in der man sich bewegen und bestenfalls sogar interagieren kann. Dem gegenüber steht Augmented Reality. Hier wird die reale Welt mit zusätzlichen Inhalten, wie beispielsweise Textinformationen, Bildern oder 3D-Modellen, überlagert.

VIRTUAL REALITY (VR) VERSUS AUGMENTED REALITY (AR)

Das Ziel der Virtual Reality ist, dass der Anwender nach kurzer Zeit nicht mehr wahrnimmt, dass er sich in einer Scheinwelt befindet. Dabei werden im Idealfall sämtliche Sinne des Benutzers übersteuert. Benötigt werden dazu komplett verdunkelnde Brillen, Kopfhörer, eventuell Handschuhe und Kleidungsstücke, welche mit Sensoren zur Positionsortung ausgestattet sind. Ein Start-up aus den USA (FeelReal) beschäftigt sich sogar gerade mit der künstlichen Erzeugung von unterschiedlichsten Düften. Zur Zeit haben die VR-Brillen (Head Mounted Devices) wie Oculus Rift oder HTC VIVE, um nur zwei zu nennen, noch nicht die optische Qualität erreicht, um vollends zu überzeugen. Auch

high speed computer chip sets is difficult to comprehend as it all takes place on an abstract level. Currently, the major change involves our eyes and all senses. The computer graphics pioneer Ivan Sutherland researched virtual reality already in the 1960s. In the 1990s, NASA was the main driving force behind these technologies as there were diverse simulations that could not be implemented in reality or that would have been far too costly to implement.

Compared to today, all these simulations were rather clumsy and highly technological. This changed quickly, however. First, the CPU performance developed at an incredible rate and currently the performance speed of graphic cards (GPU) is increasing rapidly. This presents entirely new possibilities in the area of computer-mediated reality as very large amounts of data can be processed almost in real time. As a result, there are two dominating trends – virtual reality and augmented reality.

Virtual reality is about creating and experiencing an artificial world in which the users can move about or even interact in the best of cases. This is juxtaposed by augmented reality. Here the real world is augmented by additional information such as text information, images or 3D models.

VIRTUAL REALITY (VR) VERSUS AUGMENTED REALITY (AR)

The aim of virtual reality is for users to stop noticing that they are in an artificial world after a short period of time. Ideally, this involves all senses of the user. This requires completely obscuring goggles, headphones, and sometimes also gloves and suits equipped with sensors for tracking positions. A U.S. start-up (FeelReal) is even currently exploring the artificial creation of various scents. At this time, the VR goggles (head mounting devices – HMD) such as Oculus Rift or HTC Vive to name just two, still do not offer a visual quality that is fully acceptable. The wear comfort also needs some improvement as heat development, weight and cables to the computer still limit their optimal use. However, the technical deficiencies become secondary as soon as test subjects are presented with tasks and moving

den Tragekomfort gilt es zu verbessern, denn Hitzeentwicklung, Gewicht und Kabelstränge zum Computer schränken die Nutzung noch ein. Die technischen Mängel treten aber in den Hintergrund, sobald ein Proband Aufgaben und bewegte Bilder präsentiert bekommt. Sein Fokus wandert auf die Interaktion mit der neuen Umgebung. Eine zentrale Rolle bei der Weiterentwicklung spielt auch die zeitliche Verschiebung zwischen der realen Bewegung und dem computergenerierten Bild. Zuerst muss die Position des Benutzers ermittelt, dann das entsprechende Bild berechnet und dann wieder an die Brille gesendet werden. Im Idealfall 90 bis 120 Mal pro Sekunde. Diese minimale zeitliche Verschiebung kann das Gleichgewichtsempfinden stören und Übelkeit hervorrufen. Erstaunlicherweise kann man sich daran gewöhnen. So haben wir uns im Selbstexperiment etwa 25 Minuten in einem relativ einfachen Entdeckungsspiel bewegt, welches eine deutliche Zeitverschiebung aufwies. Je länger man die Brille trug, desto weniger störend war der Effekt. Doch die Überraschung kam nach dem Ablegen der Brille. Wir kämpften im Anschluss mehrere Minuten lang mit einer Zeitverschiebung in der realen Welt.

Das Erlebnis ist heute bereits mehr als eindrücklich. Aber was sind die Vorteile von Virtual Reality gegenüber eines normalen Fernsehbilds oder Computerspiels? Hier möchte ich ein Zitat von *WIRED*-Senior Kevin Kelly aus dem Jahre 2016 anfügen:

«Menschen erinnern sich bei Virtual Reality-Erlebnissen nicht an etwas, das sie gesehen haben, sondern an etwas, das ihnen widerfahren ist.»

Dies ist mit der Reaktion auf die Methode des Storytellings vergleichbar. Hirnstrommessungen zeigen, dass hier weitaus mehr Gehirnregionen angeregt werden als beim Betrachten von TV-Sendungen. Virtual Reality wird im Bereich der Immobilienvermarktung seine zentrale Rolle finden. Seit fünfzehn Jahren beschäftigen wir uns im Team mit der optimalen Darstellung von Architekturprojekten aller Art. Dabei setzen wir uns ständig

images. Their focus turns to the interaction with the new environment. A central theme for further development is also the latency between the real movement and the computer-generated image. First, the position of the user needs to be determined, then the according image calculated and in turn transmitted to the goggles. Ideally, this takes place 90 to 120 times per second. This minimum time lapse, however, can affect the sense of balance and cause nausea. Surprisingly, users can get used to it. As a self-experiment, we moved around for about 25 minutes in a relatively simple discovery game that had significant latency. The longer one wore the goggles, the less noticeable was the effect. The real surprise came once the goggles were off. We had to struggle for a few minutes with a time lapse in the real world.

The experience is already more than impressive today. Yet what are the advantages of virtual reality as opposed to a normal television image or computer game? At this point I would like to present a 2016 quote by the founding executive editor of *WIRED* magazine:

"People remember VR experiences not as a memory of something they saw but as something that happened to them."

This is comparable to the reaction to the method of storytelling. Electroencephalography shows that many more brain regions are actuated by VR than by watching TV shows. Virtual reality is sure to play a central role in real estate marketing. For the past fifteen years, we as a team have researched the optimal presentation of all types of architectural programs. Throughout this time, we constantly dealt with the megatrend Big Data. We make information of various sources (architects, landscape architects, planners, engineers and agencies) available in images that are experienced on an emotional level. Within a very short period of time, the viewers can form their own opinions regarding a project even if they are not familiar with partial aspects of it. Yet I venture to make the following statement:

mit dem Megatrend Big Data auseinander. Wir machen Informationen aus unterschiedlichsten Quellen (Architekten, Landschaftsarchitekten, Planer, Ingenieure und Agenturen) emotional in Bildern erlebbar. Innerhalb kürzester Zeit kann sich der Betrachter seine eigene Meinung zu einem Projekt bilden, auch wenn er sich in Teilbereichen nicht auskennt. Und trotzdem wage ich folgende Behauptung:

«Konventionelle Visualisierungen werden an Bedeutung verlieren.»

Der größte Teil der Arbeit eines 3D-Spezialisten besteht darin, eine komplette Szene am Computer aufzubauen, mit Materialien zu versehen, zu möblieren, zu belichten und am Ende das Resultat von einem Computer berechnen zu lassen. Somit ist der Schritt nicht mehr weit, daraus ein Erlebnis zu entwickeln. Dank Virtual Reality ist es heute bereits möglich, diese Räume erlebbar und begehbar zu machen. Und so wird das Storytelling dank der Unterstützung von Software aus der Spieleindustrie eine völlig neue Bedeutung im Bereich der virtuellen Wohnungsbesichtigung erhalten.

«Der virtuelle Berater öffnet mir die Tür und begleitet mich durch die Neubauwohnung. Das Kaminfeuer flackert, es riecht leicht nach frischer Farbe und Eschenrauch. Die Fenster stehen offen und ich spüre eine angenehme Brise. Ob TV oder Küche, alles lässt sich interaktiv bedienen. Auch technische Erläuterungen zu den Geräten kann mir mein Berater geben. Auf die Frage, ob denn der dunkle Eichenboden den Raum nicht zu stark verdunkle, erscheinen auf meinem Visier alternative Beläge, welche ich per Fingerbewegung auf den Boden wischen kann. Um wirklich sicher zu sein, wie die Lichtverhältnisse mit dem helleren Boden aussehen, wechsle ich kurz die Tageszeit auf Dämmerung und kann so die Raumwirkung erleben. Und ja, das Chesterfield Sofa, welches mir so am Herzen liegt, kann ich auch gleich platzieren, um zu sehen, ob das Wohnzimmer groß genug ist – und vielleicht ist das dunkle Parkett doch stimmungsvoller... »

"Conventional visualization will lose in significance."

The major part of the work of a 3D specialist consists of creating a complete scene on the PC, determine the materials and furnishings, provide the lighting, and eventually have the outcome processed by a computer. This is but a short step from turning it into an experience. Thanks to virtual reality we are already able to allow users to access and experience these rooms today. This way, with the support of software from the gaming industry, storytelling will gain entirely new significance for virtual tours of apartments.

"The virtual consultant opens the door for me and accompanies me through the new building. Fire is glowing in the fireplace, there is a slight smell of fresh paint and ash wood smoke. The windows are open and I can feel a pleasant breeze. Whether the TV or the kitchen, everything can be operated interactively. My consultant can also give me technical instructions for the devices. In answer to my question of whether the dark oak floor does not make the room too dark, alternative floor covers appear on my visor that I can sweep to the floor by a finger movement. To be really sure of how the illumination is affected by the lighter-colored floor, I briefly switch the time of day to dusk to experience the effect on the room. And yes, I can immediately position the Chesterfield couch that I love so much to see whether the living room is big enough – and maybe the dark parquet flooring creates a nicer atmosphere after all..."

In the end, any assistance offered by the provider that supports the buying decision of the client will be welcomed. The earlier the buyers can realistically, informative and emotionally experience the project, the better and easier becomes its financing and the quicker construction can commence. When it comes to newly constructed building projects in particular, buyer safety is a key question to which virtual reality can provide one of the answers.

Am Ende wird jede Unterstützung auf der Anbieterseite willkommen sein, welche den Kaufentscheid des Kundens unterstützt. Je früher ein Projekt möglichst realistisch, informativ und emotional erlebbar gemacht wird, desto besser und einfacher die Finanzierung und desto schneller kann mit dem Bau begonnen werden. Und gerade beim Verkauf von Neubauprojekten geht es oft auch um Sicherheit auf der Käuferseite – und Virtual Reality wird eine der Antworten darauf sein.

AUGMENTED REALITY – MEHR ALS NUR POKÉMON GO FÜR DIE BAUSTELLE

Das zweite große Thema aus dem Bereich 3D-Technik ist die erweiterte Realität, auch Augmented Realitiy (AR) genannt. Dabei wird die reale Welt mit zusätzlichen Inhalten überlagert. Es braucht dazu lediglich ein Smartphone und ist somit für eine breite Masse bereits verfügbar. Lego lancierte bereits im Jahr 2014 eine App, mit der man das zusammengebaute Modell auf jeder Legopackung virtuell betrachten konnte. Das aktuellste und gerade populärste Beispiel ist Pokémon Go. Zwei Welten werden miteinander verschmolzen und die Realität wird dank dem Smartphone zur Spielarena. Auch da gibt es Head Mounted Devices für anspruchsvollere Anwendungen. Die großen Hoffnungsträger sind hier die Firma Magic Leap und die Hololens von Microsoft. Microsoft hat das Projekt Holoportation gestartet, welches bereits heute die Kommunikation im dreidimensionalen Raum mit Menschen auf der ganzen Welt ermöglicht. Man kann seine Geschäftspartner, Kunden oder auch seine Familie zu sich «beamen», die Szenen aufzeichnen und sogar als Miniatur Freunden beim Abendessen zeigen. Die Brillen sind zur Zeit noch in der Entwicklungsphase und eher unhandlich. Dies wird sich aber ändern. Wenn man aktuelle Forschungsprojekte, unter anderem von Google, anschaut, welche sich mit einer neuen Generation Kontaktlinsen beschäftigen, die AR-Fähigkeiten haben sollen, dürfte es bald der Vergangenheit angehören, bei einem Networking-Event nach einem Namen zu ringen. Denn auf der Netzhaut werden nicht nur der Name, sondern auf Wunsch auch das ganze Linkedin- oder Facebook-Profil angezeigt.

AUGMENTED REALITY – MORE THAN JUST POKÉMON GO FOR THE CONSTRUCTION SITE

The second large area of 3D technology is augmented reality (AR). The real world is enhanced or augmented by additional contents. All that is required is a smartphone, which makes the technology already available for a large group of people. Lego already offered an app in 2014 with which the assembled model could be virtually seen on each Lego package. The most recent and currently most popular example is Pokémon Go. Two worlds are merged with each other and reality becomes a play area thanks to the smartphone. There are also HMD for more demanding AR applications. The most promising are Magic Leap and the Hololens by Microsoft. Microsoft launched the Holoportation project that already allows the communication in three-dimensional space with people around the world today. Users can "beam" their business partners, customers or even family members to their side, record the scenes and even show them in miniature format to friends during dinner. The goggles are still in the development phase and rather unwieldy. This will change, however. When looking at current research projects, for example by Google, which focus on a new generation of contact lenses with AR capacities, it should soon be a thing of the past to struggle for a name in a networking event. This is because not only the name but, if required, the complete LinkedIn or Facebook profile can be displayed on the retina.

The question is how this innovation can be used in the real estate sector. A simple example could be the augmentation of a real estate brochure or architectural plans. With the help of AR devices, such as a smartphone, users not only see the layout but an entire 3D model. In the same way, additional information such as the 3D models of engineers and planners can be included (BIM = building information modeling). This way, complex topics can be discussed as a team, errors detected, and solution recommendations developed. The prerequisite is a precisely designed 3D model as well as the understanding and acceptance of the planning team.

Augmented Reality: Scannen Sie den QR-Code und erleben Sie das Projekt «Nova Brunnen, HRS» in 3D (nur iOs-Geräte)
Augmented reality: scan the QR code and experience the "Nova fountain, HRS" project in 3D (iOs devices only)

Da drängt sich die Frage auf, wie diese Innovationen im Immobilienbereich Verwendung finden sollen. Ein einfaches Beispiel kann die Augmentierung einer Immobilienbroschüre oder von Architekturplänen sein. Durch AR-Geräte, wie beispielsweise einem Smartphone, sieht man nicht nur den Grundriss, sondern man kann ein ganzes 3D-Modell abbilden. Auf dieselbe Weise lassen sich auch weitere Angaben wie die 3D-Modelle der Ingenieure und Planer überlagern (BIM = Building Information Modeling). So können komplexe Themen im Team besprochen, Fehler gesucht und aufgezeigt sowie Lösungsvorschläge erarbeitet werden. Voraussetzungen dafür sind ein präzise aufgebautes 3D-Modell sowie das Verständnis und die Bereitschaft des Planungsteams.

Nehmen wir einmal an, es existiert ein detailliertes 3D-Modell. Darin sind sämtliche Informationen von allen Planern enthalten. Man bräuchte noch eine entsprechende AR-Brille, eine präzise und intelligente Ortung und der Architekt kann mit der Bauherrschaft bereits vor Projektstart das Gebäude an Ort und Stelle betrachten und allfällige Änderungen besprechen oder die städtebauliche Setzung überprüfen. Während des Bauprozesses werden die Vorteile aber noch deutlicher: Der Baumeister braucht weder Plan noch Senkblei. Durch seine AR-Brille sieht er am Boden leuchtend den Grundriss eingezeichnet. Ebenso die vertikale Kante der Wand. Der Bauarbeiter hat somit beide Hände frei für seine Arbeit. Die Arbeit im Akkord kann beispielsweise durch ein Belohnungssystem unterstützt werden und im Idealfall die Motivation jedes Handwerkers positiv beeinflussen. Das Ausmessen entfällt komplett und die Bauleitung hat immer die Kontrolle. Auch Gebäudesimulationen wie der Wärmefluss oder das Strömungsverhalten der Luft können so direkt vor Ort simuliert werden. Aus all diesen Gründen – und anderen, die heute noch im Verborgenen liegen – wird auf dem Bau der Zukunft irgendwann kein Weg mehr an 3D-Modellen und Augmented Reality vorbeiführen.

Let's assume we have a detailed 3D model. It contains all the information by all planners. Now all that is needed are corresponding AR goggles and precise and intelligent positioning to allow the architect together with the owners to view the building on location even before the start of the project to discuss required changes or check its urban development location. The advantages become even more obvious during the construction process – master builders no longer need plans or plummets. Looking through their AR goggles they see the layout illuminated on the ground along with the vertical edge of the wall. This frees both hands of workers for their tasks at hand. The piece-work can be supported by an award system, for example, and ideally positively affect the motivation of each worker. Measuring is no longer needed and the construction supervisor is always in control. Similarly, building simulations such as thermal flow or the flow properties of air can be simulated directly on location. For all these reasons, and many more that we are not aware of today, construction in the future will at one point or another not be able to do without 3D models and augmented reality.

BIM – BAUEN WIRD 3D

BIM ist die Abkürzung für Building Information Modeling (deutsch: Gebäudedatenmodellierung) und beschreibt eine Methode zur Optimierung der Planung, Ausführung und Bewirtschaftung von Gebäuden, idealerweise über den gesamten Lebenszyklus eines Gebäudes. Alle relevanten Gebäudedaten werden digital erfasst, kombiniert und vernetzt mittels eines 3D-Modells, in dem technische Informationen hinterlegt werden, wie zum Beispiel Produktangaben, Kosten, Maßinformationen oder Details. Es werden nicht Punkte oder Polygone konstruiert, sondern intelligente Elemente wie Wände, Stützen, Fenster, Türen etc. Über die Anbindung an eine Datenbank kann der Benutzer jederzeit aktualisierte Gebäudeinformationen abfragen. Die Planung am dreidimensionalen Modell ermöglicht allen beteiligten Arbeitsgruppen (Architektur, Ingenieurwesen, Haustechnik, Facilitymanagement) über die Verknüpfung der einzelnen Modelle effizienter zu planen, zu simulieren und Konstruktionsfehler zu vermeiden.

«Verschiedene Szenarien für Optimierungsmöglichkeiten lassen sich schnell und einfach erstellen.»

Worin besteht der Vorteil einer Planung im Raum und welche Chancen eröffnen sich damit in der Zukunft? Mit einer intelligenten Verknüpfung der Bauteile und Räume hat man jederzeit die Kontrolle über das Raumprogramm und die Kosten. Verschiedene Szenarien für Optimierungsmöglichkeiten lassen sich schnell und einfach erstellen. Ein wichtiger Vorteil liegt aber auch im Bereich der Kostenoptimierungen. Es gibt zum Beispiel Stahlbauunternehmen mit hochspezialisierter Software, welche im Vergleich zu konventionellen Konstruktionsplanungen mit bis zu 30 % Materialeinsparungen arbeiten. Diese Vorteile sind nur mit dreidimensionalen Modellen möglich. Sie bieten jedem Planer die Möglichkeit, sein Projekt zu optimieren, seien dies zeitliche Prozesse, Materialeinsatz, Kosten oder andere Faktoren. Planungsfehler können bereits frühzeitig erkannt und vermieden werden. Ich möchte aber noch einen Schritt weitergehen.

BIM – BUILDING IN 3D

BIM is short for building information modeling, which is a method for the optimization of the planning, implementation and management of buildings, ideally across the entire life cycle of a building. All relevant building data is digitally recorded, combined and merged into a 3D model that contains technical information such as product information, costs, dimensions, or other details. It does not consist of points or polygons, but rather of intelligent elements such as walls, supports, windows, doors, etc. A link to a database allows users to access up to date building information at any time. The implementation of planning on a three-dimensional model allows all involved work groups (architecture, engineering, building services, facility management) to link the individual models for more efficient planning and simulation while avoiding construction errors.

"Different scenarios for optimization possibilities can be quickly and easily prepared."

What are the advantages of spatial planning and what are its possibilities for the future? The intelligent linking of construction elements and rooms offers permanent control of the space allocation plan and costs. Different scenarios for optimization possibilities can be quickly and easily prepared. Another key advantage is cost optimization. For example, there are steelwork companies with highly specialized software that operate with up to 30 % material savings compared to conventional construction planning. These advantages are only made possible by three-dimensional models. They offer each planner the opportunity to optimize projects in terms of time, material use, costs, and other factors. Planning errors can be detected and eliminated at an early stage. But I would like to take this one step further. Digitalization continues to conquer the construction sector as well. In Asia, many high rises are constructed by robots – floor by floor. The increased knowledge gained from 3D printing will also strongly influence construction in the

Mithilfe von Aufnahmen einer Drohne können 3D-Modelle berechnet werden (Limmatfeld, Zürich)

The photos taken by a drone can be used to calculate 3D models (Limmatfeld, Zurich)

Die Digitalisierung hält auch in der Baubranche weiterhin Einzug. In Asien werden bereits Hochhäuser in großen Teilen von Robotern aufgebaut – Geschoss für Geschoss. Auch die steigenden Erfahrungen aus dem 3D-Druck werden das Bauen der Zukunft stark beeinflussen. Somit sind 3D-Modelle zukünftig unabdingbar, denn Computer verarbeiten dreidimensionale Daten und keine Pläne.

PROGRAMMIEREN STATT MODELLIEREN

Der Trend an Architekturfakultäten geht mittlerweile stark in Richtung dreidimensionales Arbeiten. Doch denke ich, dass das Programmieren von prozeduralen Modellen massiv an Bedeutung gewinnen wird. Große Industrieroboter bauen Mauerwerke mit höchster Präzision und organischen Geometrien, Drohnen konstruieren Hängebrücken und riesige 3D-Drucker bauen ganze Siedlungen. 3D-Modelle bilden die Grundlagen für all diese Prozesse und teilweise übersteigen sie bereits heute die zeichnerischen Fähigkeiten begabter 3D-Experten. Regeln definieren und logische Abhängigkeiten entwickeln steht dem konventionellen Zeichnen von Plänen gegenüber. Ersteres braucht zu Beginn noch viel Zeit, doch wenn die Logik einmal definiert ist, kann man mit wenigen Parametern das ganze Gebäude verändern oder das Öffnungsverhalten der Fassade beeinflussen. Künstliche Intelligenz wird hier ihren Beitrag leisten.

future. This makes 3D models indispensable in the future since computers process three-dimensional data and not plans.

PROGRAMMING INSTEAD OF MODELING

The trend at architectural departments is currently strongly in favor of three-dimensional work. Yet I believe that the programming of procedural models will vastly gain in significance as well. Large industrial robots build brickwork with the highest precision and organic geometry, drones construct suspended bridges, and giant 3D printers build entire residential estates. 3D models constitute the base for all these processes and occasionally already exceed the drawing capacities of skilled 3D experts. The definition of rules and the development of logical dependencies is juxtaposed to the conventional drawing of plans. The first still initially requires plenty of time, but when the logic has been defined, one can use a limited number of parameters to alter the entire building or affect the opening behavior of the facade. Artificial intelligence will contribute to this process.

INNOVATION – EIN BIVALENTES THEMA

Neue Technologien, wie auch die daraus resultierenden Veränderungen, rufen neben einer ersten Begeisterung immer auch Ängste hervor. Aktuell können wir nur ahnen, wohin die Reise geht. Virtual und Augmented Reality werden nicht nur auf dem Bau- und dem Immobiliensektor ihre Spuren hinterlassen, sondern in vielen Bereichen. Der Arbeitsplatz der Zukunft wird seine Ortsgebundenheit weitgehend verlieren, denn für Besprechungen und Meetings kann man einfach eine VR-Brille aufsetzen und schon befindet man sich mitten in der Besprechung. Erste Plattformen wie Virtual Desktop sind nur der Anfang. Dies wird nachhaltige Auswirkungen auf unser Mobilitätsverhalten haben. Viele Geschäftsreisen werden wegfallen und auch der Pendlerverkehr der Zukunft wird anders aussehen. Dies kann soweit gehen, dass selbst Verkehrsnetze nicht mehr ausgebaut werden müssen. Die Unaufhaltbarkeit dieser Innovationen mag auf viele bedrohlich wirken. Man kann versuchen, sie zu verhindern oder zu behindern, doch die VR- und AR-Systeme werden in unserem Alltag Einzug halten. Wenn nicht über uns, dann spätestens über unsere Kinder, welche bereits heute ganz selbstverständlich und spielerisch mit diesen neuen Technologien umgehen.

«Der Arbeitsplatz der Zukunft wird seine Ortsgebundenheit weitgehend verlieren.»

WIEVIEL TECHNOLOGIE VERTRÄGT DER MENSCH?

Zur Zeit drängen unzählige neue Technologien auf den Markt und es gibt kaum einen Geschäftsanlass, bei dem der Begriff Digitalisierung nicht im Zentrum steht. Bei einem erfolgreichen Projekt, egal in welchem Bereich, sollte die Technologie nie alleine im Vordergrund stehen. In den kommenden Jahren wird unser Alltag noch stärker von Computern bestimmt, gleichzeitig wird aber auch die Bedienung viel einfacher werden und die Technik wieder vermehrt in den Hintergrund treten. Denken wir zurück an die ersten Betriebssysteme, welche über Lochkarten und Textzeilen gesteuert wurden. Die erste Computermaus war

INNOVATION – AN AMBIVALENT TOPIC

After the initial euphoria, new technologies and the changes resulting from them always also cause fears. Currently we can only guess where this is taking us. Virtual and augmented realities will not only affect the construction and real estate sectors, but many other sectors as well. The workplace of the future will mostly no longer be tied to a location, as conference and meeting participants will simply don their VR goggles and find themselves in the middle of everything. Initial platforms such as Virtual Desktop are only the beginning. This will have significant impact on our mobility behavior. Many business trips will no longer be necessary and commuting will also take different forms in the future. This can be to such an extent that traffic hubs will no longer be developed further. The inevitability of these innovations may seem threatening to many people. They can try to prevent or block them, but VR and AR systems will become parts of our everyday life. If not through us then no later than through our children who handle these technologies naturally and playfully already today.

"The workplace of the future will mostly no longer be tied to a location."

HOW MUCH TECHNOLOGY CAN HUMANS HANDLE?

Currently, a vast number of new technologies are crowding the market and there is hardly a business context in which the word digitalization is not somewhere at the core. Nevertheless, for a successful project in any sector technology should not be the sole focus. In the coming years our everyday life will be even more affected by computers, at the same time, their handling will become much easier and the technology increasingly become secondary. Just think back to the first operating systems that were controlled by punch cards and text lines. The first computer mouse was a breakthrough, but today there are already systems that are controlled by gestures and voice. New technologies should support concepts and visions, make ideas easier to understand, or emotionally emphasize information, but

ein Durchbruch, doch bereits heute gibt es Systeme, die über Gesten und Sprache gesteuert werden. Neue Technologien sollen Konzepte und Visionen unterstützen, Ideen verständlich machen oder Informationen emotional hervorheben, aber nie sich selbst dienen. Sie sind immer klar unterzuordnen: Nur weil man etwas tun kann, heißt das nicht, dass es auch wirklich Sinn macht. Darum sollte man sich zuerst immer ein Konzept erarbeiten – gerade in der Immobilienvermarktung. Die Lage, die Zielgruppe, ihre Bedürfnisse und ihr Verhalten müssen ermittelt und überprüft und erst in einem nächsten Schritt die entsprechenden Mittel gewählt werden. Für meine Arbeit ist es von zentraler Bedeutung, stets eine breite Übersicht über neue mögliche Methoden für die Vermarktung von Immobilien zu haben, doch noch wichtiger ist es, die richtige Wahl zu treffen, um die Vision oder das Vermarktungskonzept zu unterstützen. So kam es schon einmal vor, dass ein Kunde am Ende von einem Modellbauer ein wundervolles Innenraummodell im Maßstab 1:20 bauen ließ, weil das einfach mehr der Zielgruppe und der Projektidee entsprach – und es war ein Erfolg.

they should never be self-serving. They must always be clearly subordinated – just because something can be done does not mean that it actually makes sense. This is why it is essential to first develop a concept – especially in real estate marketing. The situation, the target group, its needs and behavior, must be determined and verified before selecting the appropriate means as a second step. It is of central importance to my work to always have an extensive overview of newly available methods for marketing real estate, but it is even more important to make the right choices to support the vision or marketing concept. There were incidences where a customer asked a model maker to construct a wonderful interior design model at a scale of 1:20 because this was simply more in line with the target group and the project idea – with great success.

DIE IMMOBILIENBRANCHE UND DIE DIGITALE TRANSFORMATION
THE REAL ESTATE SECTOR AND DIGITAL TRANSFORMATION

SVEN RUOSS

Sven Ruoss, Business Developer
Sven Ruoss, Business Developer

DIE IMMOBILIENBRANCHE UND DIE DIGITALE TRANSFORMATION

Die Digitalisierung ist allgegenwärtig. Es vergeht kaum ein Tag, an dem nicht ein entsprechender Zeitungsartikel publiziert, eine Konferenz diesbezüglich abgehalten, ein Blogbeitrag geschrieben oder eine Studie veröffentlicht wird. Buzzwords wie Industrie 4.0, Internet of Things, Big Data, 3D-Drucker oder Smart Home sind in aller Munde. Wer heute immer noch glaubt, bei der Digitalisierung gehe es lediglich darum, eine mobile Website zu entwickeln oder eine Social-Media-Präsenz aufzubauen, irrt gewaltig. Die genannten Technologien haben in den letzten Jahren grundlegende Veränderungen in der Art und Weise, wie wir miteinander kommunizieren, arbeiten und leben in Gang gesetzt. Die weit verbreitete Annahme, dass es bei der

THE REAL ESTATE SECTOR AND DIGITAL TRANSFORMATION

Digitalization is omnipresent. There is hardly a day without a related newspaper article being published, a conference being held on the topic, a blog entry written, or a study published. Buzz words like Industry 4.0, Internet of Things, Big Data, 3D printers, or smart home are heard everywhere. Anyone who still believes that digitalization is limited to the development of a mobile website or setting up a social media presence is very wrong. In the past few years, the above technologies have initiated key changes in the way we communicate with each other, they way we work, and the way we live. The widely held assumption that digital transformation is only about technology has long since become outdated. The technology is merely

digitalen Transformation ausschließlich um Technologie geht, ist längst überholt. Die Technologie ist lediglich die notwendige Voraussetzung für die Transformation in die digitale Welt. Digitale Technologien werden Wertschöpfungsketten, operative Prozesse, Organisationsstrukturen, ja die Unternehmenskultur per se verändern. Es entstehen komplett neue Geschäftsmodelle. Unternehmen wie Uber und Airbnb haben unmissverständlich gezeigt: Egal wie analog eine Branche ist, es kann jederzeit ein Start-up auf den Markt kommen und das traditionelle Businessmodell in wenigen Jahren auf den Kopf stellen. Auch die Immobilienbranche ist von der Digitalisierung erfasst. Schon heute drängen branchenfremde Firmen wie Google oder Samsung in die Bau- und Wohnungsindustrie. Die digitale Transformation greift gnadenlos in die bisher geltenden Spielregeln ein, eröffnet aber auch neue, spannende Möglichkeiten.

Bei der digitalen Transformation geht es nicht nur um die Einführung neuer Technologien, sondern immer auch um einen Wandel der Unternehmenskultur und -struktur sowie des Individuums selbst. Mit der fortschreitenden Digitalisierung werden nicht nur Geschäftsmodelle, sondern konkret Aufgaben und Arbeitsabläufe einzelner Mitarbeiter verändert.

the required prerequisite for the transformation into the digital world. Digital technologies become value creation chains, while operative processes, organizational structures, even the entire corporate culture are changing as such. This results in entirely new business models. Companies such as Uber and Airbnb have unmistakably shown that no matter how analog a sector, a start-up may be launched anytime to turn the traditional business model upside down. The real estate sector is also affected by digitalization. Today already, companies from other sectors such as Google or Samsung are entering the construction and residential industry. Digital transformation mercilessly disrupts the previous rules of the game while also opening up new and exciting possibilities.

Digital transformation is not only about the introduction of new technologies but also about a change of the corporate culture and structure and individuals themselves. Progressive digitalization not only changes business models but more specifically also tasks and work processes of individual employees.

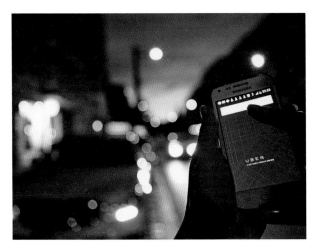 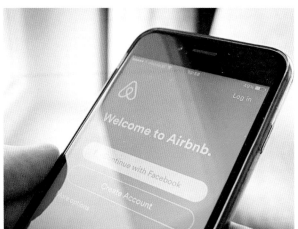

Analoge Branchen im Aufbruch: Hotellerie (Airbnb) und Fahrdienste (Uber)
Analog sectors in transitions: hotels (Airbnb) and driving services (Uber)

«Wer nicht digital
denkt, ist raus!»

"Digital is not the future,
it is the present!"

Unternehmensstruktur

Auf Basis der digitalen Technologien entstehen für das Individuum, den Staat, die Gesellschaft und Unternehmen unterschiedlichste Möglichkeiten, diese zu nutzen. Individuen kommunizieren mit ihrem Smartphone und entsprechenden Apps in Echtzeit miteinander; relevante Nachrichten verbreiten sich in wenigen Minuten über die ganze Welt. Auch der Staat kann sich digitale Technologien bei verschiedenen Aufgaben zunutze machen. So werden beispielsweise in der Schweiz immer mehr Steuererklärungen digital eingereicht. Schließlich sind insbesondere auch für Unternehmen die Möglichkeiten der Digitalisierung vielschichtig. Diese reichen von der Optimierung einzelner Prozesse bis hin zur Implementation komplett neuer, digitaler Geschäftsmodelle. Rund drei Viertel der Unternehmen in der Schweiz gehen davon aus, dass die digitale Transformation in den nächsten Jahren eine große Auswirkung auf ihre Branche haben wird. Auch in der Immobilienindustrie kann davon ausgegangen werden, dass die Digitalisierung einen Strukturwandel bewirken wird und zwar in sämtlichen Bereichen – vom Bau über die Vermarktung, die Bewirtschaftung und den Betrieb bis zur Umnutzung. Für die Unternehmen bedeutet das, die großen Chancen der digitalen Transformation bestmöglich zu nutzen.

«Rund drei Viertel der Unternehmen in der Schweiz gehen davon aus, dass die digitale Transformation in den nächsten Jahren eine große Auswirkung auf ihre Branche haben wird.»

Unternehmenskultur

Die Geschwindigkeit der digitalen Transformation hat alle überrascht: das Individuum, den Staat, die Gesellschaft und nicht zuletzt die Unternehmen. Um die Herausforderungen der digitalen Transformation im erforderlichen Tempo zu meistern, reichen bewährte Strategien nicht mehr aus. Eine hohe Agilität und radikale Offenheit gegenüber neuen Geschäftsmodellen sind unabdingbar für die Akteure der digitalen Transformation.

Corporate structure

Digital technologies offer various opportunities for individuals, the state, society, and companies to use them. Individuals communicate with each other in real time via their smartphones and apps, relevant news spread across the globe within a few minutes. The state can also utilize digital technologies for various services. For example, in Switzerland an increasing number of tax declarations are submitted digitally. Finally, for companies in particular, digitalization offers a host of possibilities. These range from the optimization of individual processes to the implementation of entirely new digital business models. Three out of four Swiss companies expect digitalization to have a major effect on their sector within the next few years. In the real estate sector also, it can be assumed that digitalization will cause a structural change in all areas – from construction to marketing, building management and use, to re-use. For companies this implies making the best possible use of the major opportunities offered by digital transformation.

"Three out of four Swiss companies expect digitalization to have a major effect on their sector within the next few years."

Corporate culture

The speed of digital transformation has surprised everyone: individuals, the state, society and last, but not least, companies. To master the challenges of digital transformation at the required speed, standard strategies are no longer sufficient. High agility and radical openness to new business models are essential for the digital transformation players. The partially bureaucratic governance structures of Old Economy constitute an obstacle to this process. Digitalization is not only accompanied by extensive change, but requires all participants to undergo a cultural change as well. While individuals have to learn to adjust to the permanent change in different lifestyle aspects, companies are also requested to develop a motivating and supportive framework that allows interdisciplinary teams to

Die teilweise bürokratischen Governance-Strukturen der Old Economy stellen dabei ein Hindernis dar. Die Digitalisierung bringt nicht nur weitreichende Veränderungen mit sich, sondern fordert von allen Beteiligten einen Kulturwandel. Während Individuen lernen müssen, mit dem permanenten Wandel in unterschiedlichsten Lebenswelten umzugehen, sind auch die Unternehmen angehalten, einen motivierenden und förderlichen Rahmen zu entwickeln, sodass interdisziplinäre Teams kooperativ an Projekten arbeiten können. Führungskräfte werden erkennen müssen, dass ihre Praktikanten in spezifischen Themen fitter sind als sie. Die Dimension «Kultur» wird bei der digitalen Transformation zum entscheidenden Erfolgsfaktor. Denn auch in der Digital Economy gilt: Der Erfolg einer jeden Strategie hängt davon ab, wie konsequent sie umgesetzt wird. Jedes Unternehmen muss seine Hausaufgaben machen und für sich entscheiden, inwiefern es seine Kultur der digitalen Transformation anpassen möchte. Nicht immer ist das Aufspringen auf einen kurzfristigen Trend empfehlenswert. Mit Blick auf eine langfristige Digitalisierung wird eine Anpassung notwendig sein; und sei es auch mit einem Gegenmodell zur Digitalisierung.

Individidium

Der Mensch steht im Zentrum der digitalen Transformation. Er ist gleichzeitig Anwender von digitalen Technologien, Mitarbeiter, Mitglied der Gesellschaft wie auch Kunde. Seine Ansprüche haben sich in den letzten Jahren stark verändert. Freuten sich Mitarbeiter früher über das Privileg, vom Arbeitgeber ein Blackberry zu erhalten, sind sie heute enttäuscht, wenn sie das Modell, welches sie bevorzugen, nicht selbst auswählen dürfen. Früher waren Kunden zufrieden, wenn sie Informationen über ein Unternehmen im Internet fanden. Heute echauffieren sie sich, sobald ein Produkt nicht mit einem Klick über das Smartphone bestellbar ist. Diese neuen Bedürfnisse und Ansprüche stehen im Zentrum der digitalen Transformation. Gleichwohl gibt es auch bei der digitalen Transformation eine Gegenentwicklung.

cooperatively work together on projects. Managers will have to realize that their trainees are more adept in specific areas than they are. The "culture" dimension becomes a key success factor in digital transformation. This is because in the digital economy it is also true that the success of any strategy depends on how consistently it is implemented. Each company must do its homework and decide for itself to which degree it wants to adjust its culture to the digital transformation. It is not always recommended to leap onto a short-term trend. When it comes to long-term digitalization some adjustment will be necessary, even if it consists a counter-model to digitalization.

Individual

Human beings are at the center of digital transformation. They are simultaneously users of digital technologies, employees, members of society, and customers. Their demands have considerably changed in the past few years. While employees used to be thrilled about the privilege of receiving a Blackberry, today they are disappointed if they cannot choose the model they prefer. Customers used to be satisfied if they found information about a company on the Internet. Today they are upset if a product cannot be ordered with a single click on the smartphone. These new needs and demands are at the center of digital transformation. At the same time, a counter-development in digital transformation is also taking place.

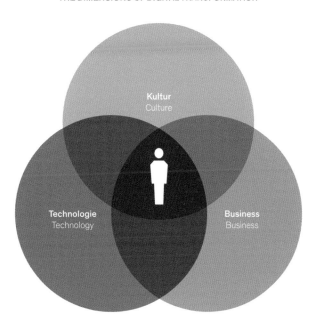

DEFINITION VON DIGITALER TRANSFORMATION

Die beiden Begriffe «digital» und «Transformation» geben schon erste Indizien dafür, dass es sich um einen Wandel handeln muss, der durch digitale Technologien ausgelöst wird. Unter der digitalen Transformation wird die Reise in das digitale Zeitalter verstanden. Dabei ist die digitale Transformation das höchste Level des digitalen Wissens und baut auf der digitalen Kompetenz und der digitalen Nutzung auf. Digitale Transformation setzt digitale Informations- und Kommunikationstechnologien ein, um die Performance von Unternehmen und Organisationen zu erhöhen. Bei der digitalen Transformation geht es um die Transformierung und die Weiterentwicklung der Unternehmensprozesse, des Kundenerlebnisses und der Geschäftsmodelle.

DEFINITION OF DIGITAL TRANSFORMATION

The two terms "digital" and "transformation" already indicate that it is some form of change initiated by digital technology. Digital transformation denotes the journey to the digital era. It is the highest level of digital knowledge based on digital competence and digital use. Digital transformation applies digital information and communication technologies to improve the performance of companies and organizations. Digital transformation is about the change and further development of corporate processes, the customer experience, and business models.

DIE ZIELE DER DIGITALEN TRANSFORMATION UND DIE IMMOBILIENBRANCHE
THE TARGETS OF DIGITAL TRANSFORMATION AND THE REAL ESTATE SECTOR

ZIELE DER DIGITALEN TRANSFORMATION

Weshalb erbringen Firmen enorme Anstrengungen, um sich digital zu transformieren? Die Hälfte der Unternehmen in der Schweiz glaubt, dass die digitale Transformation für sie in den nächsten 24 Monaten erfolgskritisch wird. Um ihre Wettbewerbsfähigkeit zu steigern und weiterhin am Markt zu bestehen, stellen sich immer mehr Unternehmen digital auf. Prinzipiell gibt es drei Ziele der digitalen Transformation: Erhöhung der Kundenbindung (externe Möglichkeit), interne Effizienzsteigerung (interne Möglichkeit) und Umsatzsteigerung durch neue Produkte und Dienstleistungen (externe Möglichkeit).

Erhöhung der Kundenbindung

Schon heute gibt es weltweit mehr Mobiltelefone als Zahnbürsten. Die Art und Weise, wie Menschen Informationen suchen, sich austauschen und untereinander kommunizieren, hat sich in den letzten Jahren mit dem Aufkommen von Social-Media-Plattformen und mobilen Endgeräten wesentlich verändert. Die neue digitale Interaktion von Kunden mit Unternehmen hat umfassende Auswirkungen auf Marketing, Vertrieb und Service. Auch das Immobilienmarketing wird zusehends digitaler. Neue Kanäle wie Online und Mobile werden erschlossen und bieten spannende Möglichkeiten, Kunden bereits in einer Presale-Phase besser anzusprechen. Die Immobilie wird zu einer eigenen Marke mit dem passenden Lebensgefühl aufgebaut, um so den Kunden vom Anfang bis zur Fertigstellung der Liegenschaft zu binden. Virtuelle Rundgänge in Wohnräumen unterstützen das Vorstellungsvermögen von potenziellen Käufern oder Mietern und verbessern das Kundenerlebnis.

«Die neue digitale Interaktion von Kunden mit Unternehmen hat umfassende Auswirkungen auf Marketing, Vertrieb und Service.»

Gleichzeitig können dank vermehrt verfügbarer Daten auch akkuratere Kundenanalysen durchgeführt werden, die dazu beitragen, Klienten und das Marktumfeld besser zu kennen

TARGETS OF DIGITAL TRANSFORMATION

Why do companies exert major efforts to transform themselves digitally? Fifty percent of Swiss companies expect digitalization to be crucial to their success within the next 24 months. To increase their competitiveness and survive on the market, an increasing number of companies are undergoing digitalization. Digital transformation has three basic aims: increasing customer loyalty (external possibility), increasing internal efficiency (internal possibility) and increasing revenues through new products and services (external possibility).

Increased customer loyalty

Today already more mobile phones than tooth brushes exist around the world. The way in which people search for information, exchange it and communicate with each other has changed considerably in recent years with the advent of social media platforms and mobile end devices. The new digital interaction of customers with companies has extensive effects on marketing, sales, and service. Real estate marketing is also increasingly becoming digital. New channels such as online and mobile applications are being developed and offer exciting opportunities for addressing customers already in the pre-sale phase. The real estate property has turned into its own brand with the associated lifestyle to ensure customer loyalty from the beginning to the completion of construction. Virtual tours of residences enhance the imagination of potential buyers or tenants and improve the customer experience.

"The new digital interaction of customers with companies has extensive effects on marketing, sales, and service."

At the same time, the increasingly available data can also be used to carry out more accurate customer analyses that contribute to a better understanding of the clients and market environment. Digital users leave traces with every click. These provide companies with information of which real estate the

und zu verstehen. Bei jedem Klick hinterlässt der digitale Nutzer Spuren. Diese geben dem Unternehmen Aufschluss darüber, für welche Immobilien der potenzielle Käufer sich interessiert sowie die Möglichkeit, ihm alternative Projekte vorzustellen, die ihm gefallen könnten. Eine reine Analyse des Ist-Zustandes wird künftig jedoch nicht mehr ausreichen. Entscheidend wird es sein, die Daten der Zukunft dahingehend zu interpretieren, um beispielsweise eine Aussage treffen zu können, in welcher Region es in kommender Zeit eine Nachfrage nach 3,5-Zimmer-Wohnungen geben wird. Über Smart Metering, Hausautomation und intelligente Energiesysteme lassen sich schon heute spannende Informationen zu Bewohnern sammeln, die dazu dienen, Mieter mit maßgeschneiderten Produkten und Dienstleistungen zu versorgen.

Interne Effizienzsteigerung

Interne Effizienzsteigerung ist auch in der Immobilienbranche ein zentraler Treiber für nachhaltiges Wachstum. Dabei lassen sich zwei Hebel unterscheiden: einerseits die Reduktion der Kosten, andererseits die Produktivitätssteigerung. Schon heute hat die Automatisierung Einzug auf den Baustellen erhalten: Erste Roboter und Drohnen sind bei Bauprojekten bereits im Einsatz. Bei Bauprojekten sind verschiedenste Akteure von unterschiedlichen Unternehmen tätig. Häufig kommt es zu Prozessbrüchen zwischen den einzelnen Unternehmen, was zu ineffizientem Zeit- und Kostenaufwand führt. Eine unternehmensübergreifende Vernetzung von Geschäftsprozessen verschiedener Akteure würde hier Abhilfe schaffen. Im Bereich des Liegenschaftenhandels wurde mit dem elektronischen Grundbuch bereits ein erster Schritt getan.

Umsatzsteigerung durch neue Produkte und Dienstleistungen

Von der Digitalisierung angestoßene Innovationen können sowohl inkrementell als auch radikal sein. Durch inkrementelle digitale Innovationen werden Produkte und Dienstleistungen weiterentwickelt und verbessert. Durch radikale Innovationen entstehen komplett neue digitale Produkte oder Dienstleistungen. So wird es zukünftig vielleicht ein Facebook der Immobi-

potential buyers are interested in coupled with the possibility of presenting them with alternative projects that may be to their liking. However, in the future a pure analysis of the status quo will no longer be sufficient. It will be important to interpret the data of the future in such a way that allows, for example, making a prediction of in which area there will be demand for 3.5-room apartments in the near future. Concepts such as smart metering, home automation, and intelligent energy systems already allow you to collect useful information about residents to provide tenants with customized products and services.

Increased internal efficiency

Increased internal efficiency is also a central driver for sustainable growth in the real estate sector. It consists of two approaches: the reduction of costs on the one hand and increased productivity on the other. Automation has already been introduced to construction sites – the first robots and drones are already in use. Very diverse stakeholders of different sectors are active in construction projects. Quite often there are process discrepancies among the individual companies resulting in wasted time and expenditures. Cross-company networking of business processes of the different players would resolve this issue. In the area of landed property trade, the electronic land register is already a first step in that direction.

Increased revenues through new products and services

Innovations initiated by digitalization can be both incremental and radical. Incremental innovations lead to the further development and improvement of products and services. Radical innovations consist of entirely new digital products or services. For example, in the future there may be a real estate Facebook in which key data, qualitative evaluation or qualitative portfolio reports of properties are stored. Another new digital product could be an online running costs monitor – after entering the apartment data, it generates a running cost comparison with an according range data while a real time dashboard supports the residents in monitoring the individual ecological target data.

lien geben, worin Kennzahlen, qualitative Bewertungen oder qualitative Portfolioberichte von Immobilien abgelegt werden. Auch ein Online-Nebenkostenmonitor könnte ein neues digitales Produkt darstellen: Nach Eingabe der Wohnungsdaten erhält man einen Nebenkostenvergleich mit entsprechenden Rangedaten und ein Echtzeit-Dashboard unterstützt die Bewohner, die individuellen Ökologieziele zu überprüfen.

DER DIGITALE LEBENSZYKLUS VON IMMOBILIEN

Die Digitalisierung macht auch vor der Immobilienbranche keinen Halt. In der Schweiz arbeiten nahezu 600'000 Vollzeitbeschäftigte in diesem Wirtschaftszweig — vom Bau über die Vermarktung, die Bewirtschaftung und den Betrieb bis zur Umnutzung. Der gesamte Gebäudepark Schweiz besteht aus ca. 2,5 Millionen Einheiten. Der Erstellungswert aller Bauten (Hoch- und Tiefbau) liegt bei rund 3'355 Milliarden Franken. Im Jahr 2011 generierte die Immobilienbranche eine Bruttowertschöpfung von rund 99 Milliarden Franken, was 18 % des Schweizerischen Bruttoinlandprodukts (BIP) entspricht. Die Zahlen unterstreichen die Bedeutung der Immobilienindustrie als wichtigen Wirtschaftsfaktor für die Schweiz

Der Lebenszyklus einer Immobilie lässt sich in sechs Phasen unterteilen. Am Anfang steht ein unbebautes Grundstück. Entsteht eine Idee, was darauf realisiert werden könnte, geht häufig ein entsprechendes Konzept hervor und die Klärung der Finanzierung. In der zweiten Phase des Immobilienzyklus steht die Planung im Zentrum. Auf Basis der Planunterlagen folgt in der dritten Phase die Bauausführung. Die Immobilie erwacht zum Leben. In der vierten Phase geht es um die Nutzung und Bewirtschaftung. In dieser längsten Phase wird in der Liegenschaft gelebt, in ihr gearbeitet, sie wird gepflegt und unterhalten. Der Lebenszyklus der Immobilie endet mit dem Rückbau. Das Immobilienmarketing stellt eine konstante Begleitung eines Lebenszyklus einer Immobilie — von der Idee bis zum Rückbau — dar und wird als sechste Phase bezeichnet. Sämtliche Phasen werden von der Digitalisierung tangiert.

THE DIGITAL LIFE CYCLE OF PROPERTIES

The real estate sector is also affected by digitalization. In Switzerland, nearly 600,000 people are employed full time in this sector — from construction via marketing, management and operation up to re-use. The overall building sector of Switzerland consists of approx. 2.5 million units. The construction value of all buildings (structural and civil engineering) is around 3.355 billion Swiss francs. In 2011, the real estate sector generated a gross added value of around 99 billion Swiss francs, which is 18 % of the Swiss gross domestic product (GDP). These numbers highlight the significance of the real estate industry as a key economic factor in Switzerland.

The life cycle of a property can be divided into six phases. First there is an empty plot of land. Once there is an idea of what may be implemented on it, it is usually followed by an according concept and determination of the financing. The second phase of the real estate cycle consists of planning. The third phase of construction is based on the plan documents. The property comes to life. The fourth phase consists of use and management. This is the longest phase of the property during which people live in it, work in it, take care of it and maintain it. Finally, the life cycle of a property ends with its demolition. Real estate marketing constantly accompanies the entire life cycle of a property, from the concept to the demolition, and is described as the sixth phase. All phases are affected by digitalization.

DER LEBENSZYKLUS EINER IMMOBILIE
THE LIFE CYLCE OF A PROPERTY

6

IMMOBILIENMARKETING
REAL ESTATE MARKETING

Analyse Markt, Entwicklung Zielgruppen, Entwicklung Markenwerte
Market analysis, target group development, brand values development

1

IDEE, KONZEPTION,
FINANZIERUNG
IDEA, CONCEPTUAL
DESIGN, FINANCING

5

RÜCKBAU
DEMOLITION

Analyse und Überprüfung Ist-Situation
Analysis and verification of the actual situation

4

NUTZUNG,
BEWIRTSCHAFTUNG
USE, MANAGEMENT

2

PLANUNG
PLANNING

3

BAUAUSFÜHRUNG
CONSTRUCTION
IMPLEMENTATION

Markenpflege mittels PR-Aktionen mit den Bewohnern, klare Kommunikation innen und außen, allfällige Wiedervermittlung
Brand management via PR campaigns with residents, clear internal and external communication, potential renewed listing

Planung Kommunikationsmaßnahmen, grafische und textliche Umsetzung der Werbemittel
Planning of communication measures, creation of advertising material graphics and text

Entwicklung Positionierung, Persönlichkeit, Name, Claim, Corporate Design
Development of the positioning, personality, name, claim, corporate design

Phase 1: Idee, Konzeption, Finanzierung

Die Standortwahl ist für die Immobilienbranche von entscheidender Bedeutung. Dazu werden heute computergestützte Standortsimulationen eingesetzt. Diese ermöglichen, mehr relevante Entscheidungs- und Umweltvariablen zu berücksichtigen, was zu einer Simulation mit deutlich höherem Detaillierungsgrad führt. Weiter sorgen die computergestützten Standortsimulationen dafür, Fehlentscheide bei der Standortwahl zu minimieren. Auch in puncto Finanzierung sind im digitalen Zeitalter neue Möglichkeiten entstanden. Über Crowdfunding-Plattformen wird für Immobilienprojekte Eigenkapital gesammelt. Das Investorenpooling sowie die Abwicklung der Finanzströme übernehmen heute Plattformen wie Exporo, BrickVest oder Crowdhouse.

Phase 2: Planung

In der Entwicklungs- und Planungsphase wird durch Building Information Modeling (BIM) die digitale Wertschöpfungskette revolutioniert und der Planungs- und Bauprozess wesentlich verändert. Durch Virtual Reality werden geplante Gebäude bereits in einer frühen Phase umfassend erlebbar gemacht. Auf Grundlage des BIM-Computermodells lassen sich mittels 3D-Drucker schnell und preiswert Miniatur-Prototypen erstellen. Die Bauprozesse werden simuliert und sämtliche Stakeholder eines Bauprojektes greifen auf ein zentrales Modell zu. Damit ist sichergestellt, dass immer mit den aktuellsten und identischen Daten gearbeitet wird. Nimmt der Architekt in seinem Baumodell eine Veränderung vor, so werden automatisch alle relevanten Parameter angepasst und bei den Modellen der betroffenen Fachexperten aktualisiert. Das Business Information Modeling führt zu Kosteneinsparungen, Zeitersparnissen und einer Vereinfachung im Planungsprozess. Zudem wird die Qualität verbessert, da allfällige Fehler nun bereits in der Planungsphase zutage kommen, die früher erst in der Bauphase entdeckt wurden.

Phase 3: Bauausführung

Die Baustelle der Zukunft wird digital. Digitale Tools helfen, den Kosten- und Zeitdruck zu mindern. Baumaschinen und Geräte

Phase 1: idea, conceptual design, financing

The choice of location is of key importance in the real estate sector. Today, computer-based location simulation programs are used for this purpose. These allow the inclusion of more relevant environmental variables, resulting in a simulation with much greater details. In addition, computer-based location simulations prevent faulty decisions when selecting locations. In the area of financing also many new possibilities have been created in the digital era. Crowd funding platforms are used to collect equity for real estate projects. Today, platforms such as Exporo, BrickVest or Crowdhouse handle the investor pooling and the financial flow.

Phase 2: planning

In the development and planning phase, building information modeling (BIM) revolutionizes the digital value creation chain and significantly changes the planning and construction process. Virtual reality presents a comprehensive insight into planned buildings at an early stage already. Based on the BIM computer model, miniature prototypes can be quickly and inexpensively created with 3D printers. The building processes are simulated and all stakeholders of a construction project access a central model. This ensures that everyone is always working with the latest identical data. If the architect initiates a change in his/her construction model, all relevant parameters are automatically adjusted and updated in the models of the concerned specialists. BIM results in cost and time savings and simplifies the planning process. In addition, the quality is improved as errors that were previously found in the construction phase are already detected in the planning phase.

Phase 3: construction implementation

The construction site of the future is digital. Digital tools help reduce cost and time pressure. Construction equipment and machinery are increasingly equipped with radio frequency identification (RFID) tags. These present a current overview of which equipment and machinery is at what construction site or available in the warehouse. The system supports the site foreman in putting together a list of required materials. The

werden vermehrt mit Radio-Frequency-Identification (RFID) Tags ausgestattet. Diese ermöglichen einen aktuellen Überblick darüber, welche Maschinen und Geräte sich auf welcher Baustelle befinden oder im Lager vorhanden sind. Das System unterstützt den Polier darin, die Liste des benötigten Materials zusammenzustellen. Die Arbeiter wiederum erhalten auf ihren Smartphones eine Liste der erforderlichen Maschinen und Geräte und laden diese auf dem Werkhof auf. Auf der Baustelle wird nicht mehr mit unterschiedlichen Papierversionen der Baupläne gearbeitet. Sämtliche Projektinvolvierte können digital auf den aktuellsten Bauplan zugreifen. Bei einer Videokonferenz über das Smartphone schließlich tauschen sich Experten, die nicht auf der Baustelle sind, über Unvorhergesehenes aus, analysieren und diskutieren. Wurden vor nicht allzu langer Zeit Rapporte von einem Polier mit Papier und Stift ausgefüllt, danach umständlich und ineffizient von der Administration abgetippt, werden diese heute digital in der Cloud erfasst. Diese kleinen Beispiele illustrieren, inwieweit die Digitalisierung bereits im Alltag einer Baustelle angekommen ist und das tägliche Arbeiten erleichtert.

«In Dubai rechnet man damit, dass bis 2030 gut 25 % aller Gebäude aus dem 3D-Drucker kommen.»

Schon heute spielt der 3D-Drucker bei der Bauausführung eine immer wichtigere Rolle. Zukünftig sollen ganze Gebäude gedruckt werden. In Dubai steht bereits das erste, voll funktionsfähige Haus, dessen Teile vom 3D-Drucker stammen. Der Druck des 250 Quadratmeter großen Gebäudes dauerte lediglich 17 Tage. In zwei Tagen wurden die Elemente zusammengesetzt. Die Kosten lagen bei rund 140'000 Euro. Dubai rechnet damit, dass bis 2030 gut 25 % aller Gebäude aus dem 3D-Drucker kommen. Das 3D-Druckverfahren hat gegenüber dem herkömmlichen Hausbau einige Vorteile. Aktuell geht man von einer Reduktion von rund 60 % beim Material, einer Einsparung von 70 % der Zeit und 80 % der Arbeitskraft aus.

workers in turn receive to their smartphones a list of required equipment and machinery to upload at the operation center. At the construction site various paper versions of the building plans are no longer used. Everyone involved in the project can digitally access the most recent building plan. Finally, during a video conference on their smartphones the experts who are not on location exchange information about unforeseen events to analyze and discuss. While in recent times reports were filled out with pen and paper by the foreman and then elaborately and inefficiently typed by the administration, today they are digitally recorded in the Cloud. These small examples illustrate to what degree digitalization has already reached the everyday operations of a construction site to facilitate daily tasks.

"In Dubai, it is expected that by 2030 a good 25 % of all buildings will be created by 3D printers."

Today already, 3D printers play an increasingly important role in construction. In the future entire buildings are expected to be printed. Dubai already witnessed the debut of the first fully functional house whose parts were created by a 3D printer. Printing the 250-square-meter building took only 17 days and the elements were assembled in two days. The costs were around 140,000 euro. In Dubai, it is expected that by 2030 a good 25 % of all buildings will be created by 3D printers. Compared to conventional building, the 3D printing process offers a number of advantages. Currently it is estimated that it saves 60 % of materials, 70 % of time and 80 % of labor.

Phase 4: Nutzung, Bewirtschaftung

Mit fortschreitender Digitalisierung steigen auch die Anforderungen der Mieter. So sind in letzter Zeit verschiedenste Anpassungen in der Nutzungsphase initiiert worden. Neue Objekte können virtuell besichtigt werden. Über spezifische Tools hat der Interessent die Möglichkeit, seine zukünftige Wohnung bereits einzurichten und über Augmented oder Virtual Reality in 3D durch seine eingerichtete Wohnung zu spazieren. Der Bewerbungsprozess erfolgt nicht mehr physisch, sondern elektronisch und Vertragsabschlüsse werden vermehrt papierlos vorgenommen. Wohnungsübergaben und -abnahmen werden vollständig digitalisiert. Auf Tablets kann man die Bauteil-Restlebensdauern automatisch berechnen und Mängel direkt auf dem digitalen Grundriss markieren. Der Mieter unterzeichnet das Protokoll digital und erhält das Dokument automatisch per Mail zugesandt. Über ein Portal können die Bewohner jederzeit auf Echtzeitangaben zu ihrem Verbrauch von Heizöl, Strom und Wasser zugreifen oder unkompliziert diverse Services wie Fensterreinigung, Wäscheservice oder Reparaturen in Auftrag geben. Immer häufiger werden Wohnungen smart. Das bedeutet, über das Internet of Things werden Gegenstände mit Sensoren und Intelligenz ausgestattet, sodass Geräte untereinander kommunizieren können. Diese Heimautomation bringt einen deutlichen Mehrwert. Smart Home hat eine Optimierung des Energieaufwands zur Folge sowie eine Erhöhung der Sicherheit.

Phase 5: Rückbau

Alles Leben hat ein Ende. So auch das von Immobilien. Doch gerade an die Rückbauphase wird zu Beginn des Projekts häufig zu wenig gedacht. Die Informationslage über eingebaute Materialien ist entsprechend dürftig. Das Business Information Model bringt auch in dieser letzten Phase Vorteile. Mit einer guten Informationslage können die Kosten eines Rückbaus reduziert werden. Daher ist auch für die Rückbauphase entscheidend, dass sämtliche objektrelevante Informationen über das virtuelle Gebäudemodell (BIM) erfasst, gepflegt und verteilt werden.

Phase 4: use, management

With increased digitalization, the expectations of tenants also increase. For example, recently various adjustments to the utilization phase have been initiated. New buildings can be viewed virtually. Using specific tools, interested parties have the opportunity to already furnish their future home and walk around their furnished apartment in 3D via augmented reality or virtual reality. The application process no longer takes place physically but electronically and contracts are increasingly paper-free. Handover and inspection of apartments will be fully digitized. Tablets can be used to automatically calculate the remaining service life of construction elements and mark faults directly on the digital layout. The tenant signs the protocol digitally and receives the document automatically per e-mail. A portal allows residents to constantly access real time information about their use of fuel oil, electricity, and water or conveniently request services such as window cleaning, laundry service or repairs. Apartments are increasingly becoming smart. This means that objects are equipped with sensors and intelligence via the Internet of Things, allowing them to communicate with each other. This home automation constitutes a substantial added value. The energy consumption of smart homes is optimized, while their safety is also increased.

Phase 5: demolition

All life comes to an end. This is also true for real estate. Yet at the outset of the project the demolition phase is often not given much thought. The information available about the used materials is accordingly scarce. The business information model also offers advantages in this final phase. With sufficient information the costs of demolition can be reduced. This is why it is also crucial for the demolition phase that all relevant building information is entered, updated and shared through the virtual building model (BIM).

Phase 6: Ständige Begleitung durch das Immobilienmarketing

Die Zeitachse des Immobilienmarketings verläuft parallel zu den geschilderten fünf Phasen. Gutes Immobilienmarketing begleitet den Lebenszyklus einer Immobilie von der ersten Idee bis zum Rückbau. Bereits in der ersten Phase werden der Markt, das Umfeld, die Zielgruppen, die Preisbereitschaft und das Projekt analysiert. Basierend auf diesen Erkenntnissen werden Zielgruppen und Markenwerte entwickelt. Die Grobkosten für das Immobilienmarketing können in dieser Phase bereits abgeschätzt werden. In der zweiten Phase werden die Positionierung, die Persönlichkeit, der Name, ein passender Claim sowie das Corporate Design (Logo, Schriften, Farben, Manual) entwickelt. Dies geschieht mit Hilfe von Personas (fiktive Personen), die typische Anwender der für die Immobilie definierten Zielgruppe repräsentieren.

«Personas verdeutlichen wichtige Eigenschaften der Zielgruppe und helfen bei der Positionierung.»

Personas verdeutlichen wichtige Eigenschaften der Zielgruppe und helfen bei der Positionierung. Während der Bauphase werden die passenden Kommunikationsmaßnahmen geplant. Der Kommunikationsplan umfasst Angaben, was wann wo und zu welchen Kosten kommuniziert werden soll. Auf Basis der kommunikativen Leitidee werden geplante Werbemittel wie Website, Broschüre, Plakate, Anzeigen, Social Media etc. grafisch und textlich umgesetzt. Während der Nutzungsphase geschieht die Markenpflege mittels PR-Maßnahmen und Aktionen mit den Bewohnern. Jede Kommunikation – sowohl gegen innen als auch gegen außen – soll die kommunikative Leitidee stärken. In der Rückbauphase werden die Ist-Situation, das Marktumfeld, die Zielgruppen, die Preisbereitschaft, die Nachfrage sowie die Bedürfnisse analysiert beziehungsweise überprüft. Das Immobilienmarketing soll den Entscheidungsprozess dahingehend prägen, wie die Zukunft der Immobilie aussehen könnte. Je nach Beantwortung dieser Frage geht die Arbeit im Immobilienmarketing mit Phase 1 oder Phase 4 weiter.

Phase 6: constant support by real estate marketing

The timeline of real estate marketing is parallel to the described five phases. Successful real estate marketing accompanies the life cycle of a property from the initial idea to the demolition. In the first phase already, the market, the environment, the target groups, the pricing options, and the project are analyzed. This information is used to define target groups and brand values. The rough costs of real estate marketing can already be estimated in this phase. In the second phase, the positioning, the personality, the name, a suitable claim, and the corporate design (logo, fonts, colors, manual) are developed. This takes place with the help of personas (fictive persons) that represent typical users of the target group that was defined for the property.

"Personas highlight key characteristics of the target group and help with positioning."

Personas highlight key characteristics of the target group and help with positioning. The appropriate communication measures are planned during the building phase. The communication plan contains information of what is communicated when where and at what cost. Based on the central communication theme, the graphic design and copy of planned advertising media such as the website, brochures, posters, advertisements, social media, etc. are implemented. During the utilization phase, brand management involves PR measures and campaigns involving the residents. Any type of communication, whether internal or external, is intended to strengthen the central communication theme. In the demolition phase, the actual situation, the market environment, the target groups, the pricing options, the demand, and the needs are analyzed or verified. Real estate marketing should influence the decision process regarding the future of the property. Depending on the answer to this question, real estate marketing proceeds with phase 1 or phase 4.

FAZIT UND AUSBLICK

Die digitale Transformation hat schon so manche Branche umgekrempelt und sie verändert auch die Immobilienindustrie. Die modernen technologischen Entwicklungen stellen in jeder Phase des Lebenszyklus eines Bauobjektes die Weichen neu. Computergestützte Standortsimulationen helfen bei der Standortwahl und mindern Misserfolge. Durch Building Information Modeling (BIM) wird der Planungsprozess nachhaltig revolutioniert. Auch das Immobilienmarketing wird von der Digitalisierung beeinflusst. Online-Kanäle bieten spannende Möglichkeiten beim Aufbau von konsistenten und nachhaltigen Markenwelten, die in der digitalen Welt eine immer wichtigere Rolle einnehmen. Nicht nur Echtzeitdaten stehen bei der Vermarktung zur Verfügung, sondern auch simulierte Zukunftsdaten. Modelle werden mittels 3D-Druck schnell und präzise hergestellt und fortlaufend angepasst. Und schließlich kann ein Interessent sein Traumobjekt nicht nur virtuell und in 3D begehen, sondern über Virtual Reality bereits komplett nach seinem Gusto einrichten. Zur Zeit klaffen Anspruch und Wirklichkeit noch auseinander, dennoch: Der Wandel wird kommen. Alle Beteiligten tun gut daran, aktiv an den positiven Auswirkungen der Digitalisierung auf die Immobilienbranche mitzuarbeiten. Neben den Erleichterungen für die Architekten, Bauingenieure, Elektroplaner, Elektroinstallateure, Immobilienhändler und Gebäudetechniker bedeutet Smart Home denn auch für jeden einzelnen, gemütlicher und entspannter zu wohnen. Viele Innovationen im Wohnbereich werden in Zukunft unaufdringlich stattfinden und unser tägliches Tun erleichtern. Smart Home wird uns darin unterstützen, uns auf das Wesentliche zu konzentrieren: Das reale Leben miteinander, und das findet schließlich immer noch analog statt.

CONCLUSION AND PROSPECTS

Digital transformation has already turned some sectors upside down and is also affecting the real estate industry. Modern technological advances reset the tracks for every phase of the life cycle of a construction project. Computer-based location simulation helps with the selection of the location and reduce errors. Building information modeling (BIM) sustainably revolutionizes the planning process. Real estate marketing is also affected by digitalization. Online channels offer exciting opportunities for setting up consistent and sustainable brand identities that play an increasingly important role in the digital world. Marketing not only uses real-time data but also simulated future data. Models are quickly and precisely created with 3D printing and constantly adjusted. Finally, interested buyers can not only access their dream property virtually and in 3D, but also furnish it completely at will via virtual reality. Currently, expectations and reality are still at odds, nevertheless: the change will come. All involved are well advised to actively participate in the positive effects of digitalization on the real estate sector. In addition to facilitating the work of architects, civil engineers, electrical designers, electricians, real estate dealers, and building service engineers, smart home means more comfortable and relaxed homes for everyone. In the future, many innovations in the home will be introduced unobtrusively and facilitate our everyday activities. Smart homes will support us in focusing on the essential – real life interaction, which takes place on an analog level after all.

MARKETING. BRANDING. ARCHITEKTUR.
MARKETING. BRANDING. ARCHITECTURE.

PROF. DR. CARY STEINMANN

Prof. Dr. Cary Steinmann, Professor für Marketing und Markenführung
Prof. Cary Steinmann, Professor of Marketing and Brand Management

MARKETING. BRANDING. ARCHITEKTUR.

Was ist eigentlich Marketing? Marketing bedeutet hölzern übersetzt «Vermarktung», mit anderen Worten und etwas überholt «zu Markte tragen», neudeutsch «go to market». Anglizismen sind übrigens im Management und of course auch im Marketingmanagement sehr beliebt. Das klingt lässiger, riecht nach internationaler Kompetenz und täuscht Weitsicht vor.

Marketing heißt eben auch ganz banal «zum Kauf anbieten» und zwar so, – das ist die quintessentielle Raffinesse der subtilen Suggestion – «dass der Käufer das Angebot als wünschenswert empfindet» (American Marketing Association).

MARKETING. BRANDING. ARCHITECTURE.

What is marketing? In the literal sense of the word, marketing means to introduce something to a market or to "go to market." Incidentally, the use of English marketing terminology is very popular in the marketing and marketing management sector of Germany and other countries. The English terms are used because they sound more casual, hint at international expertise, and simulate an extended horizon.

Essentially, on a very mundane level, marketing means "offering something for sale" in such a way that (here comes the quintessential cleverness of subtle suggestion) the "offerings have value for customers" (American Marketing Association).

Marketing wurde aus der Not erfunden. Früher, bevor es Marketing gab, verkauften sich die Produkte von selbst. Die Nachfrage war größer als das Angebot, wie zum Beispiel heute noch auf dem klassischen Wochenmarkt: Kommst du um 12 Uhr, sind die Stände leergekauft, Kartoffeln weg, Rüebli weg. Alles weg. Marketing braucht es da keins, lediglich den sogenannten Abverkauf. Circa Anfang der 1950er-Jahre kippte diese «goldene Regel» der Vermarktung ins Gegenteil, es gab mehr Angebote als Nachfrage: Die offerierten Produkte und Dienstleistungen wurden verbreitert und vertieft, Konsumenten wurden analysiert, neue Segmente (Gruppen von Verbrauchern mit ähnlichen faktischen und/oder psychologischen Daten) wurden durchaus subtil und verfeinert erschlossen und so weiter: Marketing war geboren. Die Frage lautet seit dann bis heute: Wie kann ich in einem Überangebot mein Produkt derart positionieren und kommunizieren, dass bei der angesteuerten Zielgruppe das verführerische Bedürfnis geweckt wird, eben genau mein Produkt haben zu wollen.

Wie machen wir Marketing? Erstens müssen wir den Menschen verstehen, das ist schon sehr komplex. Zweitens den Konsumenten im Menschen, das ist auch komplex, aber überschaubar. Wir wenden die Motivforschung an, erstellen Verhaltensanalysen, Fokusgruppen, Interviews, Clinics (Arbeit mit serienreifen Prototypen oder Konzepten), machen natürlich ganz viel Desk-Research (Google sei Dank) etc. Was nichts anderes bedeutet als: viel Markt- und Konsumentenforschung, je mehr, desto besser. «Show me the data», heißt die zwingende Frage eines jeden vernünftigen Markenstrategen. Das hilft uns, Komplexitäten zu reduzieren und maximal zu verstehen. Dann und nur dann können wir eine Marketingstrategie bauen. Ohne Strategie kein Erfolg, ganz einfach.

Aus dem Bauch heraus geht es natürlich auch, aber die Chance, damit an die Wand zu fahren, ist gewaltig groß. Nicht jeder ist ein bisschen Steve Jobs.

Wie machen wir also eine Strategie? Wir müssen fünf einfache Fragen stellen und diese auch möglichst fokussiert

Marketing emerged from a specific need. In earlier times, before the era of marketing, products sold themselves. The demand was greater than the supply, as can be still seen today on traditional farmer's markets: If you come at noon, the stands are sold out, the potatoes are gone and so are the carrots. All gone. This does not require marketing, only so-called end of line sales. Around the beginning of the 1950s this "golden rule" of marketing was reversed as there was more supply than demand. A greater range and more specialized products and services were offered, customers were analyzed, new segments (groups of consumers with similar lifestyle and/or psychological profiles) were discovered in a rather subtle and refined manner, and so forth: in short, marketing was born. Since that time and to this day, the main question is: In a surplus of supply how can I position and communicate my product in such a way that it evokes in my selected target group the alluring desire to want precisely my product.

How do we practice marketing? First, we must understand human beings, which is already quite complex. Second, understand the consumers inside the human beings, which is also complex, but manageable. We use motivational research, prepare behavior analyses, conduct focus groups, interviews, clinics (working with prototypes or concepts that are ready to go into serial production); of course conduct plenty of desk research (thanks to Google), etc. Which essentially means plenty of market and consumer research, the more the better. "Show me the data" is the key demand of any sensible brand strategist. This helps us reduce and ultimately understand complexities. Then and only then can we construct a marketing strategy. No strategy, no success. It's that simple.

Of course relying on gut feelings is also possible, but this offers an enormous chance of failing miserably. Not everyone has Steve Jobs' instincts.

Then how do we go about creating a strategy? All we have to do is pose five simple questions and find focused answers to them. Yet being focused, i.e. "simple" is more complicated than you

beantworten. Denn fokussiert, also «einfach» zu sein, ist komplizierter, als man denkt, denn Spreu und Weizen müssen getrennt werden, übrig bleiben darf nur, was hochgradig relevant ist. Im Gegenteil dazu bleibt festzuhalten, dass kompliziert zu sein sehr einfach ist. Man mache einfach ein großes Puff und schon ist alles megakompliziert. Hilft aber eben nichts. Also, auf geht's:

1. Wo sind wir?
2. Warum sind wir dort, wo wir sind?
3. Wo könnten wir sein?
4. Wie kommen wir dorthin?
5. Kommen wir dorthin?

Die erste einfache Frage lautet: Wo sind wir? Was eine Art Retrospektive impliziert, wie im Serienkrimi der Catch Up «was bisher geschah…» Wir analysieren die Daten und jene, die wir nicht haben, müssen wir uns eben beschaffen. Alle sinnvollen Daten, meinungsfrei und falls nötig eisenhart.

Das gilt für den Markt für Kaugummis, Damenbinden, Autos. Und natürlich genauso für Immobilien. Expertise in der Analyse und insbesondere der Interpretation wird zum entscheidenden Faktor der strategischen Einschätzung eines Projektes: Welches sind die Konsumentenbedürfnisse (Flächen, Grundrisse, Materialien, Farben) und wie lassen sich diese inszenieren (Branding, Dokumentation, Web, Beschriftung)?

Die zweite einfache und zugleich tiefsinnige Frage lautet: Warum sind wir dort, wo wir sind? Die Interpretation. Diese sinnsuchende Nachfrage nach den Gründen des Seins, präzise über den Hebel «Warum», dieses Aufdecken muss schonungslos sein. Warum sind wir nur Nummer drei im Markt und weit von der Spitze weg? Schönreden hilft nichts, die Hosen müssen runter. Und selbst wenn wir bereits super erfolgreich sind, können wir uns immer noch verbessern und müssen halt die kleinen Probleme benennen. Oder als Nummer 7 oder tragische Nummer 17 eben die großen Probleme. Was ist ergo das Tolle an der Frage nach dem «Warum»? Es ist die menschlichste aller Fragen, sie bedeutet Neugier, was wiederum strategisch hoch

would think, because the wheat must be separated from the chaff, and only things that are relevant to a high degree may be retained. In return, it should be said that being complicated is very simple. You just create a great puff and suddenly everything is exceptionally complicated. But that won't do. Well, here we go:

1. Where are we?
2. Why are we where we are?
3. Where could we be?
4. How do we get there?
5. Are we getting there?

The first simple question is: Where are we? This implies a sort of retrospective, such as the catch up in a series "previously on…" We analyze the data and whatever data we don't have has to be procured somehow. All meaningful data must be collected, free of any opinions and tough as nails, if required.

This is equally true for the markets for chewing gum, sanitary pads, cars, and, of course, real estate. Analysis and especially interpretation expertise becomes a key factor of the strategic assessment of a project – what are the consumer needs (square footage, layouts, materials, colors) and how can these be presented (branding, documentation, web, labeling)?

The second simple and at the same time profound question is: Why are we where we are? The interpretation. The truth-finding questioning of the reason for being, precisely triggered by the question "why," this uncovering must be brutally honest. Why are we only number three on the market and far from the top? Sugarcoating won't do, we have to let our pants down. Even if we are exceptionally successful already, there is always room for improvement and we have to explore the minor problems. Or as number 7 or even a tragic number 17, the major problems. Then what is so great about the question "why"? It is the most human of all questions, it indicates curiosity, which in turn is highly strategically relevant. Curiosity implies conceptual thinking all the way up to being scientific. Get it?

relevant ist. Neugier impliziert konzeptionelles Denken bis hin zur Wissenschaftlichkeit. Kapish?

Wenn wir also wissen, wo wir sind und warum dem so ist, stellen wir die nächste einfache Frage: Wo könnten wir sein? Realistisch, mit Augenmaß, kein Wunschkonzert, eine Stärken-Schwächen-Analyse mit der Suche nach Potenzialen und gegebenenfalls Risiken. Wo könnten wir realistischerweise sein, wenn wir das Maximum richtig machen würden?

Und nun zur wichtigsten unserer fünf magischen Strategiefragen: Wie kommen wir dorthin? Was müssen wir tun, was lassen, was ändern, wo investieren, wo Hilfe holen. Die Frage nach dem «Wie und Wohin» verkörpert natürlich die strategische Kernfrage, die Quintessenz, das Alles-oder-Nichts. Mit anderen Worten: Was wird uns die Zielgruppe antworten müssen, wenn wir sie nachts um drei wachrütteln und zu unserer neu positionierten Marke, unserem neuen strategischen Konzept befragen werden?

«Neugier impliziert konzeptionelles Denken bis hin zur Wissenschaftlichkeit.»

Und, wenn wir sauber arbeiten und keinen Blindflug veranstalten wollen, fragen wir uns etwas später und hoffentlich öfters, am besten regelmäßig: Kommen wir dorthin? Funktioniert die Strategie, erreichen wir die Zielgruppe, wird die Botschaft verstanden. Wiederum Marktforschung, Tracking, Panels, falls möglich toute la Boutique. Also einmal mehr: Show me the data. Und wenn wir kein Konzern, sondern ein KMU sind, dann sprechen wir einfach mal mit den wichtigen Kunden, regelmäßig, als Referenz. Indizien statt Beweise, aber auch schon mal gut.

Damit das klar ist: Wir paraphilosophieren hier im Kontext «Marketing und Immobilien»: Ein Daten-Tracking für eine neue Eiscreme weist weniger Komplexitäten auf als ein mittelgroßes Immobilienprojekt, und sei dies alleine wegen der Unterschiede

Once we have established where we are and why this is the case, we pose the next simple question: Where could we be? Realistically speaking, with a sense of proportion, not expecting a bowl of cherries, it is a strengths and weaknesses analysis in search of opportunities and potential risks. Where could we realistically be if we ultimately did everything right?

And now for the most important of our five magic strategy questions: How do we get there? What do we have to do, to stop, to change, where to invest, where to get support. Of course the question about the how and where to represents the strategic core question, the quintessence, the all-or-nothing. In other words – what will our target group reply, if we wake it up at 3 am and ask about our newly positioned brand or our new strategic concept?

"Curiosity implies conceptual thinking all the way up to being scientific."

If we work correctly and do not want to go on a wild-goose chase, we ask ourselves a little later and hopefully frequently, preferably regularly: Are we getting there? Is the strategy working, are we reaching the target group, is the message understood? Once again through market research, tracking, panels, the entire kit and caboodle, if possible. Thus once more: Show me the data. And if we are not a group of companies, but a small or medium-sized enterprise we simply talk to the key customers regularly as a reference. Indications instead of evidence, but acceptable.

Just to make things clear – we are semi-philosophizing here within the context of "marketing and real estate." Data tracking for a new brand of ice cream is less complex than for a medium-sized real estate project if only due to the different time line durations. Add to that the elements of public space, visibility, cultural change, design trends.

in der Länge der Zeitachsen. Plus öffentlicher Raum, Einsehbarkeit, kultureller Wandel, Designtrends.

Cut!

Wir halten fest: Marketers sind erstens Zielgruppenversteher, zweitens Ideenentwickler für das «Habenwollen» seitens der Zielgruppe und drittens Strategiefragensteller, siehe oben.

Die Strategie ist letztendlich das «Was». Die Umsetzung das «Wie». Das Konzept das «Waswie». Dieses müssen wir immer präzise unterscheiden. Das «Was» ist die Positionierung und also der Inhalt. Das «Wie» hingegen ist die Form, die Umsetzung, die Dramatisierung.

So weit, so klar.

Marketing = Strategie + Idee. Ist ja leicht. Die Strategie muss klar, fokussiert und kraftvoll sein und gerne um etwas positiv Irritierendes angereichert – «Disruption» heißt das Modewort, das wir hier aber möglichst vermeiden wollen. Zu abgelutscht. Zeitgeistiges Marketing braucht also unbedingt einen positiven kleinen Schock: «Huch, das hätte ich so nicht erwartet.» Eine klare und fassbare Strategie zu haben ist ja kein Selbstzweck, sondern soll maximal helfen, die Zielgruppe zu erkennen, sie zu erreichen und ihre Bedürfnisse ideal zu befriedigen. «Zielgruppe» klingt blöd, oder? Die Gruppe, auf die wir zielen… das hat was Martialisches. Typisch Männersprache. Marketing trieft nur so von derartigen Begriffen, zum Beispiel «Marktpenetration» (sic!) oder eben «Bedürfnisbefriedigung». Marketing ist immer noch Männerdomäne, auch darum die etwas affige Sprache. Aber zum Glück drängen immer mehr Frauen ins Marketinghaus, weibliche Werte werden zunehmend relevant. Emotionalität, Harmonie und Einfühlung sind keine vermeintliche Schwäche mehr, au contraire.

Und nun auf direktem Weg zur ewigen Frage des Marketings – und allenfalls des Lebens: Können Bedürfnisse geschaffen werden oder müssen sie bereits latent vorhanden sein und wer-

Cut!

We recapitulate: Marketers are firstly target group savvy, secondly develop concepts to create a "want to own" urge in the target group, and thirdly adept at posing strategic questions, see above.

The strategy constitutes the "what." The implementation constitutes the "how." The concept constitutes the "what how." We must always precisely distinguish this. The "what" is the positioning, i.e. the content. The "how" on the other hand is the form, the implementation, the dramatization.

So far, so clear.

Marketing = strategy + idea. That's easy. The strategy must be clear, focused and powerful and often enhanced by a positively irritating concept – "disruption" is the trendy word for this, which we would rather avoid here. Too worn out. Contemporary marketing therefore necessarily needs a minor positive shock – "Oops, I wasn't expecting that." Having a clear and defined strategy is not an end in itself but intends to maximally support recognizing, reaching and ideally fulfilling the needs of target groups. "Target group" sounds rather stupid, doesn't it? The group that is our target… sounds rather martial. Typical male language. Marketing is filled with such terms, for example "market penetration" (sic!) or "need satisfaction." Marketing is still a male dominated domain, which explains the rather apish language. Luckily, more and more women are entering marketing and feminine values are increasingly becoming relevant. Emotionality, harmony and empathy are no longer perceived as weaknesses, rather the contrary.

And now we proceed directly to the eternal question of marketing – and possibly even life: Can needs be created or do they have to be present in a latent state and are therefore only be "brought to life" by marketing? Did anyone have a latent need for an iPhone? There were enough smartphones around, Nokia was big in the game, so was Motorola, Blackberry very much so

den also durch das Marketing «wachgeküsst»? Hatte irgendjemand ein latentes Bedürfnis nach einem iPhone? Smartphones gab es genug, Nokia war fett am Ball, Motorola auch, Blackberry sehr und niemand außer den evangelisierten Apple-Fans hatte auf ein Telefon aus Cupertino gewartet. Gab es ein latentes Bedürfnis nach Tamagotchis? Nach Pokémon Go? Natürlich nicht. Selbstverständlich aber können Bedürfnisse abgerufen werden, ihre Erdung finden sie immer irgendwo auf der Pyramide der Bedürfnisse des guten alten Maslow. Die Tamagotchis lassen sich an das Bedürfnis des Kümmerns binden sowie einen gewissen sozialen Kontext erkennen.

too, and no one except for die-hard Apple fans was waiting for a telephone from Cupertino. Was there a latent need for Tamagotchis? For Pokémon Go? Of course not. However, it goes without saying that needs can be traced, they always boil down to some place on good old Maslow's hierarchy of needs. Tamagotchis can be linked to the need for caring in combination with a certain social context.

We can generally always refer to the basic needs (eating, drinking, sleeping, and sex), safety is a huge need that can accommodate almost everything. From a marketing point of view,

DIE BEDÜRFNISPYRAMIDE NACH ABRAHAM MASLOW
ABRAHAM MASLOW'S HIERARCHY OF NEEDS

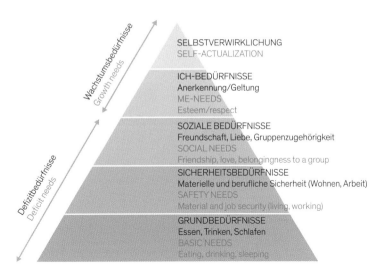

Auf die Grundbedürfnisse (Essen, Trinken, Schlafen und Sex) können wir uns in der Regel immer beziehen, Sicherheit ist ein Riesenbedürfnis in das fast alles gepackt werden kann. Soziale Bedürfnisse sind aus Marketingsicht geradezu eine selbsterfüllende Prophezeiung (Facebook und Tinder bis hin zu «Akademiker und Singles mit Niveau»). Die Maslowschen Individualbedürfnisse wie Stärke, Erfolg und insbesondere

social needs are practically a self-fulfilling prophecy (Facebook and Tinder up to online dating services). The individual needs according to Maslow, such as power, success and especially independence and freedom are also an open door for marketers. The needs for esteem, prestige and importance are passive components of self-esteem because other people fulfill them for us, and they are a virtual dream world for the creation of

Ohne Markierung kein Wiedererkennen – funktioniert bei Produkten ebenso gut wie bei Rindern

Without labeling no recognition – this applies to products the same as for cattle

Unabhängigkeit und Freiheit sind für Marketers ebenfalls ein offenes Scheunentor. Die Wünsche nach Ansehen, Prestige und Wichtigkeit sind passive Komponenten der Selbstachtung, weil andere Menschen diese für uns erfüllen; für die Kreation von Produkten und Dienstleistungen stellen diese geradezu eine Traumwelt dar. Und wie haben wir es mit den Bedürfnissen nach Selbstverwirklichung und gar mit den Luxusbedürfnissen? Der marketingstrategische Placebo-Effekt lässt grüßen.

Ach ja, die ewige Frage nach dem Leben, dem Universum und dem ganzen Rest. Wir könnten zynisch sein und (Show-me-the-data) sagen: 42. Tun wir aber nicht.

Also ja, Bedürfnisse können geschaffen werden (Manager mit Midlife-Crisis fährt am Wochenende Harley-Davidson). Und ja, Bedürfnisse sind im weiteren Sinne im Kontext der Sozialisierung in unserer postmodernen Welt des Konsums bereits vorhanden beziehungsweise erlernt. Ein Neugeborenes hat gemäß Maslow ein paar Grundbedürfnisse. Essen, Trinken, Schlafen, ganz viel Schlafen und eben auch Stoffe ausscheiden (terminus technicus: Exkretion), that's it. Alles andere kommt später dazu. Sicherheit. Aufmerksamkeit. Zuneigung. Selbstwert. Wie gesagt, Sozialisierung. Und die ist an der Goldküste des Zürichsees eben anders als im sozial schwachen Stadtquartier Zürich Seebach. Logo.

Ein zweites Standbein einer schneidigen Vermarktung ist die Markierung, neudeutsch «Branding», was sich vom Brandzeichen ableitet, also die Kennzeichnung von Herdenvieh. In den unendlichen Weiten der Steppen Nordamerikas wurden die umherziehenden Rinder gebrandmarkt, um sie später, von Cowboys eingefangen, dem richtigen Besitzer zuordnen zu können. Wenn wir im Marketing erfolgreich sein wollen, brauchen wir nicht nur ein tolles Produkt oder eine ebensolche Dienstleistung (oder beides), sondern ebenso eine starke Marke und eine strategisch klare Markengestaltung, alles gemäß unserer integrierten Strategie (siehe oben), was wir letztendlich als Positionierung bezeichnen: Das Vorstellungsbild in den Köpfen der Zielgruppe. Das ist durchaus sehr

products and services. And what about the needs for self-actualization or even the luxury needs? With compliments by the marketing strategy placebo effect.

Oh yes, the eternal question about life, the universe, and everything else. We could be cynical and (show me the data) say: 42. But we won't.

Ok then yes, needs can be created (see a manager going through a midlife crisis riding a Harley Davidson on the weekend). And yes, in the extended sense within the context of socialization in our post-modern world of consumption needs are already present or previously learned. According to Maslow, a newborn has a few basic needs. Eating, drinking, sleeping, lots of sleeping, and secreting substances (technical term: excretion), that's it. Everything else is added later. Safety. Attention. Affection. Self worth. As stated earlier, socialization. This takes a different form on the Goldcoast of Lake Zurich than in the socially weak city quarter of Zurich Seebach. Naturally.

A second pillar of spirited marketing is so-called branding, which is derived from the brands applied to mark cattle. On the endless prairies of North America, roaming cattle was branded to allocate it to the proper owners when it was caught later by cowboys. If we want to be successful in marketing, we not only need a great product or service (or both) but also an equally powerful brand and a strategically clear brand design, all in line with our integrated strategy (see above), which we ultimately describe as positioning the image in the heads of the target group. This is certainly very important. To a luxury car brand it is highly relevant to know what the rich and beautiful in Monte Carlo think, feel and know about the brand. Not what people in the Bümpliz quarter of Berne, Switzerland think. The term image is derived as a liberal interpretation of Sigmund Freud (coupled with a bit of C. G. Jung) from the Latin term Imago ("imagine").

It goes without saying that branding is part of the image. Brands such as Apple and Google are cool. They are conspicuous, evoke emotions, have a brand concept, motivate the desire to

wichtig, für eine Luxusautomarke ist es hoch relevant, was die Schönen und Reichen in Monte Carlo über die Marke denken, fühlen und wissen. Nicht, was die Leute in Bern Bümpliz meinen. Dieses Vorstellungsbild bezeichnen wir frei nach Sigmund Freud (und ein bisschen C. G. Jung) als (lat.) Imago («stelle dir vor») und verneudeutscht eben Image.

Selbstverständlich ist das Branding Teil des Images. Brands (vulgo: Marken) wie Apple und Google sind cool. Sie fallen auf, wecken Emotionen, haben eine Markenidee, motivieren zum Habenwollen, vermitteln immer klar die Markenwerte und sind sehr, sehr einprägsam. Schwache Marken haben das alles nicht. Oder jeweils nur ein bisschen. Und das reicht eben nicht, ein bisschen schwanger geht auch nicht. Kodak. Nokia. Bümpliz.

Eine starke Marke können wir sofort verstehen, inhaltlich wie formal. Was und wie. Ein wichtiger Bestandteil der Markenführung kann die physische Inszenierung der Marke im Raum darstellen. Wie sieht der sogenannte Point of Sale (Verkaufsort) vor Ort aus, wo befindet er sich, wie sieht die architektonische Umsetzung aus? Bleiben wir bei der Übermarke Apple: Der Store an der Fifth Avenue in NYC ist die fünft meist fotografierte Sehenswürdigkeit New Yorks. Vor der Brooklyn Bridge, vor der Freiheitsstatue.

Dieses ist keine «Weisheit» aus irgendeinem Blog, sondern die hochwissenschaftliche Erkenntnis einer breit angelegten Studie basierend auf Fotografien auf der Plattform Flickr, welche an der renommierten Cornell Universität durchgeführt wurde.

«Die Markierung beziehungsweise Kennzeichnung des Etwas nennen wir Branding und ist integrierter Bestandteil einer starken Markenstrategie.»

Also, nochmals und von vorne. Marketing ist das Vermarkten von etwas über die Ansprache virulenter Bedürfnisse der Zielgruppe. Die Markierung beziehungsweise Kennzeichnung des

own, always clearly convey the brand values, and are very very memorable. Weak brands have none of these attributes. Or only a little of each. But this is not enough, just like a little pregnant is also not possible. Kodak. Nokia. Bümpliz.

We can immediately comprehend a powerful brand in terms of content and form. What and how. The physical presentation of the brand can be an important component of brand management. What does the so-called point of sale (sales location) look like, where is it, what is its architectural implementation? Let's stay with the super brand Apple: Its store on Fifth Avenue in NYC is the city's fifth most photographed landmark. Beating the Brooklyn Bridge and the Statue of Liberty.

This is not a piece of "wisdom" from some obscure blog, but actually the highly scientific outcome of a large-scale study of photographs posted on the Flickr platform, carried out by the renowned Cornell University.

"The marking or labeling of something is called branding and is an integral component of a powerful marketing strategy."

Ok, let's take it again from the top. Marketing is the promotion of something by addressing the viral needs of the target group. The marking or labeling of something is called branding and is an integral component of a powerful marketing strategy. Branding should reflect and enhance the strategy. See Chanel, see Virgin, see GoPro.

The creation of a brand reflects the respective self-conception and the market conception of those who create it. The self-conception refers to the mission of the brand that is designed, its inner convictions and its attitude towards things. In 1926, Messrs. Gabrielsson and Larson founded Volvo (Latin for "I roll," yes this is how beautiful branding can be) with a focus on the protection of passengers, especially child safety.

Starke Marke, starke Inszenierung: der Apple Store an der Fifth Avenue in New York

Strong brand, strong staging – the Apple Store on Fifth Avenue in New York

Etwas nennen wir Branding und ist integrierter Bestandteil einer starken Markenstrategie. Das Branding sollte die Strategie reflektieren und verstärken. Siehe Chanel, siehe Virgin, siehe GoPro.

Die Kreation einer Marke reflektiert das jeweilige Selbstverständnis und das Marktverständnis derer, die die Marke gestalten. Das Selbstverständnis bezieht sich auf die Mission der zu gestaltenden Marke, ihrer inneren Überzeugung, ihrer Haltung zu den Dingen. Die Herren Gabrielsson und Larson gründeten 1926 Volvo (lat. «ich rolle», ja, ja, so schön kann Branding sein) mit Fokus auf dem Insassenschutz, insbesondere der Kindersicherheit.

Larry Page und Sergey Brin bauten eine Suchmaschine, die nichts Böses will («don't be evil»). Den Namen entlehnten sie der höheren Mathematik (Googol = zehn Sexdezilliarden = sehr, sehr große Zahl), die Farben im Logo wurden von Lego mehr als nur inspiriert, weil die beiden übrigens Lego-Fans waren und sind. Und nein, zu Apple sagen wir hier jetzt nichts. Das ist, was die Marke will. Ihre Idee, ihr vermitteltes Lebensgefühl, ihre Attitude.

Das Marktverständnis bezieht sich auf die Hausaufgaben, die zur Etablierung einer neuen Marke gemacht wurden – oder nicht: Wo sind wir, warum, was wäre…, Sie wissen schon. Und wenn der Markt dechiffriert, analysiert, kategorisiert und strukturiert ist und die eigene Marke richtig zugeordnet wird, dann lässt sich die Marke im Markt positionieren, siehe oben: Positionierung gleich möglichst klare, trennscharfe und einzigartige Vorstellung in den Köpfen und in den Herzen der Zielgruppe. Das ist, was die Marke kann. Im Kontext des Wettbewerbes, realistisch aber mit Verve.

Architektur kann ein starkes Marketinginstrument sein (siehe Apple Stores, siehe BMW-Vierzylinder München, siehe Centre Pompidou Paris). Mit Betonung auf kann, oft wirkt die Kunst des Bauens überfordert und bleibt beliebig, weil sie die Markenstrategie bestenfalls skizziert. Falls überhaupt.

Larry Page and Sergey Brin built a search engine that has good intentions ("don't be evil"). They derived its name from higher mathematics (Googol = ten sexdecilliard = a very very large number), the colors of the logo were more than inspired by Lego because both founders were and continue to be Lego fans. And no, we will not go into Apple here. This is what the brand wants. Its idea, its conveyed lifestyle, its attitude.

The market conception refers to the homework that was conducted for the establishment of a new brand – or not: where are we, why, what if,… you know what we mean. Once the market has been decoded, analyzed, categorized and structured, and the own brand has been correctly allocated, the brand can be positioned on the market, see above: positioning equals a preferably clear, distinguished and unique image in the heads and hearts of the target group. That is what a brand can do. Within the context of the competition, realistic but with verve.

Architecture can be a powerful marketing tool (see Apple Stores, see the BMW "four cylinder" headquarters in Munich, or the Centre Pompidou in Paris). We deliberately used the term can, as the art of architecture is often overtaxed and remains random because the marketing strategy sketches it vaguely at best. If at all.

On the other hand, marketing can be a razor-sharp tool of architecture, if it is understood correctly (see above) and properly dosed.

Real estate marketing should be staged and sometimes even dramatized on three dimensions of the juxtaposition of self-conception and market conception. These dimensions consist of the physical and spatial location of a project, the lifestyle of the target group of the construction project (inside-out), and the esthetic interaction with the constructed space, i.e. the architecture.

Last but not least, love it or leave it – we know that polarization is very good in the marketing context. If your brand is hated

Marketing hingegen kann ein messerscharfes Instrument der Architektur sein, richtig verstanden (vgl. oben) und richtig dosiert.

Immobilienmarketing sollte jeweils auf drei Dimensionen im Spannungsfeld des Selbstverständnisses und des Marktverständnisses inszeniert oder bisweilen sogar dramatisiert werden. Diese Dimensionen umfassen die physische und räumliche Lage eines Projektes, den Lifestyle der Zielgruppe des Projektes (Inside-Out) und die ästhetische Auseinandersetzung mit dem gebauten Raum, vulgo der Architektur.

Zu Guter letzt, love it or leave it: Wir wissen, dass Polarisieren im Marketing sehr gut ist. Wenn deine Marke geliebt und gehasst wird, dann macht sie vieles richtig. Die Liebhaber sind Fans, Markenbotschafter, Storyteller. Die Hasser projizieren Neid und Missgunst, was toll ist. Aufmerksamkeit überall. Das Gegenteil ist: «ja, nett». Das ist tödlich im Wettbewerb.

and loved then it is doing a good job. The lovers are fans, brand ambassadors, storytellers. The haters project envy and resentment, which is great. Attention everywhere. The opposite would be: "Yes, nice." This is deadly in the competitive sense.

PROZESS
PROCESS

MARKEN MIT SEELE

Im Fokus unserer Marketingstrategien steht immer der Mensch mit seinen Bedürfnissen, mit seinen Werten und Ansprüchen – mit seiner ganzen Persönlichkeit. Unabhängig davon, ob es sich bei der zu verkaufenden Immobilie um ein exklusives Dreifamilienhaus am Zürichberg oder eine zukunftsorientierte Minergie-Siedlung am Bodensee mit über 160 Wohnungen handelt: Der Ausgangspunkt des Immobilienmarketings ist immer der potenzielle Käufer oder Mieter.

«Im Fokus unserer Marketingstrategien steht immer der Mensch.»

Immobilienmarketing-Projekte haben alle eines gemeinsam: Sie kreieren Marken auf Zeit. Und unsere Aufgabe als Marketer ist es, diese mit einer Seele zu füllen. Wobei die Marke am einen oder anderen Ort auch zum Synonym der postalischen Adresse werden kann und die Frage nach dem «wo wohnst du» mit: im Atrium oder im Witenzelg beantwortet wird. Übergeordnetes Ziel ist jedoch primär eine effiziente Vermarktung – mit hohem Identifikationspotenzial, einer klaren und adäquaten Kommunikation sowie einer hoch professionellen Vermarktung. Die durchschnittliche Projektdauer beträgt circa 24 Monate, ab Markenlancierung bis Ende der Vermarktung beziehungsweise dem Zeitpunkt der Bezugsbereitschaft. In dieser Zeit müssen die eingesetzten Maßnahmen Bekanntheit aufbauen, Vertrauen gewinnen und Verkäufe oder Vermietungen generieren. Zum Erfolg verdammt, denn am Schluss zählen keine Emotionen, sondern Zahlen.

SPIELERISCHE ANALYSE

Im Rahmen der persönlichkeitsfokussierten Analyse nähern wir uns auf spielerische wie systematische Weise den kommunikationsrelevanten Schwerpunkten – im Optimalfall in enger Zusammenarbeit mit der Bauherrschaft, den Projektentwicklern, den Architekten und den Immobilienvermarktern. Das Resultat spiegelt zielgenau die verschiedenen Vorgaben und Werte der Anspruchsgruppen wider und erzeugt eine verbindliche Basis für

BRANDS WITH A SOUL

The focus of our marketing strategies is always on human beings with their needs, values and expectations – their entire personality. Regardless of whether the real estate for sale consists of an exclusive three-family house near Zürichberg, Zurich or a futuristic Minergie estate near Lake Constance with over 160 apartments – real estate marketing is always based on the potential buyer or tenant.

"The focus of our marketing strategies is always on human beings."

Real estate marketing projects all have one thing in common – they create brands for a specific time period. Our duty as marketers is to fill this brand with a soul. Within this process the brand can also become synonymous for the postal address and the question of "where do you live" is answered by: in the Atrium or in Witenzelg. The basic aim, however, is efficient marketing with high identification potential, clear and adequate communication, and highly professional marketing. The average project duration is around 24 months, from the launch of the brand to the end of marketing or the time the building is ready for occupancy. Within this period of time the applied measures must create awareness, gain trust and generate sales or lease agreements. Condemned to succeed, because at the end of the day it is about figures and not about emotions.

PLAYFUL ANALYSIS

Within the scope of the personality-focused analysis we playfully and systematically approach the communication-relevant themes – preferably in close cooperation with the owners, the project developers, architects, and real estate marketers. The outcome precisely reflects the various prerequisites and values of the stakeholders and creates a solid foundation for the real estate marketing strategy. We base our work on three basic value factors: location, lifestyle, and architecture. These are filled with the project-specific attributes and weighted according to their relevance. As a result, only factors that have singular char-

die Immobilienmarketing-Strategie. Dabei arbeiten wir mit drei grundlegenden Wertefaktoren: Lage, Lifestyle und Architektur. Diese werden mit den projektspezifischen Attributen gefüllt und nach Relevanz gewichtet. So bieten sich für die anschließende Vermarktung im Rahmen der drei Faktoren primär jene an, welche einzigartige Ausprägungen aufweisen – die Reduktion auf die kommunikationsrelevanten uniquen Merkmale. Zur Veranschaulichung nachstehend ein Anwendungsbeispiel:

acteristics are primarily chosen for the subsequent marketing – through reduction to the communication-relevant unique features. To illustrate, we present an application example below:

DAS LAGE-LIFESTYLE-ARCHITEKTUR-MODELL VON FELIX PARTNER
THE LOCATION-LIFESTYLE-ARCHITECTURE MODEL OF FELIX PARTNER

A: Lage

Zentral gelegen, gute Verbindungen, Grenze Stadt und Land, Naherholungsraum, schnell überall, Natur direkt vor der Haustür, qualitativ gewachsener Ort, tiefe Steuerbelastung etc.

B: Lifestyle

Angebot der Stadt liegt zu Füßen (gute Anbindung), breit gefächertes Angebot an Freizeit- und Outdooraktivitäten, gut ausgebautes Vereinswesen.

C: Architektur

Hoher Standard, modern, eigenständig und doch ins Gesamtbild passend.

Fazit

Hervorstechende Merkmale sind hier vor allem bei der Lage zu finden und gehen in Richtung Verkehrsanbindung, Standortqualität, Erholungsraum vor der Haustür, kurze Wege, tiefe Steuern.

A: Location

Centrally located, good traffic infrastructure, on the border between city and countryside, recreational facilities within easy reach, quick access everywhere, nature at the doorstep, qualitatively grown community, low tax burden, etc.

B: Lifestyle

All offers of the city accessible (good traffic connection), wide range of leisure and outdoor activities, good local club and public life structure.

C: Architecture

High standard, modern, independent yet incorporated into the overall structure.

Conclusion

Characteristic features are primarily present in the location and tend towards traffic connection, location quality, leisure area at the doorstep, short connections, low taxes.

PROZESSE IMPLEMENTIEREN

Prozesse definieren und implementieren, klare Arbeitsabläufe einrichten und Strukturen bilden sind das A und O eines erfolgreichen Projektmanagements. Auch bei uns. Trotz aller kreativen Freiheit und allem interdisziplinären Denken. Oder vielleicht gerade deshalb. Unsere Abläufe sind im Grundsatz klassisch aufgebaut, mit einzelnen Positionen, die uns in der Gesamtbetrachtung besonders wichtig sind.

IMPLEMENTING PROCESSES

Defining and implementing processes, setting up clear work processes and creating structures are the essence of successful project management. Also for us. Despite all creative liberties and interdisciplinary thinking. Or maybe because of that. Basically, our processes are set up classically with individual points that are especially important to us in the overall consideration.

DAS PROZESSMODELL DES IMMOBILIENMARKETINGS VON FELIX PARTNER
THE PROCESS MODEL OF REAL ESTATE MARKETING OF FELIX PARTNER

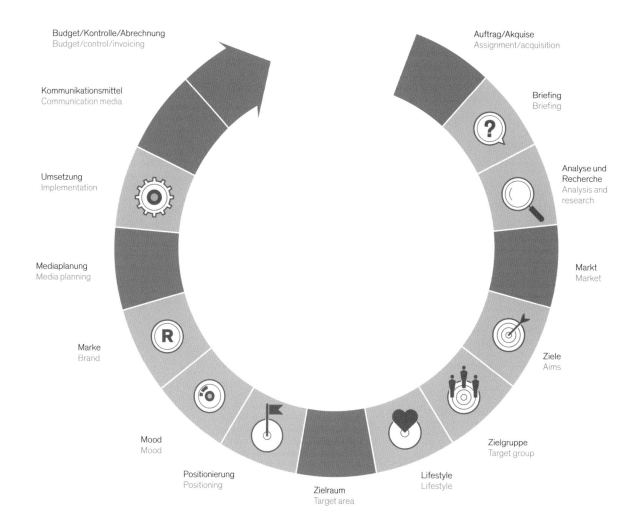

Budget/Kontrolle/Abrechnung
Budget/control/invoicing

Kommunikationsmittel
Communication media

Umsetzung
Implementation

Mediaplanung
Media planning

Marke
Brand

Mood
Mood

Positionierung
Positioning

Zielraum
Target area

Lifestyle
Lifestyle

Zielgruppe
Target group

Ziele
Aims

Markt
Market

Analyse und Recherche
Analysis and research

Briefing
Briefing

Auftrag/Akquise
Assignment/acquisition

Briefing

Der Start eines jeden Projekts beginnt mit dem Briefing vom Kunden. Dieses wird gründlich studiert und hinterfragt. Durch das Hinterfragen ergeben sich meist offene Punkte, die geklärt werden müssen und in unserem Rebriefing enden. So haben wir die Gewähr, auf der bestmöglichen Ausgangslage zu arbeiten und über alle Informationen, soweit vorhanden, zu verfügen.

Analyse und Recherche

Alle Informationen werden zerlegt und mit den jeweiligen internen Fachstellen geprüft. Wo nötig (so gut wie immer), wird zusätzlich am Ort des Bauvorhabens recherchiert: Was ist besonders dort, wie sieht es wirtschaftlich und politisch aus, gibt es ein Konkurrenzumfeld, wie ist die Lage einzustufen, für welche Menschen eignet es sich, wie hoch ist die Kaufkraft der Umgebung, ist das geplante Projekt dort, so wie angedacht, sinnvoll umsetzbar? Viele Fragen führen zu vielen Antworten und zu viel Wissen. Und Wissen ist Mehrwert. Ergänzend ziehen wir zu unseren eigenen Recherchen aktuelle Marktdaten und wissenschaftliche Erkenntnisse aus verschiedenen Bereichen hinzu – zum Beispiel aktuelle Zielgruppen-Milieu-Analysen oder Standort- und Marktanalysen, um eine möglichst lückenlose Datenbasis für die strategischen Entscheide zur Verfügung zu haben. Aus dieser Fülle an gesammelten Informationen erarbeiten wir im Anschluss als Basis zur Weiterarbeit eine Verdichtung – wir nennen es die Essenz – und formulieren daraus unseren Kerngedanken, der Teil jedes Projekts ist.

Ziele

Die genaue Definition der Ziele ist für uns matchentscheidend und für eine klare Strategie unabdingbar. Denn nur so wissen wir, mit welchen Schwerpunkten wir den Mitteleinsatz gestalten müssen und welche Phase in welchem Zeitabschnitt zum Tragen kommt. Wenn es ein Ziel ist, bis zum Rohbau die Hälfte aller Einheiten zu verkaufen, um die weitere Finanzierung zu sichern, agieren wir anders, als wenn die Gelder bereits gesprochen sind und auf die Bezugsbereitschaft die ersten Verkäufe getätigt werden müssen.

Briefing

Each project begins with the briefing by the customer. We carefully study and examine it. The examination usually results in some unresolved issues that must be clarified and end up in our rebriefing. This guarantees us that we are commencing work from the best possible starting position and that we have all available information.

Analysis and research

All information is dissected and examined by the respective internal specialized departments. If required (practically every time) we additionally research on location at the intended construction site – what makes it special, what is the economic and political situation, is there a competitive environment, how can the location be assessed, for which persons is it suitable, what is the buying power of the area, can the planned project be feasibly implemented as intended? Many questions result in many answers and plenty of knowledge. And knowledge is added value. We complement our own research by current market data and scientific findings from various areas, for example current target group milieu analyses or location and market analyses to obtain a complete as possible data basis for strategic decisions. We then condense the wealth of collected information into what we call the essence that constitutes the basis for our subsequent work, and from which we formulate our core concept that is part of each of our projects.

Aims

A precise definition of aims is of key importance to us and essential to a clear strategy. This is the only way for us to determine what to focus the employed means on and which phase plays a role during which time segment. If the aim is to sell half of all units by the time of the completion of the shell of the building to secure further financing, we operate differently than when the funds are already secured and sales must only be initiated once the structural work is completed.

Zielgruppe

Das klare Wissen, an wen wir uns richten, ist uns ebenso wichtig wie die Verkaufsziele selbst. Der Zielgruppe kommt strategische Bedeutung zu, denn letztlich erhoffen wir uns bei ihr die größten Chancen auf einen erfolgreichen Verkauf oder eine Vermietung. Ergo muss alles aufeinander abgestimmt sein. Das neue Umfeld muss genauso passen wie die Architektur, die Ausstattung, die Grundrisse oder das Preisgefüge. Wir müssen die Bedürfnisse der potenziellen Käufer und Mieter kennen und objektiv beurteilen. Unsere Nähe zu den Architekten, zur Bauherrschaft und zum Immobilienmakler verschafft uns diesbezüglich einen großen Vorteil. Und wir entdecken unsere Zielgruppe bis ins Detail, beschreiben sie, setzen uns mit ihren Lebensphasen auseinander und identifizieren uns mit ihr. Damit gerade die Identifikation etwas einfacher fällt, nehmen wir uns einen Menschen aus der Zielgruppe heraus, geben ihm einen Namen, einen Beruf, eine Herkunft, ein Leben und sprechen darüber. Diese Beschreibung wird für uns zum verbalen, emotionalen Moodboard, zu dem sich jeder intern am Projekt Beteiligte ein eigenes, subjektives Bild machen kann. Und sie dient der Reflektion zu allem, was wir an Gedankenspielen durchgehen. So sehen wir sehr schnell, ob etwas passt, ob es die richtigen Bedürfnisse abdeckt, die definierten Wunschvorstellungen erfüllt und dem Lifestyle nahe kommt oder eben nicht. Und was ganz wichtig ist: Durch diese Personifizierung nehmen wir unsere Zielgruppe ernst.

Target group

The clear knowledge of who we are addressing is as important to us as the sales targets themselves. The target group has a strategic importance as, after all, we expect it to offer the greatest chances of successful sales or rental agreements. Therefore, everything must be well coordinated. The new environment must be suitable along with the architecture, the finishing, the layouts and the price range. We must know the needs of potential buyers and tenants and evaluate them objectively. Our close association with the architects, owners and real estate agents gives us a significant advantage in this regard. We also explore the members of our target group to the minutest detail, describe them, examine their life phases and identify with them. To make identification a little easier, we select an individual of the target group, give him or her a name, a vocation, a background, and a life and discuss them. This description serves us as a verbal emotional mood board for which everyone who is internally involved in the project can create their own subjective image. It also serves as a reflection of everything we brainstorm. This allows us to quickly discover if something is right, if it fulfills the right needs and defined expectations and matches the lifestyle or not. And a very important aspect: this personification allows us to take our target group seriously.

Lifestyle

Innerhalb der Zielgruppe bilden wir homogene Cluster und beschreiben zu jedem Cluster eine mögliche Persönlichkeit. Wie er oder sie aussieht, welchen Lifestyle er oder sie pflegt, welchen Beruf die Person ausübt und wie sie ihre Freizeit gestaltet oder welche Gewohnheiten sie hat. Dazu suchen wir passende Bilder, schaffen eine komplette Persönlichkeit und prüfen, ob das Resultat zum Angebot passt. So erhalten wir Gewissheit darüber, ob das Angebot die Bedürfnisse potenzieller Kunden abdeckt.

Lifestyle

We create homogenous clusters within the target group and describe a possible personality for each cluster. What he or she looks like, what his or her lifestyle, job and leisure activities are, as well as any habits and preferences. We look for suitable images, create a complete personality, and check whether the result matches the offer. This confirms to us whether the offer fulfils the needs of potential customers.

Positionierung

Jede Marke sollte Stärken und Qualitäten in sich tragen und für eine klare Zielgruppe sowie geografisch definiert sein. Idealerweise grenzt sie sich auch zu den Mitbewerbern ab und zeichnet sich durch Alleinstellungsmerkmale aus. So sehen wir das. Nimmt man eine der zahlreichen Begriffsdefinitionen, so gehen diese mit unterschiedlichen Formulierungen in dieselbe Richtung. Hier ein Beispiel aus dem Wirtschaftslexikon: «Ziel der Positionierung – als einer Strategie – ist es, den Abstand (Distanz) zwischen den von den potenziellen Interessenten wahrgenommenen Eigenschaften eines Objektes und den von ihnen für ideal betrachteten Ausprägungen der Objekteigenschaften zu minimieren. Soll ein neues Objekt in den Markt eingeführt werden, so ist das Ziel, das Objekt so zu gestalten, dass es möglichst den Idealvorstellungen der potenziellen Käufer (Idealprodukt) entspricht.» Erarbeitet wird die Positionierung bei uns über das Markensteuerrad (siehe Abbildung). Wir beschreiben sehr klar und in Stichworten die vier Quadranten Markennutzen, Markenkompetenz, Markentonalität und Markenbild und leiten daraus dann eine stimmige Aussage ab, die für die angestrebte Zielgruppe relevant ist.

Positioning

Each brand should contain strengths and qualities. It should be defined geographically and for a clear target group. Ideally, it defines potential distinction areas from our competitors and develops unique selling points. This is our take on things. If one looks at the many definitions of positioning, they all contain the same basic information stated in different ways. Following is a rough translation of the entry in a German business dictionary: The aim of positioning as a strategy is to minimize the discrepancy between the properties of an object as perceived by potentially interested parties and the object characteristics that are perceived as ideal by them. Should a new object be introduced to the market then the aim is to design the object in such a way that it complies as much as possible with the concept of an ideal product held by the potential buyers. We develop the positioning via the brand management steering wheel (see illustration). We describe very clearly and in key points the four quadrants of brand benefits, brand competence, brand tonality and brand image to derive a coherent statement that is relevant to the desired target group.

DAS POSITIONIERUNGSMODELL FÜR DIE MARKENARBEIT VON FELIX PARTNER
THE POSITIONING MODEL FOR THE BRAND DEVELOPMENT OF FELIX PARTNER

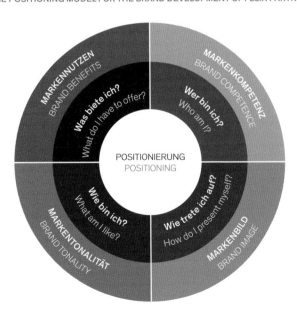

LAGE
LOCATION

OBJEKTE
OBJECTS

FARBEN
COLORS

Strategisches Moodboard als Basis für die Weiterarbeit in der Umsetzung
Strategic mood board as the basis for subsequent implementation work

Mood

Bevor wir vom strategisch-konzeptionellen in den kreativen Prozess übergehen, erstellen wir Moodboards, um ein noch besseres, intensiveres und klareres Gefühl für die Zielgruppe, das Projektumfeld sowie die Wohn- und Lebensgewohnheiten zu erhalten. Moodboards sind Bildcollagen von Stimmungen, Objekten, Orten, Pflanzen, Fortbewegungsmitteln, Menschen, Gewässern, Farben, Fotostilen etc. Das Ergebnis verwenden wir einerseits als visuell orientierte Grundlage für die Diskussion mit dem Kunden, denn Bilder sagen oft mehr als viele Worte und an Worten bleibt man oft hängen. Andererseits ist es für uns die Basis zur Weiterarbeit in der Kreativphase. Wie bei der Personenbeschreibung innerhalb der Zielgruppe können wir in der internen Zusammenarbeit das Moodboard jederzeit als Referenz heranziehen und prüfen, ob eine Umsetzung in die passende Richtung geht, ob die Bildwelt stimmig ist, ob zentrale Punkte hervorgehoben sind.

Marke

Aufbauend auf die Positionierung, die Zielgruppenpersönlichkeiten, die Moodboards und die umfassenden Analysedaten kreieren wir die Leitidee, auf der Name, Claim, Basisargumentation sowie Bild- und Farbwelten der Marke auf Zeit aufbauen, wie sie schlussendlich in der Kommunikation nach außen angewendet wird. Dazu gehören auch die zielgruppengenaue und budgetadäquate Wahl der Kommunikationskanäle und die Anpassung der Messages und des Kommunikationsdesigns an das jeweilige Medium.

Umsetzung

Die Ausgestaltung der Website, der Verkaufsdokumentation, der Inserate und anderen verkaufsunterstützenden Maßnahmen erarbeiten wir bis zur Druck- und Programmiervorstufe inhouse. Dabei nehmen wir die aktuellen Entwicklungen der digitalen Transformation, von den wachsenden Möglichkeiten im Bereich der Augmented Reality über den veränderten Medienkonsum bis hin zu den neuen Lebenswelten der Menschen, in unsere Strategien und Ideenentwicklungen mit auf.

Mood

Before we proceed from the strategic-conceptional to the creative process, we create mood boards to get an even better, more intense and clearer feel for the target group, the project environment, as well as the living and lifestyle habits. Mood boards are image collages of moods, objects, plants, means of transportation, people, bodies of water, colors, photo styles, etc. We use them on the one hand as a visual basis for our discussions with customers as pictures often say more than words and one can get hung up on words. On the other hand, they serve as the basis for our work in the creative phase. Similar to the description of persons within the target group, we can use the mood board anytime in our internal work as a reference and check whether the implementation is headed in the right direction, if the images are harmonious, and if central issues are highlighted.

Brand

Based on the positioning, the target group personalities, the mood boards, and the comprehensive analysis data, we create the basic idea as the foundation for the name, claim, basic argumentation, as well as image and color schemes of the temporary brand the same way in which it is externally communicated in the end. This also includes the target-group-specific and budget-based choice of communication channels as well as the matching of the messages and the communication design to the respective medium.

Implementation

We prepare the website design, sales documentation, advertisements and other sales promotion measures in-house up to the pre-print and pre-programming stage. We incorporate the current developments of digital transformation from increased augmented reality options up to the ramifications on media consumption and the changing living environments of people into all our strategies and idea development processes.

PROJEKTE
PROJECTS

AUTHENTISCHES JUGENDSTILHAUS IN ZÜRICH WIEDIKON

AUTHENTIC ART NOUVEAU HOUSE IN ZURICH WIEDIKON

PROJEKTNAME: «Rotach»
IMMOBILIE: Mehrfamilienhaus mit 12 Wohnungen im Eigentum
STANDORT: Rotachstrasse 22, 8003 Zürich, Schweiz
AUFTRAGGEBER: Fundamenta Group AG, Zug, Schweiz
ARCHITEKTUR: Linearch GmbH, Zürich, Schweiz
VERMARKTUNG: 2015
AUSZEICHNUNGEN: Iconic Awards 2015, Communication Winner
und Real Estate Award 2015 Schweiz, Nomination in der Kategorie
Vermarktung, 2. Platz durch Publikumswahl

PROJECT NAME: "Rotach"
PROPERTY: Multi-party residential building with 12 condominiums
LOCATION: Rotachstrasse 22, 8003 Zurich, Switzerland
CLIENT: Fundamenta Group AG, Zug, Switzerland
ARCHITECTURE: Linearch GmbH, Zurich, Switzerland
MARKETING PERIOD: 2015
RECOGNITIONS: Iconic Awards 2015, Communication Winner and
Real Estate Award 2015 Switzerland, nominated in the category marketing,
2nd place by audience vote

EIN ERLEBNIS AN EPOCHEN-BESCHREIBENDEN ZEITZEUGEN

EXPERIENCE HISTORIC
WITNESSES OF A SPECIAL ERA

DIE BASIS

Die Grundlage für das Immobilienmarketing bildet ein Bau aus dem vorletzten Jahrhundert in einer begehrten Zürcher Lage. Das Gebäude versammelt eine Blüte an epochenbeschreibenden Zeitzeugen, außen wie innen: Holzelemente wie die Treppen, Geländer oder Wandtäfelungen, Fischgratparkett, aber auch Stuckaturen, Glas- und Metallarbeiten. Die sehr attraktive Lage wird durch viele Angebote in direkter Nähe und den sehr guten Anschluss an die öffentlichen und privaten Verkehrswege unterstrichen. Naherholungsgebiete sind schnell zu erreichen. Der Stadtkreis Wiedikon gilt als altes und traditionelles Quartier, das Schritt um Schritt als Wohnlage neu entdeckt wird.

DIE ESSENZ

Die Immobilie an der Rotachstrasse 22 bietet eine Besonderheit: steinerne Köpfe als Wandschmuck an der Hausfassade. Und dazu ein Gebäude aus der Zeit des Jugendstils, mit vielen noch vorhandenen und intakten Zeitzeugen. Eine Kombination, die mit ihrem Charme auf viele Menschen anziehend wirkt.

Daraus leitet sich der Kerngedanke ab: Kluge Köpfe. Er spielt damit, dass die Köpfe, die vor über 100 Jahren auf der Hausfassade verewigt wurden, von damalig klugen, interessanten und bekannten Menschen stammen. So wird impliziert, dass die künftigen, neuen Eigentümer ebenfalls kluge Köpfe sein müssen, die dazu auch noch auf Wohnen mit Geschichte Wert legen.

THE BASIS

The real estate marketing is based on a building going back to the 19th century in a coveted area of Zurich. The building features a wealth of historic witnesses of its era on its exterior and interior: timber elements such as stairs, railings or wall paneling, herringbone parquet, as well as plastering, glass and metal elements. The very attractive location is complemented by a wide range of offers in the immediate vicinity and excellent public and private transportation connections. Leisure and recreation areas can be reached quickly. The urban district of Wiedikon is considered an old and traditional quarter that is recently gradually being rediscovered as a residential address.

THE ESSENCE

The building on Rotachstrasse 22 has a distinguishing feature – stone heads that decorate the walls on its facade. To boost, it goes back to the Art Deco era with many intact elements that serve as historic witnesses. This is a combination whose charm appeals to many people.

The core concept – Smart Heads was derived from this basis. It plays with the idea that the heads that were immortalized on the building's facade more than 100 years ago were of smart, interesting, and prominent persons at the time. This implies that the future new owners must also have smart heads who appreciate living alongside history.

DIE STANDORTFAKTOREN
THE LOCATION FACTORS

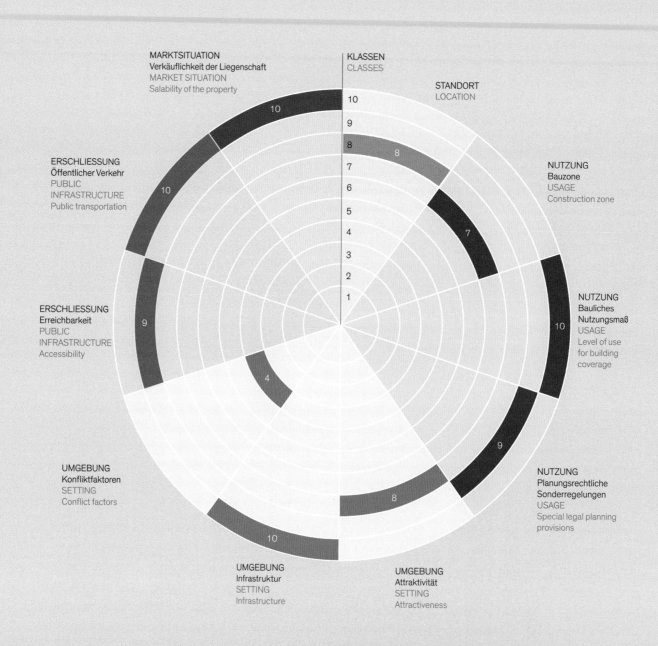

MARKTSITUATION
Verkäuflichkeit der Liegenschaft
MARKET SITUATION
Salability of the property

KLASSEN
CLASSES

STANDORT
LOCATION

ERSCHLIESSUNG
Öffentlicher Verkehr
PUBLIC
INFRASTRUCTURE
Public transportation

NUTZUNG
Bauzone
USAGE
Construction zone

ERSCHLIESSUNG
Erreichbarkeit
PUBLIC
INFRASTRUCTURE
Accessibility

NUTZUNG
Bauliches
Nutzungsmaß
USAGE
Level of use
for building
coverage

UMGEBUNG
Konfliktfaktoren
SETTING
Conflict factors

NUTZUNG
Planungsrechtliche
Sonderregelungen
USAGE
Special legal planning
provisions

UMGEBUNG
Infrastruktur
SETTING
Infrastructure

UMGEBUNG
Attraktivität
SETTING
Attractiveness

DIE STANDORTQUALITÄT VON «ROTACH»

+ Gesuchte Wohnlage

+ Attraktiv mit Abendsonne

+ Viele Angebote in direkter Nähe

+ Direkte Anschlüsse an den öffentlichen und privaten Verkehr

+ Maximale Ausnutzung möglich

− Starke Lärmbelastung

THE LOCATION QUALITY OF "ROTACH"

+ Coveted residential area

+ Attractive and exposed to the evening sun

+ Many offers in the immediate vicinity

+ Direct connections to public and private transportation

+ Maximum utilization possible

− Extensive noise pollution

DER MARKT

Durch die gute Lage und die einzigartige Ausstrahlung des Gebäudes innen wie außen kann mit einer guten Resonanz im Markt gerechnet werden. Eine moderate Preisgestaltung eröffnet zusätzliches Potenzial für jüngere und auch ältere Käufer. Es gibt im Quartier keine vergleichbaren Objekte und der Immobilienmarkt im angrenzenden Umfeld ist generell ausgetrocknet. Das bestätigt unter anderem auch das Wohnungsregister der Stadt Zürich.

DER AUFTRAG

Der Auftrag beinhaltet die Entwicklung und Umsetzung eines vorgabenfokussierten Immobilienmarketings, mit dem Kernthema, dass hier Neues im Alten entsteht. Das präsentierte Konzept umfasst die Namens- und Markenentwicklung, die Positionierung und den Claim sowie die gesamte Umsetzung im Corporate Design und den Werbemaßnahmen.

DER ZIELRAUM

– Stadt Zürich
– Nähere Agglomeration Zürich
– Kanton Zürich

THE MARKET

Due to the excellent location and unique charm of the building on the inside and outside, positive market resonance can be expected. The moderate pricing offers additional potential for younger and older buyers. There are no comparable projects in the quarter and the real estate market in the surrounding area has generally dried up. This is also confirmed by the apartment registry of the city of Zurich.

THE ASSIGNMENT

The assignment consisted of the development and implementation of prerequisite-focused real estate marketing with the central theme that something new is being created within something old. The presented concept includes the name and brand development, positioning and the claim, as well as the entire implementation of corporate design and advertising measures.

THE TARGET AREA

– City of Zurich
– Nearby Zurich vicinity
– Canton Zurich

DIE ZIELGRUPPE

Die Individualität des Gebäudes und die urbane Lage erfordern auch eine individuelle Zielgruppendefinition. Hier ist neben der Sinus-Analyse auch eine gute Portion Erfahrung und Marketinggefühl der Planer gefragt.

Quantitativ:

– Jüngere Einzelpersonen (unter 30)

– Unverheiratete Paare und Ehepaare ohne Kinder

– Unverheiratete Paare und Ehepaare nach Familienphase

– Aktive ältere Paare und Alleinstehende

– Zugezogene und Interessierte aus dem Ausland

– Mittlere Einkommensschicht (oberer Rand)

Qualitativ:

– Schätzen ein eher ruhiges Quartier

– Sind stadtorientiert

– Verkehrsanbindung (privater und öffentlicher Verkehr) ist wichtig

– Schätzen das Angebot des Quartiers mit seiner Vielfalt

– Sind eher konservativ eingestellt

Schlüsselargumente:

– Urbanes Lebensgefühl

– Gesamtinfrastruktur Einkaufen und Freizeit

– Werterhaltung und Unverbaubarkeit

– Verkehrsanbindung

– Hohe Lebensqualität

– Einzigartiges Wohneigentum

– Vielfalt im Quartier

THE TARGET GROUP

The individual nature of the building and the urban setting also required an individual target group definition. In addition to the Sinus analysis, the planners also needed a good amount of expertise and sense of marketing.

Quantitative:

– Younger individuals (aged under 30)

– Unmarried couples and couples without children

– Unmarried couples and couples after the family phase

– Active older couples and singles

– Expatriates and interested persons from abroad

– Middle income strata (top edge)

Qualitative:

– Appreciate a rather quiet quarter

– City-oriented

– Traffic connections (private and public) are important

– Appreciate the diversity of offers in the quarter

– Are rather conservative

Key arguments:

– Urban lifestyle

– General shopping and leisure infrastructure

– Value conservation and no future development around it

– Traffic connection

– High quality of life

– Unique residential property

– Diversity of the quarter

DIE SINUS-ANALYSE DER ZIELGRUPPE FÜR «ROTACH»

THE SINUS ANALYSIS OF THE TARGET GROUP FOR "ROTACH"

SOZIALE LAGE UND GRUNDORIENTIERUNG
SOCIAL STATUS AND BASIC VALUES

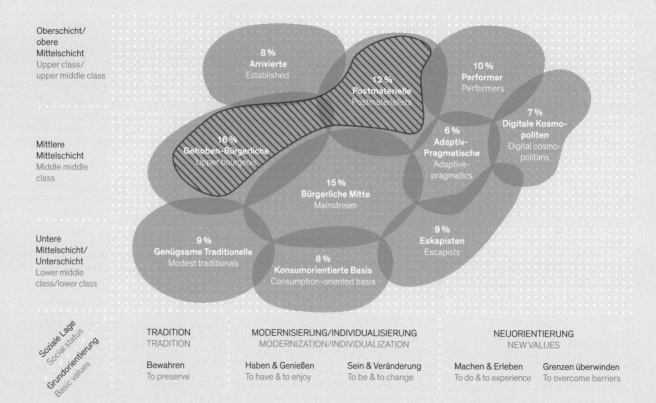

Oberschicht/
obere
Mittelschicht
Upper class/
upper middle class

Mittlere
Mittelschicht
Middle middle
class

Untere
Mittelschicht/
Unterschicht
Lower middle
class/lower class

**8 %
Arrivierte**
Established

**12 %
Postmaterielle**
Postmaterialists

**10 %
Performer**
Performers

**7 %
Digitale Kosmo-
politen**
Digital cosmo-
politans

**16 %
Gehoben-Bürgerliche**
Upper bourgeois

**6 %
Adaptiv-
Pragmatische**
Adaptive-
pragmatics

**15 %
Bürgerliche Mitte**
Mainstream

**9 %
Genügsame Traditionelle**
Modest traditionals

**8 %
Konsumorientierte Basis**
Consumption-oriented basis

**9 %
Eskapisten**
Escapists

Soziale Lage
Social status
Grundorientierung
Basic values

TRADITION
TRADITION

MODERNISIERUNG/INDIVIDUALISIERUNG
MODERNIZATION/INDIVIDUALIZATION

NEUORIENTIERUNG
NEW VALUES

Bewahren
To preserve

Haben & Genießen
To have & to enjoy

Sein & Veränderung
To be & to change

Machen & Erleben
To do & to experience

Grenzen überwinden
To overcome barriers

Die Zielgruppe des Rotach-Projekts ist mit den Sinus-Milieus nicht trennscharf abzubilden. Die einzigartigen Eigenschaften des Gebäudes, die Architektur, die Mikro- und Makrolage ergeben eine heterogene Zielgruppenstruktur, die zwischen den Sinus-Gruppen Postmaterielle und Gehoben-Bürgerliche liegt.

The target group of the Rotach project cannot be precisely delineated within the Sinus milieus. The unique characteristics of the building, the architecture, and the immediate and extended location result in a heterogeneous target group structure situated between the Sinus groups of postmaterialists and upper bourgeois.

INDIVIDUALISTEN MIT SINN FÜRS DETAIL

Das Projekt ist ein gutes Beispiel für die zunehmende Auflösung der klassischen Marktsegmentierungen. Das Gebäude zieht sehr unterschiedliche Käufer aus verschiedenen Segmenten an. Deshalb muss auch die Kommunikation offener gestaltet werden. Zum Beispiel mit einem Porträt eines jungen, urbanen Paares, das für die Individualität des Projekts steht.

Petra Kirchner ist 32 Jahre alt und arbeitet in Zürich im Kundenmanagement einer Versicherung. Sie ist seit neun Jahren mit Lukas Meyer liiert, der als Logistiker arbeitet und immer wieder auf Reisen ist. Das Paar hat sich entschieden, die bisherige Mietwohnung gegen eine Eigentumswohnung zu tauschen. Das neue Zuhause sollte nicht zu groß sein, dafür einen eigenwilligen Charakter haben und Charme ausstrahlen. Da die großgewachsene Brünette oft auch von Zuhause aus arbeitet, wären dreieinhalb Zimmer ideal. Wichtig ist die Anbindung an den Verkehr. Öffentlicher Verkehr für Petra einerseits und keine langen Stehzeiten im Straßenverkehr für Lukas, wenn der mit dem Auto losfährt. Ihr Daheim ist beiden wichtig, es ist ein Ort der Ruhe, ein Erholungs- und Rückzugsort und dieser sollte nicht in einem der lauten Quartiere liegen, sondern eher in einem traditionellen, langsam wachsenden Umfeld. Ein Quartier mit Anschluss an die Natur, mit kleinen Läden und intaktem Gewerbe, mit Nachbarn, die man kennt und wo nach 22 Uhr nur noch die Fernseher Geräusche von sich geben.

INDIVIDUALISTS WITH A SENSE OF DETAIL

The project is a good example of the ongoing disintegration of classical market segmentations. The building attracts very diverse buyers from various segments. Therefore the communication must also be more open. For example, by using a portrait of a young urban couple that represents the individuality of the project.

Petra Kirchner is 32 years old and works in Zurich in the customer management department of an insurance company. For the past nine years, she has been living with Lukas Meyer who works as a logistics specialist and often travels for his work. The couple decided to move out of their current rental apartment and buy a condominium. The new home should not be too large, preferably with a unique character and charm. As the tall brown-haired woman often works from home, three and a half rooms would be ideal. The traffic connection is key. Public transportation for Petra on the one hand and no extended traffic jams for Lukas when he takes the car on the other. Their home is very important to the couple; it is their place of quiet, for relaxation and retreat, which should not be located in one of the noisy city quarters but rather in a traditional slowly growing environment. A quarter that is linked to nature, with small stores and an intact trade industry, with neighbors they can become familiar with and where after 10 pm the only sound comes from TV sets.

GUT AUFGEHOBEN ZWISCHEN HERKUNFT UND ZUKUNFT
COMFORTABLY AT HOME BETWEEN HERITAGE AND FUTURE

DIE POSITIONIERUNG

Der Positionierungssatz «Gut aufgehoben zwischen Herkunft und Zukunft» erfolgt aus der Verdichtung des Positionierungsbeschriebs: Wer an der Rotachstrasse 22 im Zürcher Kreis 3 wohnt, will nicht zur Masse gehören, sondern in einem authentischen Gebäude aus der vorletzten Jahrhundertwende mit originellen Details gepaart mit zeitgemäßem Komfort leben. Die Käufer schätzen das lebenswerte Zürcher Quartier in einer echten Stadtwohnung mit Atmosphäre und Tradition.

DER ANALYSE-SCHWERPUNKT

Die beiden relevanten Themen im Analyse-Schwerpunkt bilden die Architektur und die Lage. Die Architektur spielt jedoch eine relevant stärkere Rolle und nimmt denn auch in der Kommunikation mehr Gewicht ein.

Der Analyse-Schwerpunkt Architektur:
- **Haus mit Geschichte**
- **Jugendstil**
- **Mix aus Moderne und Authentizität**
- **Hohe Lebensqualität**
- **Individualität**
- **Attraktives Umfeld**

THE POSITIONING

The positioning statement "Comfortably at home between heritage and future" is a condensation of the positioning description – people who live at Rotachstrasse 22 in district 3 of Zurich do not want to be part of the mainstream but want to live in an authentic building dating back to the turn of the 19th to the 20th century with unique details coupled with contemporary comfort. The buyers appreciate the living quality of the Zurich quarter in a genuine townhouse filled with a special atmosphere and tradition.

THE FOCUS OF THE ANALYSIS

The two relevant themes of the focus of the analysis are architecture and location. However, architecture plays a more relevant role and is emphasized more in the communications.

The architecture focus of the analysis:
- **A house with a history**
- **Art deco**
- **Mix of modernity and authenticity**
- **High quality of life**
- **Individuality**
- **Attractive setting**

DER NAME: «ROTACH»

Die Geschichte klingt schon im Namen mit und verweist auf die weit zurückliegenden Anfänge des traditionsreichen Quartiers Wiedikon im Zürcher Stadtkreis 3. Der Namensgeber des vornehmlich von Genossenschaftsbauten geprägten Quartiers war Uli Rotach, ein Appenzeller Freiheitskämpfer aus dem 15. Jahrhundert.

DER CLAIM: «KLUGE KÖPFE»

Der Claim lässt die architektonischen Zeitzeugen an der Gebäudefassade wieder aufleben und spielt mit der Vergangenheit des Gebäudes und den klugen Menschen, die heute darin wohnen und leben.

DIE FARBEN UND DIE TYPOGRAFIE

Die warmen Farbtöne erinnern an das alte Gemäuer, die vorhandene Fassadenstruktur und die Fassadenfarbe. Die Farbsprache unterstützt so die visuelle Umsetzung und schafft Harmonie. Die Schriften für die Titel und für die Lauftexte verbinden das Alte mit dem Modernen und spiegeln auf diese Weise die Geschichte des Gebäudes wider.

DIE IDEE: SO KLUG WIE GESTERN UND HEUTE

Die Kommunikationsidee spannt einen Bogen zwischen den klugen Köpfen von damals, die in der Fassade des geschichtsträchtigen Gebäudes verewigt wurden und jenen, die sich heute den Traum, in einem solchen Bau mitten in Zürich zu leben verwirklichen. Wer genau diese Köpfe in der Fassade sind, konnten die Marketer von Felix Partner trotz intensiver Recherche nicht herausfinden.

DAS WERBLICHE KONZEPT

Für die Umsetzung der Kommunikationsidee hauchen die Gestalter den Fassadenköpfen des Gebäudes Leben ein. Sie prägen das Logo und alle Kommunikationsmaßnahmen – nicht aufdringlich, aber omnipräsent. Der Stil des Kommunikationsdesigns ist edel und erhaben. Die zu neuem Leben erwachten Figuren begleiten die Interessenten durch das Quartier und durch die stilvoll renovierten Räume des Gebäudes.

THE NAME: "ROTACH"

The history already resounds in the name that refers back to the beginning of the traditional Wiedikon quarter in Zurich's district 3. The quarter, which is dominated by cooperative buildings, was named after Uli Rotach, a 15th century freedom fighter of Appenzell.

THE CLAIM: "SMART HEADS"

The claim revives the architectural historical elements on the building facade while toying with the history of the building and the smart people who live in it today.

THE COLORS AND THE TYPOGRAPHY

The warm hues are reminiscent of the old walls, the existing facade structure and the facade color. The color vocabulary thus supports the visual implementation and provides harmony. The fonts used for the headlines and the text copy combine old and new to reflect the history of the building.

THE IDEA: AS SMART AS YESTERDAY AND TODAY

The communication idea creates a link between the smart heads of earlier times that were eternalized in the facade of the historical building and those of today who fulfill their dream of living in such a building in the heart of Zurich. Despite in-depth research, the marketers of Felix Partner could not find out whom the heads on the facade represent.

THE ADVERTISING CONCEPT

For the implementation of the communication concept, the designers brought the facade heads of the building to life. They are featured on the logo and all communication measures, and while they are not obtrusive, they are omnipresent. The communication design is noble and grand. The revived figures accompany the potential buyers through the quarter and through the stylishly renovated rooms of the building.

DAS CORPORATE DESIGN FÜR «ROTACH»
THE CORPORATE DESIGN FOR "ROTACH"

LOGO
LOGO

TYPOGRAFIE
TYPOGRAPHY

Heroic Condensed
Adobe Garamond

AN DER ROTACHSTRASSE

An der Rotachstrasse 22 in Zürich Wiedikon werden in einem authentischen Gebäude aus der vorletzten Jahrhundertwende zwölf Wohn-Schmuckstücke verkauft. Ausgestattet mit originalen Stilmitteln, voller stimmiger und authentischer Details, kombiniert mit aktueller Moderne.

FARBEN
COLORS

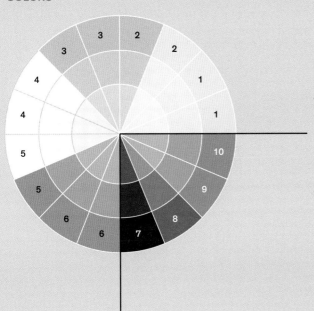

1–6

Die Farben im Corporate Design
The colors of the corporate design

7–10

Die Farben in der Bildwelt
The colors of the imagery

Smart heads live stylishly

Smart heads have distinct characters

Smart heads pamper themselves

Smart heads love beauty

DIE KOMMUNIKATIONSMITTEL

Website (Presite und Vollversion), Verkaufsbroschüre, Anzeigen, Flyer, Baureklameblache vor Ort, ausführliche Grundrisspläne in einem Maßstab von 1:100, Fassadenpläne und Gebäudeschnitt, Situations- und Umgebungsplan, Verkaufspreisliste und Kurzbaubeschrieb

THE COMMUNICATION MEDIA

Website (pre-site and full version), sales brochure, advertisements, flyers, banner advertisement on location at the construction site, detailed ground plans with a scale of 1:100, facade plans and building layout, location and setting plan, sales price list and brief construction description

Baureklameblache
Banner advertisement on location at the construction site

Website (Presite und Vollversion)
Website (pre-site and full version)

Anzeige
Advertisement

Satelliten-Anzeige
Satellite advertisement

Verkaufsbroschüre
Sales brochure

Verkaufsbroschüre
Sales brochure

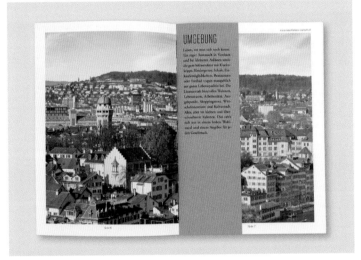

Verkaufsbroschüre
Sales brochure

Verkaufsbroschüre
Sales brochure

Verkaufsbroschüre
Sales brochure

WOHNEN ZWISCHEN HERKUNFT UND ZUKUNFT
AT HOME BETWEEN HERITAGE AND FUTURE

DIE IMMOBILIE

Das Gebäude an der Rotachstrasse 22 steht unter Denkmalschutz. Daher bleiben die Fassade und die tragende Struktur sowie Details des Treppenhauses – Malereien, Treppengeländer, Treppenstufen und deren Beläge sowie Wohnungstüren – im Original bestehen. Dank der Reparatur und Auffrischung fast aller bestehenden Holzarbeiten wie Fenstergewände, Brusttäfer, Schränke und Zimmertüren, bewahren auch die Räume ihren ursprünglichen Ausdruck. Die Struktur des Hauses und der Zimmer bleibt ablesbar, dennoch wird der Wunsch nach zusammenhängenden Wohn-Ess-Küchenräumen und großzügigeren Räumen erfüllt.

THE PROPERTY

The building on Rotachstrasse 22 is designated as a historic monument. This is why the facade and the bearing structure as well as stairway elements such as the frescoes, the stairway railings, the stairs and their covers as well as the entrance doors were maintained in their original state. Similarly, the original style of the rooms was kept intact as all existing timber elements such as window frames, front paneling, closets, and room doors of the apartments were repaired and renovated. The structure of the building and the rooms remained discernible while the contemporary desire for open living-dining-kitchen spaces and more generously proportioned rooms could be fulfilled.

Außenansicht Rotachstrasse 22
External view Rotachstrasse 22

Inspiration für den Claim: «Kluger Kopf» an der Fassade
Patron: "Smart head" on the facade

Wo früher der Estrich/Dachboden war, befinden sich heute zwei Maisonettewohnungen
The previous attic was replaced by two duplex apartments

Historisches Flair dank unverändertem Treppenhaus
The unaltered staircase has a historical flair

Einblick in 2,5-Zimmer-Wohnung mit Originalparkett
View of a 2.5-room apartment with original parquet

Hauseingang mit authentischen Wandmalereien
Building entrance with authentic frescoes

Wanddurchbrüche erzeugen ein neues Raumgefühl
Wall openings create a new spatial atmosphere

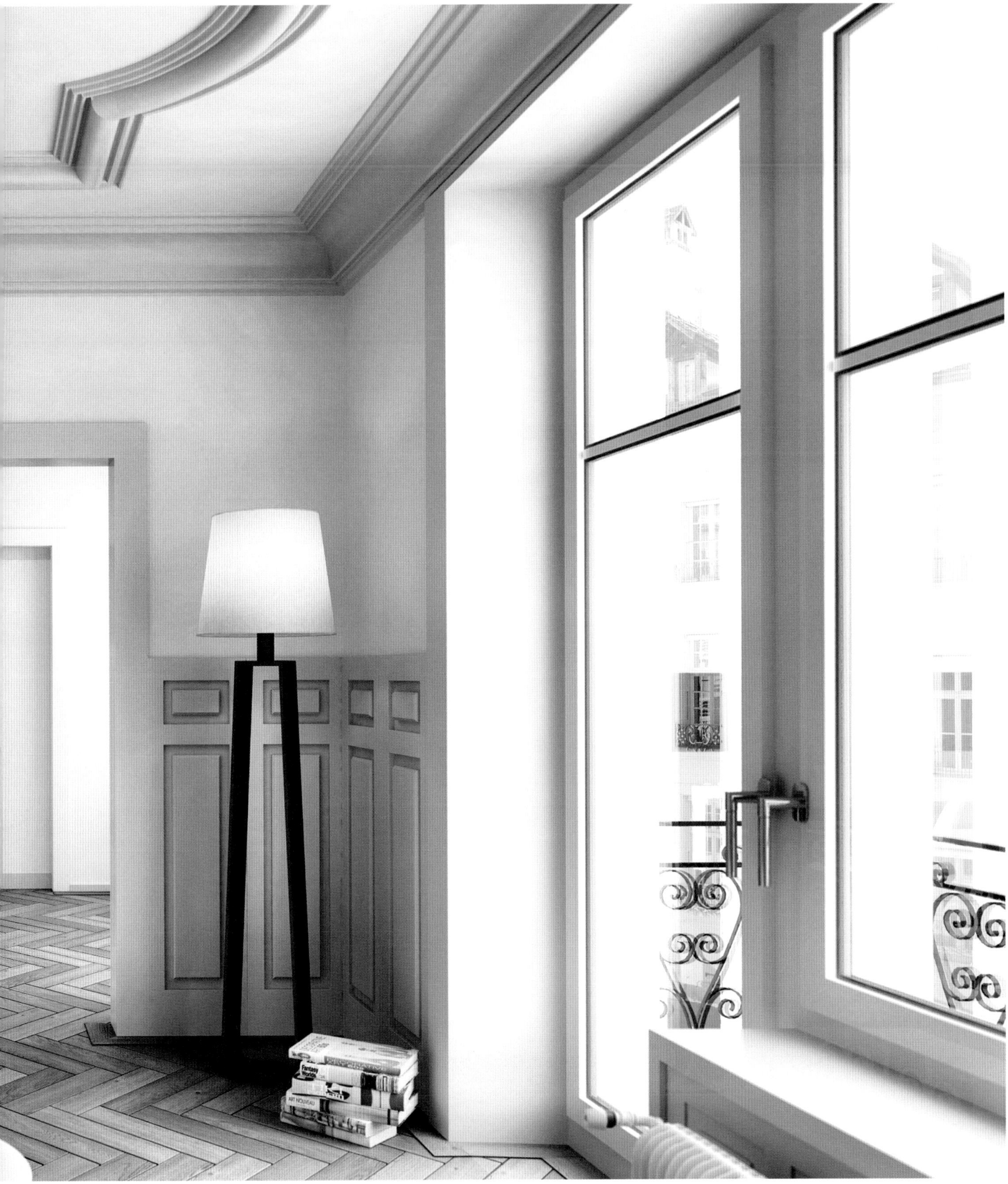

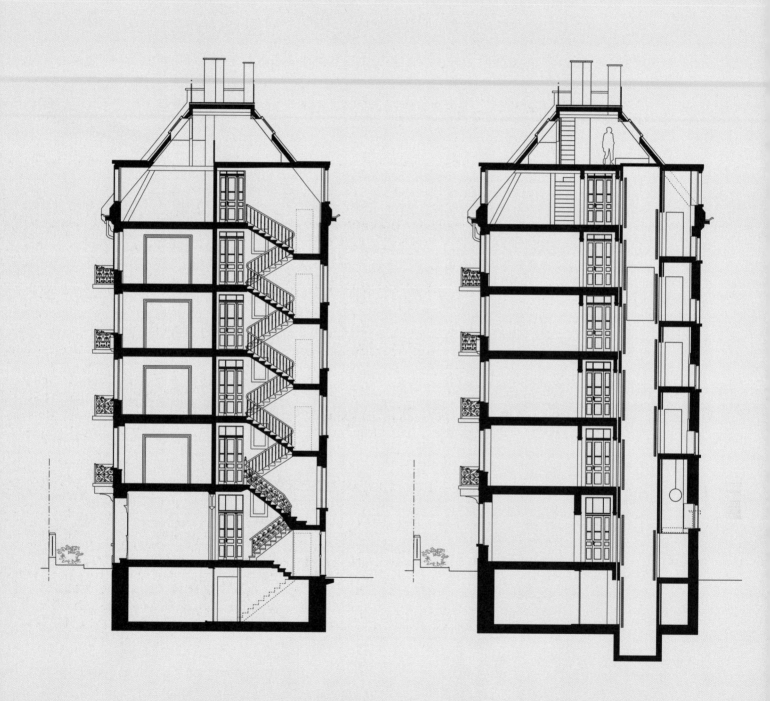

Querschnitte

Cross sections

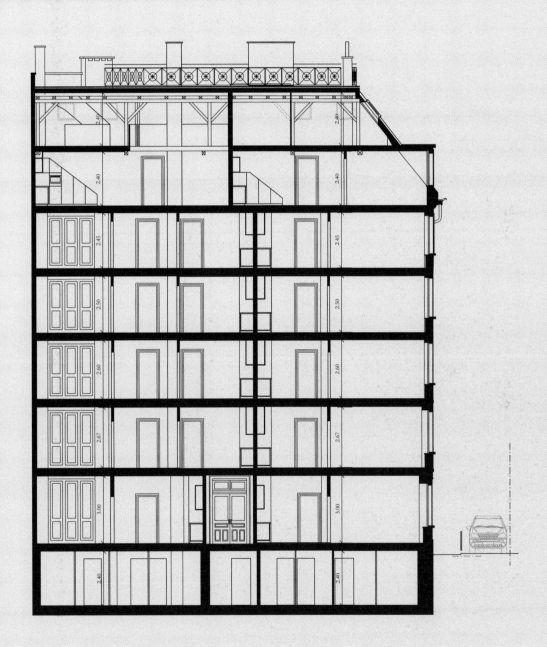

Längsschnitt
Longitudinal section

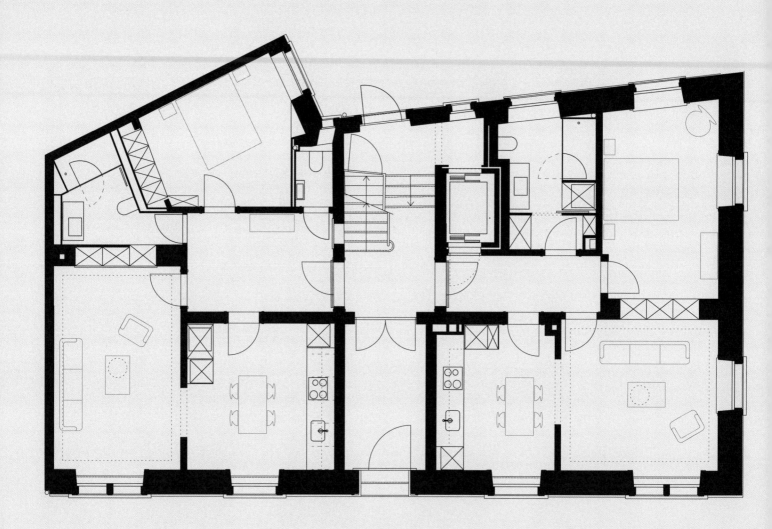

Grundriss Erdgeschoss, Eingangsgeschoss
Layout ground floor, entrance floor

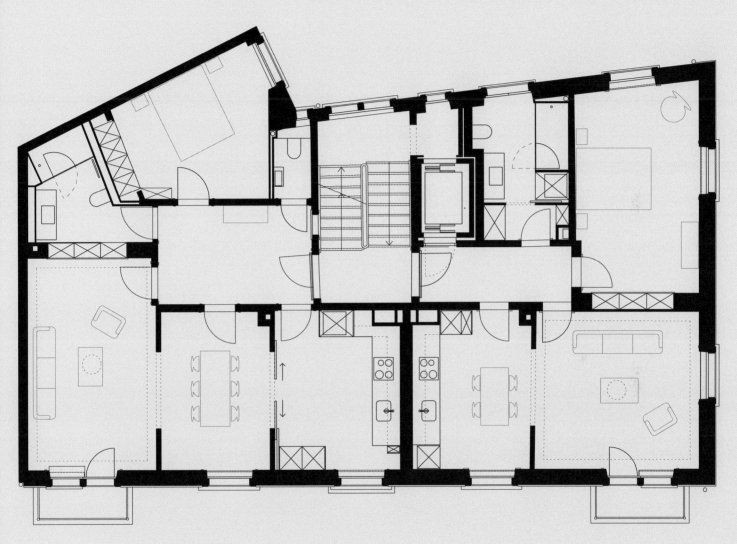

Grundriss 1.–4. Obergeschoss
Layout 2nd to 5th floor

MINERGIE-SIEDLUNG
MIT EIGENEM PARK
MIETE, EIGENTUM, GEWERBE
MINERGIE HOUSING ESTATE
WITH ITS OWN PARK
RENTAL, OWNERSHIP, TRADE

PROJEKTNAMEN: «Witenzelg Romanshorn»,
«Mein Witenzelg», «Witenzelg Work»
IMMOBILIE: 10 Mehrfamilienhäuser mit 144 Miet- und
22 Eigentumswohnungen sowie 15 Gewerbelofts
STANDORT: Reckholdernstrasse 11/13, Martina-Hälg-Strasse
1/3/5/7/15/17/19/21/23/25, 8590 Romanshorn, Schweiz
AUFTRAGGEBER: ASGA Pensionskasse Genossenschaft,
St. Gallen, Schweiz; Felix Partner Immobilien AG, Romanshorn, Schweiz
ARCHITEKTUR: Felix Partner Architektur AG, Zürich, Schweiz
VERMARKTUNG: 2015–2017

PROJECT NAMES: "Witenzelg Romanshorn,"
"My Witenzelg," "Witenzelg Work"
PROPERTY: 10 multi-party residential buildings with 144 rental
apartments and 22 condominiums as well as 15 commercial lofts
LOCATION: Reckholdernstrasse 11/13, Martina-Hälg-Strasse
1/3/5/7/15/17/19/21/23/25, 8590 Romanshorn, Switzerland
CLIENT: ASGA Pensionskasse Genossenschaft, St. Gallen, Switzerland;
Felix Partner Immobilien AG, Romanshorn, Switzerland
ARCHITECTURE: Felix Partner Architektur AG, Zurich, Switzerland
MARKETING PERIOD: 2015–2017

DA SEIN, WO DAS LEBEN GERNE WOHNT
LIVING WHERE LIFE IS PLEASURABLE

MIETE IM WITENZELG
RENTING IN WITENZELG

DIE BASIS

In Romanshorn entsteht auf dem zentral gelegenen Witenzelg-areal auf rund 20'000 Quadratmetern eine für den Kanton Thurgau und die Region wegweisende Minergie-Siedlung. Der Umwelt und seinen Bewohnern zuliebe wird das Witenzelg mit Wasser aus dem Bodensee geheizt und ist komplett autofrei. Die mit Holz verkleideten Fassaden schaffen den Sprung von außen nach innen, wo sich fließende, helle Räume mit großzügigen Außenbereichen finden. Der Standort liegt nur wenige Gehminuten vom Bodensee und vom Zentrum entfernt und alles, was man für den Alltag und darüber hinaus braucht, ist in Romanshorn gut zu finden. Inklusive einem breiten Angebot an Kultur, Sport, Bildung und Erholung.

DIE ESSENZ

Im Witenzelg wird ein echtes Stück qualitativen Raums für Menschen geschaffen: eine angenehme Atmosphäre, nachhaltige und naturorientierte Bauweise, Ökologie vor reiner Ökonomie. Im Auftritt modern, aber nicht aufdringlich und als Mittelpunkt sowie als Symbol für den Lebensraum ein wunderbarer, zum Verweilen auffordernder Park von über 7'000 Quadratmetern.

Daraus leitet sich der Kerngedanke ab: Wie das Leben gerne wohnt. Harmonisch und nutzenorientiert, mit angenehmen, mediterranen Farben, viel Natur, Offenheit und doch auch Raum für den persönlichen Rückzug innen und außen: ein qualitativer Lebensraum für Menschen.

THE BASIS

In Romanshorn, a Minergie housing estate, which is pioneering for the Canton Thurgau and the region, is being established on the centrally located Witenzelg premises on an area of approx. 20,000 square meters. For the sake of the environment and its residents, Witenzelg is heated with water from Lake Constance and is completely car-free. The facades with the timber cladding create a link between the exterior and the interior with its open light-flooded rooms and generously sized outdoor areas. The location is only a few minutes away from Lake Constance and from the city center. All necessities of daily life and beyond are conveniently found in Romanshorn, including a wide range of cultural, sports, education, and leisure facilities.

THE ESSENCE

The Witenzelg project creates a genuine high-quality space for people to enjoy life: a pleasant atmosphere, sustainable and nature-friendly construction, ecology before pure economy. Its look is modern but not obtrusive and at its heart, also acting as a symbol for the living space, there is a wonderful inviting park of over 7,000 square meters.

This is what inspired the core concept: where life is pleasurable. Harmonious and user-oriented, with pleasant Mediterranean colors, plenty of nature and open spaces, yet also with room for individual retreats on the inside and outside – a high-quality living environment.

LAGE
LOCATION

DIE STANDORTFAKTOREN
THE LOCATION FACTORS

MARKTSITUATION
Verkäuflichkeit der Liegenschaft
MARKET SITUATION
Salability of the property

KLASSEN
CLASSES

STANDORT
LOCATION

ERSCHLIESSUNG
Öffentlicher Verkehr
PUBLIC
INFRASTRUCTURE
Public transportation

NUTZUNG
Bauzone
USAGE
Construction zone

ERSCHLIESSUNG
Erreichbarkeit
PUBLIC
INFRASTRUCTURE
Accessibility

NUTZUNG
Bauliches
Nutzungsmaß
USAGE
Level of use
for building
coverage

UMGEBUNG
Konfliktfaktoren
SETTING
Conflict factors

NUTZUNG
Planungsrechtliche
Sonderregelungen
USAGE
Special legal planning
provisions

UMGEBUNG
Infrastruktur
SETTING
Infrastructure

UMGEBUNG
Attraktivität
SETTING
Attractiveness

DIE STANDORTQUALITÄT VOM WITENZELG

+ Gut bis sehr gut nachgefragte Lage

+ Seenähe

+ Attraktiv mit Abendsonne

+ Viele Angebote in Gehdistanz

+ Gut ausgebautes öffentliches Verkehrsnetz

+ Gute Anschlüsse für den Privatverkehr

+ Hohe Ausnutzung möglich

+ Wertsteigernde Wohnzone

− Eingeschränkte Aussicht

THE LOCATION QUALITY OF WITENZELG

+ Popular to very popular location

+ Near the lake

+ Attractive and exposed to the evening sun

+ Many offers within walking distance

+ Well developed public transportation network

+ Good private transportation connections

+ High utilization possible

+ Increasing value residential zone

− Limited view

DER MARKT

Das Projekt kann mit seinem Ausbau, seiner Ausstrahlung, dem Volumen und der ansprechenden, zentralen Wohnlage in See- und Zentrumsnähe als sehr gut absorbierbar eingestuft werden. Insbesondere im Vergleich mit den kurz zuvor fertiggestellten Erstvermietungsobjekten in Romanshorn und Umgebung.

DER AUFTRAG

Bei diesem Großprojekt kommt von Investmentanteilen über die Projektentwicklung, Planung und Architektur bis hin zum Immobilienmarketing alles aus dem Haus Felix Partner. Ein Prestige- und Vorzeigeprojekt für das Unternehmen, das alle interdisziplinären Vorteile nutzt, die eine solch enge und eingespielte Zusammenarbeit ermöglicht. Die Designer unterstützen die Architekten schon in der ersten Planungsphase bei der Wahl der warmen, im mediterranen Stil gehaltenen Farbkonzepte, sowohl im Innen- als auch Außenbereich. Auf diese Weise sind alle Elemente aufeinander abgestimmt und ergeben ein harmonisches Ganzes – kosteneffizient und zeitnah. Das Immobilienmarketing-Konzept beinhaltet die Namens- und Markenentwicklung, Positionierung und Claim sowie die gesamte Umsetzung im Corporate Design und den breit angelegten Kommunikationsmaßnahmen.

DER ZIELRAUM

– Stadt Romanshorn
– Kanton Thurgau
– Region Ostschweiz bis Zürich
– Grenznahe Region von Deutschland und Österreich

THE MARKET

With its development, its ambiance, size, and the attractive central location near the lake and city center, the project can be classified as excellently absorbable – especially in comparison to the recently completed first-time rental buildings in Romanshorn and the vicinity.

THE ASSIGNMENT

For this large-scale project, Felix Partner contributed everything from investment shares, planning, and architecture up to real estate marketing. It serves as a prestigious flagship project for the company that benefits from all the interdisciplinary advantages that result from the close and orchestrated cooperation approach. The designers supported the architects already in the first planning phase in the choice of the warm Mediterranean color schemes for the interior and the exterior. This resulted in a harmonious overall concept in which all elements complement each other – cost-efficiently and within a short period of time. The real estate marketing concept incorporates the name and brand development, positioning and the claim, as well as the entire implementation of corporate design and the extensive communication measures.

THE TARGET AREA

– City of Romanshorn
– Canton Thurgau
– East Switzerland region up to Zurich
– Neighboring regions in Germany and Austria

DIE ZIELGRUPPE

Die Mietwohnungen zielen auf eine heterogene, lage- und regionenbezogene Mieterschaft, ermittelt und definiert über fundierte Analysen:

Quantitativ:
– Unverheiratete Paare und Singles
– Familien mit Kindern
– Ältere Paare nach Familienphase
– Wohnhaft in der Region und im nahen Ausland (Deutschland und Österreich)
– Mittlere bis höhere Einkommen

Qualitativ:
– Schätzen Erholung am See und auf dem Land
– Suchen gute Infrastruktur mit persönlichem Flair
– Verkehrsanbindung (privater und öffentlicher Verkehr) ist wichtig
– Bodenständig und naturverbunden
– Setzen auf Bewährtes und Regionales

Schlüsselargumente:
– In der Stadt, aber mit Landcharakter
– Gute Gesamtinfrastruktur
– Gute Schulen
– Erholung durch See und Naherholungsgebiete
– Hohe Lebensqualität
– Bodenständigkeit und Regionalität

THE TARGET GROUP

The rental apartments are targeted at a heterogeneous group of tenants who are connected to the location and the region that were determined and defined by extensive analyses.

Quantitative:
– Unmarried couples and singles
– Families with children
– Older couples after the family phase
– Residents of the region and nearby other countries (Germany and Austria)
– Middle to high incomes

Qualitative:
– Appreciate relaxation near the lake and in the countryside
– Looking for a good infrastructure with a personal ambiance
– Traffic connections (private and public) are important
– Down-to-earth and nature lovers
– Traditionally and regionally oriented

Key arguments:
– In the city, but with a rural character
– Good general infrastructure
– Good schools
– Leisure and recreation by the sea and in recreation areas
– High quality of life
– Down-to-earth and regionally oriented

DIE SINUS-ANALYSE DER ZIELGRUPPE FÜR «WITENZELG ROMANSHORN»
THE SINUS ANALYSIS OF THE TARGET GROUP FOR "WITENZELG ROMANSHORN"

SOZIALE LAGE UND GRUNDORIENTIERUNG
SOCIAL STATUS AND BASIC VALUES

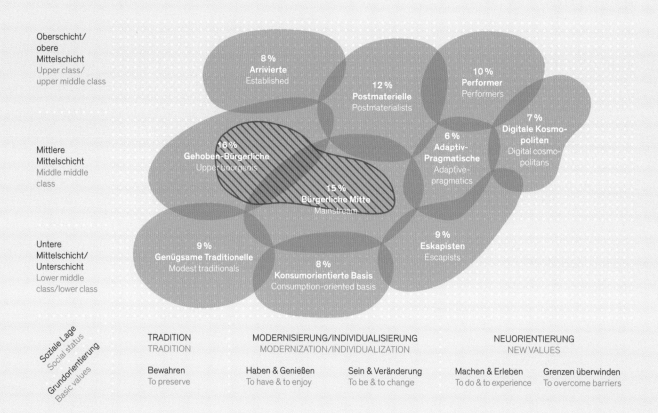

Oberschicht/
obere
Mittelschicht
Upper class/
upper middle class

Mittlere
Mittelschicht
Middle middle
class

Untere
Mittelschicht/
Unterschicht
Lower middle
class/lower class

8 %
Arrivierte
Established

12 %
Postmaterielle
Postmaterialists

10 %
Performer
Performers

7 %
Digitale Kosmo-
politen
Digital cosmo-
politans

16 %
Gehoben-Bürgerliche
Upper boourgeois

6 %
Adaptiv-
Pragmatische
Adaptive-
pragmatics

15 %
Bürgerliche Mitte
Mainstream

9 %
Eskapisten
Escapists

9 %
Genügsame Traditionelle
Modest traditionals

8 %
Konsumorientierte Basis
Consumption-oriented basis

Soziale Lage
Social status

Grundorientierung
Basic values

TRADITION
TRADITION

MODERNISIERUNG/INDIVIDUALISIERUNG
MODERNIZATION/INDIVIDUALIZATION

NEUORIENTIERUNG
NEW VALUES

Bewahren
To preserve

Haben & Genießen
To have & to enjoy

Sein & Veränderung
To be & to change

Machen & Erleben
To do & to experience

Grenzen überwinden
To overcome barriers

Lage, Architektur und Preissegment entsprechen bei der Sinus-Analyse den Ansprüchen und dem Lebensstil der bürgerlichen bis gehoben bürgerlichen Mitte.
The location, architecture and price segment are in line with the demands and the lifestyle of the mainstream and upper bourgeois milieus.

NATUR- UND TRADITIONSVERBUNDEN

Detailliert ausgearbeitete und zielgruppenadäquate Porträts wie das nachfolgende von Lisa Frick wirken bei potenziellen Mietern integrierend – vertraute Elemente aus dem eigenen Leben stärken das Gefühl, angekommen zu sein. Das erfolgreiche Marketingmittel wird auch im eigens für das Projekt entwickelten Witenzelg Magazin mit realen Porträts der ersten Mieterinnen und Mieter weitergeführt.

Lisa Frick ist 39 Jahre alt und im Thurgau zwischen See und Säntis aufgewachsen. Sie kehrt nach einigen Jahren Ostschweiz-Abstinenz zurück nach Romanshorn. Als neue Leiterin des Technischen Kundendienstes eines lokal ansässigen Energieversorgers übernimmt sie hier nun eine große Herausforderung in einer Männerbastion. Um dem Job gerecht zu werden, möchte sie nicht allzu weit weg vom Arbeitsplatz ihren Lebensmittelpunkt einrichten und sich eine Wohnung mieten. Die Wohnungsgröße ist nicht so entscheidend, drei oder vier Zimmer wären ideal, sodass ihre 19 Jahre alte Tochter sie besuchen und bei ihr übernachten kann. Wichtiger ist: Die Wohnung muss ihr gefallen und sie muss sich vom ersten Augenblick an darin wohlfühlen. Schön wäre auch etwas Weitsicht in Richtung See oder Romanshorner Wald. Überhaupt liegt ihr die Naherholung am Herzen. Kurze Distanzen zu allem, was man braucht, mal zu Fuß, mal mit dem Fahrrad unterwegs sein, das passt zu der sportlichen Frau.

VALUING NATURE AND TRADITIONS

Detailed and target group-adequate portraits like the following one of Lisa Frick address and involve potential tenants who detect familiar elements from their own life that make them feel at home. The successful marketing tool is also continued in the periodic Witenzelg magazine that was specifically developed for the project featuring real-life portraits of the first tenants.

Lisa Frick is 39 years old and grew up in the Thurgau region between Lake Constance and Säntis mountain. After living away for a few years, she is now returning to eastern Switzerland to live in Romanshorn. As the new head of technical customer service of a local utility company, she is taking on a major challenge in a male-dominated sector. To be able to focus on her job, she would like to rent an apartment not too far away from her workplace. The size of the apartment is not very important, but three or four rooms would be ideal so that her 19-year-old daughter can come to visit her and stay overnight. What is more important: the apartment must be to her liking and she must feel at home in it from the very first second. It would also be nice if it had a view of the lake or the Romanshorn forest. In general, she is interested in local recreation. Short distances so that she can get everything she wants, either by foot or by bicycle would also suit the athletic woman.

MIT FREUDE WOHNEN
PLEASURABLE LIVING

DIE POSITIONIERUNG

Witenzelg positioniert sich mit dem aus den Standort- und Marktanalysen resultierenden Fokussatz «Mit Freude wohnen». Die Freude an Wohnkomfort, Bewegungsfreiheit, Natur, nahe Infrastruktur mit See und Stadt und das gute Gefühl, dank Seewasserheizung bewusst und sorgsam mit den natürlichen Ressourcen umzugehen, stehen im Mittelpunkt der Kommunikation.

DER ANALYSE-SCHWERPUNKT

Architektur und Lifestyle sind die Analyse-Schwerpunkte für Witenzelg, welche die Kommunikation und Argumentation dominieren. Den Lifestyle betont Felix Partner noch etwas stärker, da sich mit der Seewasserheizung und dem autofreien Park im Zentrum der Überbauung überzeugend kommunizieren lässt.

Die Analyse-Schwerpunkte Lifestyle und Architektur:
– **Sehr großzügige Lebensräume**
– **Autofrei**
– **Seewassernutzung für Heizung**
– **Eigener Park**
– **Hohe Lebensqualität**
– **Seenähe**
– **Großes Angebot an Freizeit und Sport**
– **Gute Verkehrsanbindung**

THE POSITIONING

Witenzelg is positioned with the focal theme "Pleasurable living" resulting from the location and market analyses. The communication focuses on the pleasure of living comfortably, freedom of movement, nature, the convenient infrastructure incorporating both the lake and the city, and the good feeling of heating with a lake water heater and thus handling natural resources responsibly.

THE FOCUS OF THE ANALYSIS

Architecture and lifestyle are the focal points of the analysis of Witenzelg that dominate the communication and argumentation. Felix Partner emphasized the lifestyle slightly more because it can be conveyed convincingly thanks to the lake water heating and the car-free park at the center of the estate.

The lifestyle and architecture focus of the analysis:
– Very generous living spaces
– Car-free
– Lake water used for heating
– Own park
– High quality of life
– Near the lake
– Large range of sports and leisure activities
– Good traffic connection

DER NAME: «WITENZELG ROMANSHORN»

Der Flurname verspricht Nähe zur Region, zum nahen Umfeld in Romanshorn und zur Umwelt – ein Versprechen, an welchem sich auch die Planer immer wieder selber messen können.

DER CLAIM: «WIE DAS LEBEN GERNE WOHNT»

Dahinter steht der Gedanke, bewusst zu leben, ohne auf den Komfort zu verzichten, den Neubau-Mietobjekte im mittleren und oberen Segment heute bieten können. Der Claim nimmt das Gefühl der Verbundenheit zur Natur und Region aus dem Positionierungsbeschrieb auf und verstärkt dieses.

DIE FARBEN UND DIE TYPOGRAFIE

Ein angenehmes Klima, schöne Stimmungen vom See her, ein mediterraner Touch: All dies wird in den Farben aufgenommen. Ein Spiel mit dem Petrol des Sees, mit den Brauntönen der Erde, dem Gelb der Sonne und dem verwitterten Grau des Holzes. Die aus einer Familie stammende Schrift präsentiert sich dagegen zurückhaltend.

DIE IDEE: LEBENSGEFÜHL VERMITTELN

Es werden emotionale Aussagen und Porträts entwickelt und kommuniziert, die das Lebensgefühl und den Lifestyle von «Witenzelg Romanshorn», abgestimmt auf Positionierung und Zielgruppe, vermitteln. Das ist die Kommunikationsidee des Immobilienmarketings von «Witenzelg Romanshorn». Menschlich, natürlich, lebensnah.

DAS WERBLICHE KONZEPT

Die zentralen Argumente des Lifestyles und der Architektur von «Witenzelg Romanshorn» werden fokussiert und konzentriert auf die Kommunikationsmittel übertragen: Die Umsetzung der Kommunikationsidee basiert auf Effizienz und Wirksamkeit, auf der emotionalen Vermittlung des Claims «Wie das Leben gerne wohnt» – visuell und medientechnisch optimiert in Szene gesetzt.

THE NAME: "WITENZELG ROMANSHORN"

The field name promises a close connection to the region, to the vicinity in Romanshorn and to the environment – a promise that the planners can also always resort to for measuring their own performance.

THE CLAIM: "WHERE LIFE IS PLEASURABLE"

The claim is based on the concept of living consciously without having to forego the comfort offered by newly built rental buildings in the middle and top sector nowadays. The claim reiterates and boosts the feeling of connectivity to nature and the region of the positioning description.

THE COLORS AND THE TYPOGRAPHY

A pleasant climate, nice moods created by the lake, a Mediterranean touch – all these are reflected in the colors. An interplay of the petrol color of the lake, the brown hues of earth, the yellow of the sun and the faded gray of the wood. In contrast, the font that is based on a single typeface is rather understated.

THE IDEA: CONVEYING A LIFESTYLE

Emotional statements and portraits are developed and communicated that convey the attitude and lifestyle of "Witenzelg Romanshorn" matched to the positioning and target group. This is the communication idea of "Witenzelg Romanshorn" real estate marketing. Humane, natural, drawn from life.

THE ADVERTISING CONCEPT

The central arguments of the lifestyle and the architecture of "Witenzelg Romanshorn" are transferred to the means of communication in a focused and concentrated fashion. The implementation of the communication idea is based on efficiency and effectiveness, on the emotional conveyance of the claim "Where life is pleasurable" staged in a way that is optimized in visual and media technology terms.

DAS CORPORATE DESIGN FÜR «WITENZELG ROMANSHORN»
THE CORPORATE DESIGN FOR "WITENZELG ROMANSHORN"

LOGO
LOGO

TYPOGRAFIE
TYPOGRAPHY

Museo Sans

IM WITENZELG IN

Im Witenzelg in Romanshorn entsteht auf rund 20'000 m² eine mit Seewasser beheizte Minergie-Siedlung. Die zum Projekt herausgearbeitete Positionierung «So wie das Leben gerne wohnt» wird dabei als zentrale Aussage umgesetzt.

FARBEN
COLORS

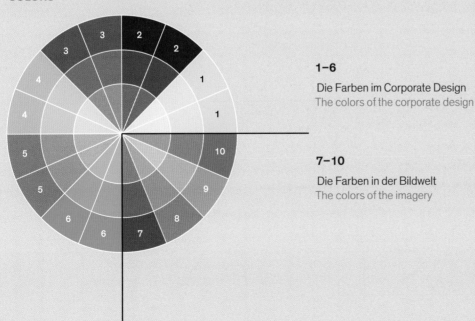

1–6

Die Farben im Corporate Design
The colors of the corporate design

7–10

Die Farben in der Bildwelt
The colors of the imagery

WIE DAS LEBEN GERNE

Where life is pleasurable

WITENZELG
ROMANSHORN

WOHNT

DIE KOMMUNIKATIONSMITTEL

Website (Presite und Vollversion), wiederkehrendes Magazin, Anzeigen, Plakate F200, Busplakate, Signaletik, Vermietungsdokumentation, Angebotsflyer, Baureklametafel, Bauwand entlang der Baustelle, ausführliche Grundrisspläne mit einem Maßstab von 1:100, Fassadenpläne und Gebäudeschnitt, Situations- und Umgebungsplan, Kurzbaubeschrieb, Preislisten, Tage der offenen Tür, Zukunftstage für Schüler, Medienarbeit und Publicity

THE COMMUNICATION MEDIA

Website (pre-site and full version), periodical magazine, advertisements, F200 posters, bus posters, directional signs, rental documentation, offer flyer, construction site advertising banner, construction wall along the construction site, elaborate ground plans with a scale of 1:100, facade plans and building layout, location and setting plan, brief construction description, price lists, open house days, future days for students, media activities and publicity

Website (Presite und Vollversion)
Website (pre-site and full version)

Baureklametafel
Construction site advertising banner

Anzeigen
Advertisements

Vermietungsdokumentation
Rental documentation

Magazin
Magazine

Give-away Zukunftstag
Give-away future day

Plakat F200
F200 poster

Plakat F200
F200 poster

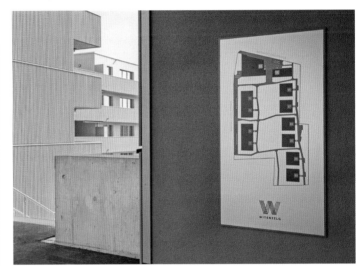

Signaletik
Directional signs

Medienarbeit und Publicity
Media activities and publicity

GEMEINSAMKEITEN UND EIGENSTÄNDIGKEITEN IM EINKLANG
PERFECT BALANCE OF COMMONALITY AND AUTONOMY

EIGENTUM IM WITENZELG
CONDOMINIUMS IN WITENZELG

DIE BASIS

Als Teil der Minergie-Siedlung im Witenzelg werden die Wohnungen der Häuser Nummer 23 und 25 an der Martina-Hälg-Strasse im Eigentum angeboten. Der Standort überzeugt durch ein einmaliges Gesamtkonzept, bei welchem Lebensqualität und Nachhaltigkeit im Zentrum stehen. Die Häuser bilden ein harmonisches Ganzes, sind auf eine gute Besonnung ausgerichtet und werden selbstverständlich ebenfalls im Sinne der Nachhaltigkeit mit Wasser aus dem Bodensee beheizt.

DIE ESSENZ

Für das Projekt hat Felix Partner einen Weg gesucht, der das Witenzelg nicht verleugnet und der neben dem bestehenden Hauptbrand «Witenzelg Romanshorn» trotzdem eigenständig bestehen kann. Der Ort ist von Lebensqualität und Nachhaltigkeit geprägt und so soll das Eigentumsgefühl verstärkt und ins Zentrum gesetzt werden.

Daraus leitet sich der Kerngedanke ab: Mein Witenzelg. Mein Zuhause. Es wird mit dem positiven Gefühl gearbeitet, ein ganz persönliches Eigentum zu erhalten, ganz genau so, wie jeder Einzelne es rund um die Themen Standortqualität, Lebensraum, Ausstrahlung, Wohlfühlzone oder Engagement für sich haben möchte.

THE BASIS

As part of the Minergie housing estate in Witenzelg, the apartments of buildings no. 23 and 25 on Martina-Hälg-Strasse are offered for sale. The location offers a compellingly unique overall concept focusing on high quality of life and sustainability. The buildings constitute a harmonious unit, are aligned for optimal sun exposure, and of course also support economic sustainability by utilizing water from Lake Constance for heating.

THE ESSENCE

For the project an approach was sought that does not negate Witenzelg and that can nevertheless hold its own next to the existing main brand "Witenzelg Romanshorn." The location is characterized by a high quality of life and sustainability and the feeling of proprietorship is strengthened and emphasized.

This is what inspired the core concept: My Witenzelg. My home. The concept is based on the positive emotion of having a very personal property that complies precisely with the way each individual wants it to be in terms of location quality, living space, ambiance, comfort zone, or commitment.

DER MARKT

Einen Teil der Wohnungen im Neubauprojekt Witenzelg als Stockwerkeigentum zu verkaufen, entspricht der Nachfrage im Markt – Lage, Ausbau- und Energiestandard entsprechen den hohen Anforderungen kaufkräftiger Interessenten. Gleichzeitig optimieren die Eigentumswohnungen die Vielfalt des Projekts Witenzelg neben den Mietwohnungen und den Gewerberäumen.

DER AUFTRAG

Das Immobilienmarketing läuft unter der Dachmarke «Witenzelg Romanshorn», ist aber speziell auf das Projekt Wohneigentum und auf dessen Zielgruppe zugeschnitten. Das Konzept beinhaltet die Namens- und Markenentwicklung, Positionierung und Claim sowie die gesamte Umsetzung im Corporate Design und in den eingesetzten Kommunikationsmaßnahmen.

DER ZIELRAUM

– Stadt Romanshorn
– Kanton Thurgau

THE MARKET

Offering some of the apartments of the new construction project Witenzelg as condominiums is a response to the market demand – the location, finishing, and energy standards are in line with the high demands of affluent potential buyers. At the same time, the condominiums optimize the diversity of the Witenzelg project in addition to the rental apartments and the commercial spaces.

THE ASSIGNMENT

Under the umbrella brand "Witenzelg Romanshorn," the real estate marketing was specifically adjusted to the condominium project and its target group. The concept incorporates the name and brand development, positioning and the claim, as well as the entire implementation of the corporate design and applied communication measures.

THE TARGET AREA

– City of Romanshorn
– Canton Thurgau

DIE ZIELGRUPPE

Für die Eigentumswohnungen definieren die Planer einzelne, sehr fokussierte Zielgruppen, angepasst an die Standort- und Marktdaten sowie die Werte und Eigenschaften der Überbauung.

Quantitativ:
– Einzelpersonen oder DINKs (double income no kids) aus der Region
– Unverheiratete Paare und Ehepaare mit ein bis höchstens zwei Kindern
– Unverheiratete Paare und Ehepaare ohne Kinder oder nach Familienphase
– Hausverkäufer (eher älter, Wohnung anstelle Haus)
– Kleininvestoren

Qualitativ:
– Schätzen Erholung am See und auf dem Land
– Suchen gute Infrastruktur mit persönlichem Flair
– Verkehrsanbindung (privater und öffentlicher Verkehr) ist wichtig
– Setzen auf Bewährtes und Regionales

Schlüsselargumente:
– Standort nahe See und Grünzonen
– Infrastruktur mit allem, was man braucht
– Für jeden Geschmack das passende Angebot
– Wenn ich will, läuft immer etwas
– Verkehrsanbindung ist wichtig

THE TARGET GROUP

The planners defined individual very precise target groups for the condominiums, matched to the location and market data as well as the values and characteristics of the buildings.

Quantitative:
– Individuals or DINKs (double income no kids) from the region
– Unmarried couples and couples with one or maximum two children
– Unmarried couples and married couples without children or after the family phase
– Home sellers (rather older, replacing a house by a condominium)
– Small investors

Qualitative:
– Appreciate relaxation near the lake and in the countryside
– Looking for a good infrastructure with a personal ambiance
– Traffic connections (private and public) are important
– Traditionally and regionally oriented

Key arguments:
– Location near the lake and nature zones
– Infrastructure offering all necessities of life
– Offers to suit any taste
– Whenever I want, things are happening
– Traffic connections are important

DIE SINUS-ANALYSE DER ZIELGRUPPE FÜR «MEIN WITENZELG»
THE SINUS ANALYSIS OF THE TARGET GROUP FOR "MY WITENZELG"

SOZIALE LAGE UND GRUNDORIENTIERUNG
SOCIAL STATUS AND BASIC VALUES

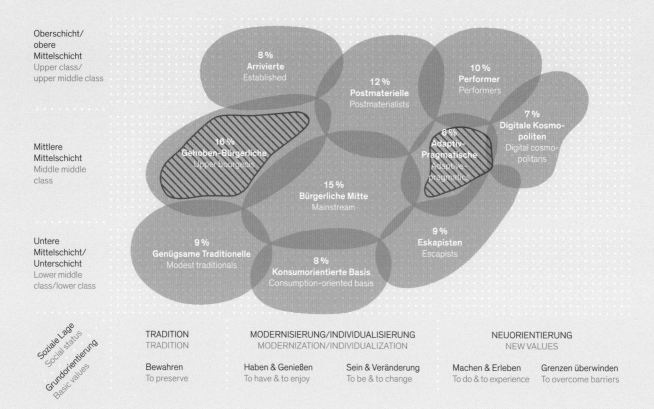

Oberschicht/
obere
Mittelschicht
Upper class/
upper middle class

8 %
Arrivierte
Established

12 %
Postmaterielle
Postmaterialists

10 %
Performer
Performers

7 %
**Digitale Kosmo-
politen**
Digital cosmo-
politans

Mittlere
Mittelschicht
Middle middle
class

16 %
Gehoben-Bürgerliche
Upper bourgeois

6 %
**Adaptiv-
Pragmatische**
Adaptive-
pragmatics

15 %
Bürgerliche Mitte
Mainstream

Untere
Mittelschicht/
Unterschicht
Lower middle
class/lower class

9 %
Genügsame Traditionelle
Modest traditionals

8 %
Konsumorientierte Basis
Consumption-oriented basis

9 %
Eskapisten
Escapists

Soziale Lage
Social status
Grundorientierung
Basic values

TRADITION TRADITION	MODERNISIERUNG/INDIVIDUALISIERUNG MODERNIZATION/INDIVIDUALIZATION		NEUORIENTIERUNG NEW VALUES	
Bewahren To preserve	Haben & Genießen To have & to enjoy	Sein & Veränderung To be & to change	Machen & Erleben To do & to experience	Grenzen überwinden To overcome barriers

Rational handelnde Menschen mit viel Sinn für Natur und Infrastruktur: Die dazu passenden
Sinus-Milieus beschreiben die Gehoben-Bürgerlichen und die Adaptiv-Pragmatischen.
Rationally acting persons who appreciate nature and a good infrastructure – the matching
Sinus milieus are the upper bourgeois and the adaptive-pragmatics.

KLUGE ENTSCHEIDER

Wie bei den Mietwohnungen stellt das Marketing auch hier mögliche Käufer der Eigentumswohnungen vor und spricht so die entsprechende Zielgruppe direkt und emotional an.

Thomas Auf der Maur ist 67 Jahre alt und seit 40 Jahren in Romanshorn ansässig. Seit er alleine lebt, wird ihm sein Einfamilienhaus zu groß und die damit verbundene Arbeit zu mühsam. Er möchte jedoch gerne seinen nächsten Lebensabschnitt weiter in der Region Romanshorn verbringen und sich sein angestammtes Umfeld nicht neu aufbauen müssen. Ebenso bevorzugt er eine Wohnung zum Kauf, die er später seinen Kindern hinterlassen kann. Er ist viel und gerne draußen, wünscht sich eine zentrale Lage, an der er nicht immer gleich das Auto nehmen muss und eine moderne Wohnung mit viel Grün im Außenbereich. Die Wohnungsgröße steht für ihn nicht im Vordergrund, ideal wäre eine großzügig geschnittene 2,5- oder eine 3-Zimmer-Wohnung.

SMART DECISION MAKERS

Similar to the rental apartments, marketing for this sector also presents possible buyers of the condominiums to directly and emotionally address the target group.

Thomas Auf der Maur is 67 years old and has been residing in Romanshorn for 40 years. Since he now lives alone, his single-family home has become too large for him and the work associated with it too strenuous. However, he would like to continue to spend the next part of his life in the Romanshorn region without having to give up his accustomed surroundings. He is looking to purchase a condominium that his children can inherit one day. He loves being outdoors and desires a central location where he does not have to take the car all the time and a modern apartment surrounded by plenty of nature. While the size of the apartment is not a chief consideration, a generously sized 2.5 or 3-room apartment would be ideal.

EIGENTUM, WIE ICH ES WILL
PROPERTY, THE WAY I LIKE IT

DIE POSITIONIERUNG

«Eigentum, wie ich es will» zielt als Positionierungssatz direkt auf das eigenständige und wohlüberlegte Denken der Zielgruppe ab. Sie handelt vernünftig und individuell. Sie weiß, was gut für sie ist, schätzt die Nähe zu ihrem sozialen Umfeld und nimmt Rücksicht auf die Umwelt.

THE POSITIONING

As a positioning statement, "Property, the way I like it" directly targets the independent and deliberate thinking of the target group. They act rationally and individually. They know what is good for them, appreciate the vicinity to their social environment, and are environmentally conscious.

DER NAME: «MEIN WITENZELG»

Der Flurname des Hauptprojekts «Witenzelg Romanshorn» bleibt als Basis bestehen. Die Ergänzung «Mein» zielt nicht nur auf das Eigentum, sondern auch auf das Selbstbewusstsein der Zielgruppe ab.

DER CLAIM: «MEIN WITENZELG. SO WIE ICH ES WILL»

Der selbstbewusste Projektname wird nochmals verstärkt und ergänzt mit einem Versprechen, sein Umfeld, sein Leben, seinen Wohnraum nach seinen eigenen Vorstellungen zu gestalten.

DIE FARBEN UND DIE TYPOGRAFIE

Vielfältig. Spielerisch. Persönlich. Individuell. Vieles unter einen Hut zu bringen und die Breite des Eigentums mit seinen vielen Möglichkeiten mit Farben zu dokumentieren wird einfach bunt. Bewusst bunt. Freude. Eigenständigkeit. Meins. Und für jeden seins. Die Schriften aber sind dafür geradezu klassisch und zurückhaltend. Klar. Reduziert.

DIE IDEE: ICH BIN WITENZELG

Plakativ, laut, direkt und ungeschminkt: So kommt «Mein Witenzelg» daher, so lebt und denkt auch seine Zielgruppe. Identifikation und Wiedererkennung wird durch die Personifizierung des Projekts geschaffen: Diese Idee lädt die neuen Eigentümer dazu ein, Witenzelg selber zu gestalten und zu definieren — so, wie sie es mit allem in ihrem Leben tun.

DAS WERBLICHE KONZEPT

Im Zentrum der Kommunikationsmittel stehen visuelle Ausschnitte des entwickelten Logos sowie kurze Schlagzeilen, die direkt die Fakten und Vorteile auf den Tisch legen. Das Layout ist plakativ, die Sprache schnell und auf den Punkt. Viel Kopf, weniger Lifestyle.

THE NAME: "MY WITENZELG"

The field name of the main project "Witenzelg Romanshorn" remains in place as the base. The addition of "My" expresses not only the proprietorship but also the self-confidence of the target group.

THE CLAIM: "MY WITENZELG. THE WAY I LIKE IT"

The self-confident project name is enhanced and complemented by the promise of shaping one's surroundings, one's life, and one's living space according to individual wishes and expectations.

THE COLORS AND THE TYPOGRAPHY

Diverse. Playful. Personal. Individual. Expressing the multitude of aspects and the broad range of possibilities offered by owning properties results in a colorful mix. Deliberately colorful. Joy. Independence. Mine. To each his own. The fonts, in return, are rather classical and understated. Clear. Unadorned.

THE IDEA: I AM WITENZELG

Striking, loud, direct, and unadorned: this is how "My Witenzelg" comes across, this is also the way its target group lives and thinks. Personification of the project aids its identification and recognition. This idea invites the new owners to design and define Witenzelg themselves — just as they do with everything in their lives.

THE ADVERTISING CONCEPT

The communication tools are based on visual excerpts of the developed logo coupled with short statements that directly and simply present the facts and advantages. The layout is striking, the language quick and to the point. Plenty of rationality, less lifestyle.

DAS CORPORATE DESIGN FÜR «MEIN WITENZELG»
THE CORPORATE DESIGN FOR "MY WITENZELG"

LOGO
LOGO

TYPOGRAFIE
TYPOGRAPHY

Theinhardt

NUR WENIGE GEHMINUTEN

Nur wenige Gehminuten vom Bodensee entfernt, bietet «Mein Witenzelg» 22 neue Eigentumswohnungen mit 2,5 bis 4,5 Zimmern und durch seinen zentralen Standort beste Voraussetzungen für Schule, Einkaufen, Freizeitgestaltung, Sport, Kultur und vieles mehr.

FARBEN
COLORS

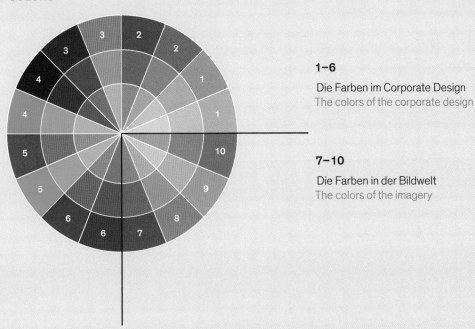

1–6

Die Farben im Corporate Design
The colors of the corporate design

7–10

Die Farben in der Bildwelt
The colors of the imagery

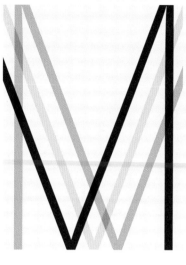

MEIN WITENZELG.
STANDORT-
QUALITÄT, WIE
ICH SIE WILL.

My Witenzelg. Location quality, the way I like it

MEIN WITENZELG.
WOHLFÜHLZONE,
WIE ICH SIE WILL.

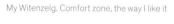

My Witenzelg. Comfort zone, the way I like it

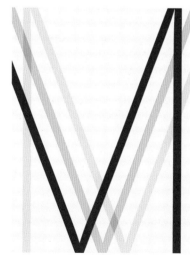

MEIN WITENZELG.
ENGAGEMENT,
WIE ICH ES WILL.

My Witenzelg. Commitment, the way I like it

My Witenzelg. Property, the way I like it

MEIN WITENZELG. EIGENTUM, WIE ICH ES WILL.

DIE KOMMUNIKATIONSMITTEL

Website, Verkaufsbroschüre, Inserate, Plakate F200, Planbroschüre, Messe-
flyer, Pläne, Informationsmaterial, Pressearbeit, Banner und Bautafel

THE COMMUNICATION MEDIA

Website, sales brochure, advertisements, F200 posters, layout brochure, trade fair flyer, plans, information material, press activities, banner and construction site sign

Bautafel
Construction site sign

Plakat F200
F200 poster

Banner
Banner

Inserate
Advertisements

Website
Website

Verkaufsbroschüre
Sales brochure

Verkaufsbroschüre
Sales brochure

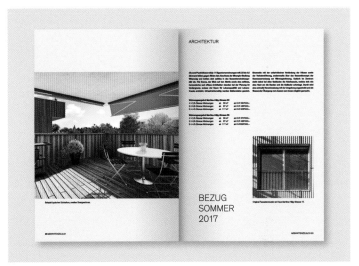

Verkaufsbroschüre
Sales brochure

Verkaufsbroschüre
Sales brochure

EINE WIN-WIN-SITUATION FÜR ALLE BETEILIGTEN
A WIN-WIN SITUATION FOR EVERYONE INVOLVED

GEWERBE IM WITENZELG
COMMERCIAL SPACES IN WITENZELG

DIE BASIS

Auf dem Witenzelg-Areal finden Jungunternehmer und etablierte Firmen einen idealen Standort. Die multifunktionalen Gewerbelofts eignen sich für Büros oder Shops genauso gut wie für Kunstateliers und werden zu tiefen Einsteigerpreisen vermietet. Das Angebot umfasst Räume von 50 bis 140 Quadratmeter in verschiedenen Preisklassen und Ausbaustandards. Das ganze Projekt setzt sich für eine starke Standortförderung von Romanshorn und dem Witenzelg und einen bunten Angebotsmix ein.

DIE ESSENZ

Gewerberäume sind an vielen Standorten schwierig zu vermieten. Es herrscht oftmals ein Überangebot, die Preise sind schlicht zu hoch oder der Angebotsmix am Standort passt nicht. Ein Angebot mit moderner Infrastruktur, in einem neuen Gebäude und dann noch zentral gelegen, soll lokale und regionale Jungunternehmer und gestandene Unternehmen ansprechen und den Standort Romanshorn stärken.

Daraus leitet sich der Kerngedanke ab: ab 66 Franken zum Erfolg. Attraktive, neue Gewerbelofts werden zu tiefen Einsteigerpreisen an neu gegründete Firmen und etablierte Unternehmen vermietet. Dank reduzierten Betriebskosten können die Gewerbetreibenden ihre finanziellen Mittel optimal einsetzen und sich noch stärker auf ihre Kernkompetenzen konzentrieren.

THE BASIS

Young and established businesses find ideal situations on the Witenzelg premises. The multi-functional business lofts are suited for offices or shops as well as art studios and are available for rent at low beginner's prices. The offer includes spaces from 50 to 140 square meters in various price categories and finishing standards. The entire project promotes the strengthening of the Romanshorn and Witenzelg location and a varied mix of offers.

THE ESSENCE

Commercial spaces are difficult to rent out in many locations. Often there is excess supply, the prices are simply too high or the mix of offers at the location is not acceptable. An offer with modern infrastructure, in a new building and centrally located to boost is intended to address local and regional young entrepreneurs and established businesses to strengthen the Romanshorn location.

This is what inspired the core concept: Success starting at 66 francs. Attractive new commercial lofts are rented at low beginning prices to newly founded and established businesses. Thanks to the low operational costs, the businesses can optimize their financial means to focus even more on their core competencies.

DER MARKT

Gewerberäume sind im Raum Romanshorn schwierig zu vermieten, denn vielerorts besteht ein Überangebot und eine Einschränkung für die betriebliche Nutzung. Meist sind nur stilles Gewerbe und Büro zulässig. Aus diesem Grund erfordert die Vermarktung von «Witenzelg Work» vom Planungs- und Verkaufsteam ein besonderes Konzept, das neue Marktbereiche erschließt.

DER AUFTRAG

Eine Business-Strategie entwickeln, wie die leerstehenden Gewerbelofts vermietet werden können – so lautet der Auftrag. Das dazu passende Konzept beinhaltet eine überraschende und aggressive Angebotsstrategie, die sich an Start-ups und gestandene Unternehmer richtet, die Namens- und Markenentwicklung, Positionierung und Claim sowie die gesamte Umsetzung im Corporate Design und in den eingesetzten Kommunikationsmaßnahmen inklusive Pressearbeit und Partnerakquisition.

DER ZIELRAUM

– Stadt Romanshorn
– Kanton Thurgau

THE MARKET

In the Romanshorn area, commercial spaces are difficult to rent out as in many areas there is excessive supply of spaces while commercial use is limited by regulations. Usually only noiseless trades and offices are permitted. The planning and sales team of "Witenzelg Work" therefore had to come up with a special concept for the marketing to reach new market areas.

THE ASSIGNMENT

The assignment was to develop a strategy for renting out the unrented commercial lofts. The associated concept incorporates a surprising and aggressive offer strategy addressing start-ups and established businesses, the name and brand development, positioning and the claim, as well as the entire implementation of the corporate design and utilized communication measures including press relations and partner acquisition.

THE TARGET AREA

– City of Romanshorn
– Canton Thurgau

DIE ZIELGRUPPE

Der Gewerbe- und Unternehmer-Mix für die Lofts soll so breit wie möglich sein, damit Durchmischung und gegenseitige Synergien geschaffen werden können. In Verbindung mit den attraktiven Finanzierungsmodellen fokussiert die Kommunikation folgende Zielgruppen:

Jungunternehmen:
– Technologiegetriebene Start-ups
– Handwerkliche Betriebe
– Freiberufler wie Berater, Fotografen, Coiffeure oder Künstler

Etablierte Firmen:
– Aus den verschiedensten Bereichen

Beeinflusser:
– Investoren
– Business Angels
– Gewerbevereine
– Startnetzwerk Thurgau
– Unternehmensberater
– Treuhänder

Argumente, die überzeugen:
– Zentrale Lage
– Attraktives Mietangebot
– Gute Verkehrsanbindung
– Neue, praktische Räume
– Standortförderung

THE TARGET GROUP

The trade and business mix for the lofts should be as varied as possible to ensure diversity and mutual synergy effects. In combination with the attractive financing models, the communication targets the following groups:

Young businesses:
– Technology-oriented start-ups
– Trades and crafts
– Self-employed entrepreneurs such as consultants, photographers, hairdressers, or artists

Established companies:
– From a variety of sectors

Influencers:
– Investors
– Business Angels
– Trade associations
– Startnetzwerk Thurgau (Thurgau start-up network)
– Business consultants
– Trustees

Compelling arguments:
– Central location
– Attractive rent offer
– Good traffic connection
– New convenient spaces
– Strengthening of the location

DIE SINUS-ANALYSE DER ZIELGRUPPE FÜR «WITENZELG WORK»
THE SINUS ANALYSIS OF THE TARGET GROUP FOR "WITENZELG WORK"

SOZIALE LAGE UND GRUNDORIENTIERUNG
SOCIAL STATUS AND BASIC VALUES

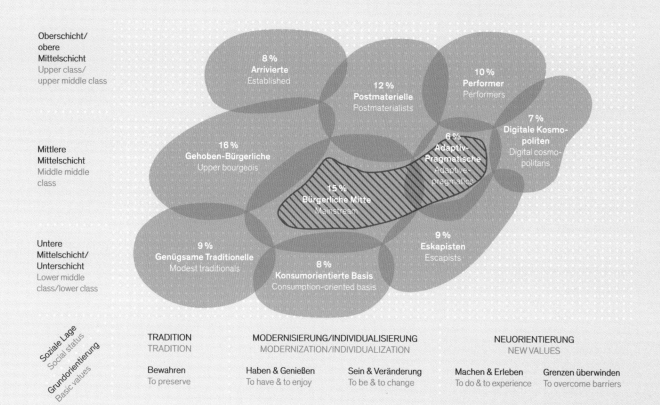

Oberschicht/
obere
Mittelschicht
Upper class/
upper middle class

Mittlere
Mittelschicht
Middle middle
class

Untere
Mittelschicht/
Unterschicht
Lower middle
class/lower class

8 %
Arrivierte
Established

12 %
Postmaterielle
Postmaterialists

10 %
Performer
Performers

7 %
Digitale Kosmo-
politen
Digital cosmo-
politans

16 %
Gehoben-Bürgerliche
Upper bourgeois

6 %
Adaptiv-
Pragmatische
Adaptive-
pragmatics

15 %
Bürgerliche Mitte
Mainstream

9 %
Genügsame Traditionelle
Modest traditionals

8 %
Konsumorientierte Basis
Consumption-oriented basis

9 %
Eskapisten
Escapists

Soziale Lage
Social status

Grundorientierung
Basic values

TRADITION
TRADITION

MODERNISIERUNG/INDIVIDUALISIERUNG
MODERNIZATION/INDIVIDUALIZATION

NEUORIENTIERUNG
NEW VALUES

Bewahren
To preserve

Haben & Genießen
To have & to enjoy

Sein & Veränderung
To be & to change

Machen & Erleben
To do & to experience

Grenzen überwinden
To overcome barriers

Unternehmer und Investoren mit klaren Zielen und hohen Ansprüchen bei Infrastruktur und Verkehrsanbindungen:
Die dazu passenden Sinus-Milieus beschreiben die bürgerliche Mitte und die Adaptiv-Pragmatischen.
Entrepreneurs and investors with clearly structured aims and high demands regarding infrastructure and traffic
connections – the matching Sinus milieus are the mainstream and the adaptive-pragmatics.

DER START IN DAS UNTERNEHMERLEBEN

Im Fokus der Kommunikation stehen Jungunternehmerinnen und -unternehmer, die mit «Witenzelg Work» durchstarten und ihren Traum leben können. Ihre Porträts, die direkt ansprechen, prägen die Kommunikation und sollen Träume und den Mut wecken, den Moment jetzt zu nutzen.

Manuel und Matthias sind beide 27 und schon zusammen zur Schule gegangen. Dann haben sich ihre Wege getrennt, der eine studierte Mathematik und der andere absolvierte eine Lehre zum Orgelbauer. Durch gemeinsame private Interessen haben sie sich vor einem Jahr wieder getroffen. Nach vielen Stunden Planung und Grundlagen schaffen haben sie sich entschieden, ein Start-up-Unternehmen zu gründen und sich als Entwickler von komplexen, webbasierten Lösungen einen Namen zu machen. Da nebst dem Startkapital die Mittel eher knapp bemessen sind, sind sie auf der Suche nach einem Standort, an dem die Infrastruktur stimmt und an dem sie konzentriert arbeiten können. Bewusst ohne den Chic von Industriebrachen und dem Charme alter Gießereihallen.

BUSINESS LAUNCH

The focus of the communication is on young entrepreneurs who are launching their own business at "Witenzelg Work" to live out their dream. Their portraits, which are immediately appealing, characterize the communication with the intention of evoking dreams and encouraging others to seize the moment.

Manuel and Matthias are both 27 years old and already attended high school together. After that, their paths diverged; one of them studied mathematics while the other was professionally trained as an organ builder. Based on their common private interests they met again a year ago and after many hours of planning and scheming, they decided to found a start-up company for the development of complex, web-based solutions. As, other than the seed money, their means are rather limited, they are in search of a location with the appropriate infrastructure where they can focus on their work. They deliberately want to avoid the style of fallow industrial areas and the charm of old foundry halls.

RAUM FÜR UNTERNEHMER
ROOM FOR ENTREPRENEURS

DIE POSITIONIERUNG

«Raum für Unternehmer» – die Aussage steht gleichzeitig für Entwicklungsraum, Raum für gelebte Träume, vielseitig nutzbaren und bezahlbaren Raum für neue Ideen. «Witenzelg Work» präsentiert sich als das Silicon Valley des Bodensees, ein Melting Pot spannender Unternehmer-Persönlichkeiten, die sich hier gegenseitig den Weg für den großen Erfolg ebnen.

THE POSITIONING

"Room for entrepreneurs" – the statement stands simultaneously for room for development, room to live out one's dreams, multiple-use and affordable room for new ideas. "Witenzelg Work" presents itself as the Silicon Valley of Lake Constance, a melting pot of interesting entrepreneurial personalities that pave each other's ways to great success.

DER NAME: «WITENZELG WORK»

Einprägsam, international, dem Geist des kreativen Potenzials der Gewerbelofts entsprechend, nimmt der Name bereits vieles vorweg, was die Kommunikation wieder aufnimmt und vertieft.

DER CLAIM: «RAUM FÜR UNTERNEHMER»

Der Claim entspricht dem Positionierungssatz und bietet direkt an, was Start-ups wie auch gestandene Unternehmer für ihre Visionen brauchen: Raum, flexibel nutz- und finanzierbar.

DIE FARBEN UND DIE TYPOGRAFIE

Das Ziel: Eine Abgrenzung zum Auftritt der Miete und des Eigentums finden. Eigenständig sein und doch eine Ergänzung. Die Farbsprache wird in der Basis beibehalten, mit starken Farbtönen ergänzt und mit Akzenten versehen. Signalcharakter schaffen und die Aktion unterstützen. Ohne Orange und ohne Rot, die im Markt zu stark besetzt sind. Typografisch wieder eine klare Reduktion und Einfachheit.

DIE IDEE: THE OFFER IS THE HERO

Jeder Jungunternehmer muss mit seinem Kapital so effizient wie möglich für die Umsetzung seiner Geschäftsideen umgehen, damit er sich durchsetzen kann. Darauf zielt «Witenzelg Work» ab. Das Konzept sieht vor, dass von der Zielgruppe akzeptierte Beeinflusser und Anlaufstellen das Angebot hinaustragen und sich als Botschafter einsetzen.

DAS WERBLICHE KONZEPT

Das Angebot steht als Key Visual bei allen Kommunikationsmaßnahmen im Zentrum. Denn 66 Franken Miete pro Quadratmeter und Jahr ist ein Anreiz für alle Unternehmer. Damit die Glaubwürdigkeit in der Zielgruppe hochgehalten wird, erzielt das Projekt über eine regionale Kooperation mit dem Startnetzwerk Thurgau (Kantonalbank, Kanton, Industrie- und Handelskammer, Gewerbe Thurgau und die Stadt Frauenfeld) einen Imagetransfer vom Beeinflusser auf das Angebot.

THE NAME: "WITENZELG WORK"

Catchy, international, in line with the commercial lofts' spirit of creative potential, the name already reveals many aspects that are repeated and intensified in the communication.

THE CLAIM: "ROOM FOR ENTREPRENEURS"

The claim is in line with the positioning sentence and directly offers what start-ups and established companies need for their visions — space that can be flexibly used and financed.

THE COLORS AND THE TYPOGRAPHY

The aim was to differentiate the offer from the presentation of the rental apartments and condominiums. As an independent entity that is at the same time complementary. The color scheme was basically maintained, with the addition of strong colors and accents. To create a beacon and support the campaign, avoiding the use of orange and red that are over-used in the market. The typography in turn was once again clearly understated and simple.

THE IDEA: THE OFFER IS THE HERO

Every young entrepreneur must handle the business capital as efficiently as possible for the implementation of the business concept to prevail. This is the aim of "Witenzelg Work." The concept involves influencers and supporters that are accepted by the target group spreading awareness of the offer and acting as its ambassadors.

THE ADVERTISING CONCEPT

The offer is at the center of all communication measures as a key visual element. This is because 66 francs rent per square meter and year appeals to all entrepreneurs. To increase the credibility among members of the target group, the project initiated a regional cooperation with the Startnetzwerk Thurgau (Thurgau start-up network involving the canton bank, canton, chamber of industry and trade, business and trade of Thurgau and the city of Frauenfeld) which resulted in an image transfer from the influencer to the offer.

DAS CORPORATE DESIGN FÜR «WITENZELG WORK»
THE CORPORATE DESIGN FOR "WITENZELG WORK"

LOGO
LOGO

TYPOGRAFIE
TYPOGRAPHY

Theinhardt

WITENZELG
WORK

FÜR DIE VERMIETUNG

Für die Vermietung von attraktiven, neuen Gewerbe-lofts im Witenzelg Romanshorn haben wir ein umfas-sendes Programm erarbeitet. So werden die Räume zu tiefen Einsteigerpreisen ab 66 Franken pro m²/ Jahr an neu gegründete Firmen abgegeben.

FARBEN
COLORS

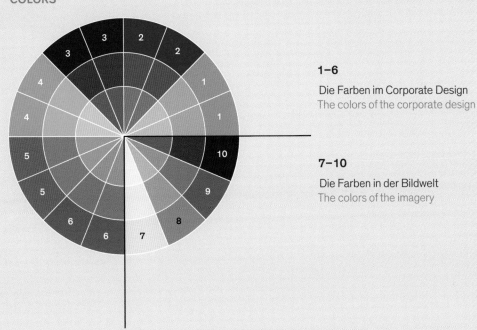

1–6

Die Farben im Corporate Design
The colors of the corporate design

7–10

Die Farben in der Bildwelt
The colors of the imagery

VERKAUFEN SIE HIER IN ZUKUNFT IHRE NEUSTEN WERKE.

This is the place where you can sell your latest work in the future

HANDELN SIE HIER IN ZUKUNFT DAS BESTE FÜR IHRE KUNDEN AUS.

This is the place where you can get the best deal for your customers in the future

NEHMEN SIE HIER IN ZUKUNFT AN IHREN KUNDEN MASS.

This is the place where you can measure your customers in the future

KREIEREN SIE HIER IN ZUKUNFT IHREN KUNDEN EINEN NEUEN LOOK.

This is the place where you can create a new look for your customers in the future

DIE KOMMUNIKATIONSMITTEL

Website, Anzeigen, Plakat F200, Broschüre, Einladungsmailing, Informationsmaterial, Pressearbeit, Werbe- und Beschriftungskonzept am Bau

THE COMMUNICATION MEDIA

Website, advertisements, F200 poster, brochure, invitation mailing, information material, press activities, advertising and lettering concept on the building

Werbung am Bau
Advertising concept on the building

Beschriftungskonzept am Bau
Lettering concept on the building

Plakat F200
F200 poster

Plakat F200
F200 poster

Website
Website

Anzeigen
Advertisements

Informationsmaterial
Information material

NACHHALTIGE, AUSSERGEWÖHNLICHE
WOHNQUALITÄT UND FLEXIBLEN RAUM
FÜR GEWERBE SCHAFFEN
CREATING SUSTAINABLE, EXCEPTIONAL
RESIDENTIAL QUALITY AND FLEXIBLE
SPACE FOR BUSINESSES

DIE IMMOBILIE

Nach außen wird die kompakte Anlage als Randbebauung definiert, wodurch in der Mitte ein großer Freiraum von über 7'000 Quadratmetern entsteht, der als komplett autofreier Park konzipiert ist. Dies wird durch eine zusammenhängende gemeinsame Tiefgarage ermöglicht, die alle Häuser miteinander verbindet. Die Bauten sind somit vom Außenraum geprägt und bilden ein harmonisches Gebäudeensemble. Das markanteste Element sind die zum Park hin orientierten, großzügigen Balkone, deren Holzverkleidung nahtlos in die Fassade übergeht.

Sechs Punkthäuser vermitteln auf der Westseite zu den bestehenden Einfamilienhäusern des Quartiers. Die beiden Längsbauten im Osten bilden den Abschluss zu den benachbarten Sportanlagen. Zwei erhöhte Volumen an der Straße im Norden formen das Eingangstor zum großzügigen Park in der Siedlungsmitte, der sich nach Süden hin zur Freihaltezone öffnet. Auf den so zur Straße hin ausgebildeten Vorplatz sind konsequenterweise auch die Gewerbenutzungen orientiert.

Das ganze Areal ist in öffentliche Bereiche wie den Park mit seinen Wegen und Rasenflächen, halböffentliche Bereiche wie die Gebäudezugänge sowie in private Bereiche wie Gartensitzplätze, Terrassen und Balkone gegliedert. Die Distanzen zwischen den Gebäuden sind besonders groß gehalten und gewährleisten daher eine gute Besonnung und auf den privaten Außenräumen viel Privatsphäre. So sind die Gartensitzplätze zum Park hin leicht erhöht angelegt und mit einer schützenden Grünbepflanzung versehen.

THE PROPERTY

On the outside, the compact estate is designed as perimeter buildings, which results in a large open area of over 7,000 square meters at the center designed as a completely car-free park. This is made possible by a common connected underground garage that connects all buildings to each other. Therefore, the buildings are characterized by the outdoors and constitute a harmonious building ensemble. The most prominent elements are the generous balconies facing the park, whose timber cladding merges seamlessly with the facade.

Six point houses on the west side create a link to the existing single-family homes of the quarter. The two longitudinal buildings to the east divide the estate from the neighboring sports facilities. Two elevated volumes on the street to the north constitute an entrance to the generously sized park at the center of the estate, which opens up on the south to the undeveloped zone. The commercial establishments all face the front courtyard that was thus created towards the street.

The entire plot is divided into public areas such as the park with its paths and grassy meadows, semi-public areas such as the building entrances, as well as private areas such as garden seating, terraces, and balconies. The distances among the buildings are particularly large and therefore ensure good sun exposure and a large degree of privacy in the private outdoor areas. The seating areas are slightly elevated towards the park and planted for visual protection.

Gesamtansicht Ensemble mit Blick vom Park nach Norden mit markanten, holzverkleideten Balkonen und Freitreppe

General view of the ensemble with view from the park towards the north with prominent, timber-clad balconies and outdoor flight of steps

Detailansicht Freitreppe
Detailed view of the outdoor flight of steps

Großes Bad mit Tageslicht
Large bathroom with daylight

Großzügige, südorientierte Dachterrasse im 4. Obergeschoss
Generous south-oriented roof terrace on the 5th floor

Sehr heller und offener Wohn-/Essbereich
Very bright and open living/dining area

Einblick in typische 2,5-Zimmer-Wohnung
View of a typical 2.5-room apartment

Zurückhaltende, zeitlose Materialisierung
Understated timeless materials

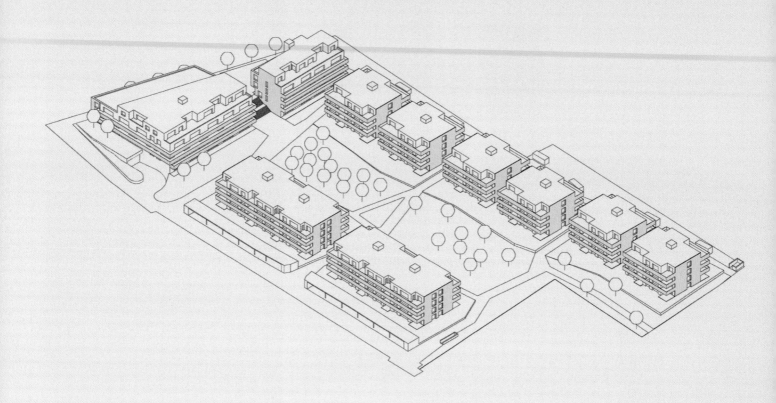

Axonometrie
Axonometric projection

Gesamtplan 1. Obergeschoss
General layout 2nd floor

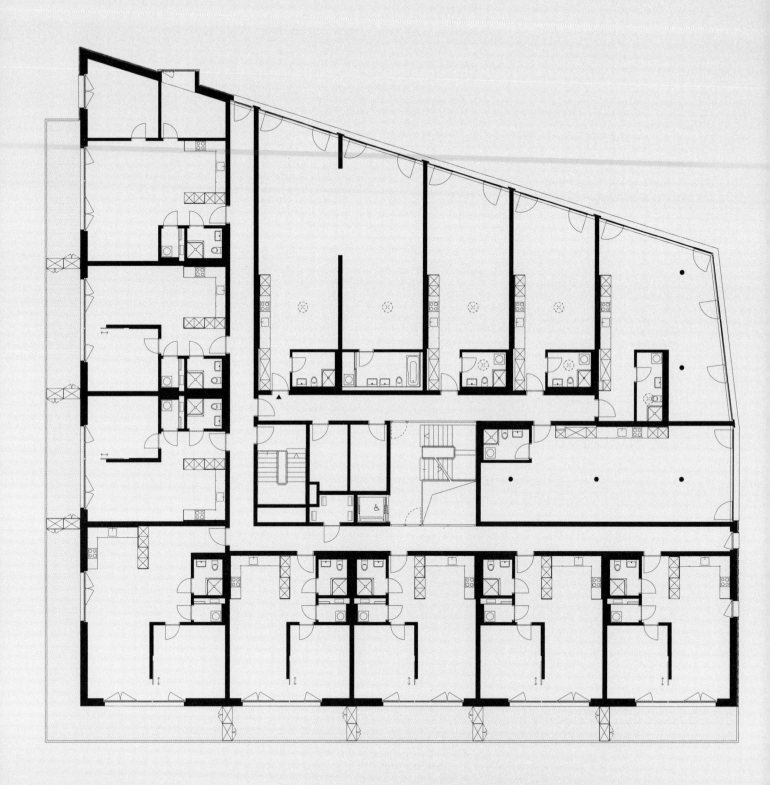

Grundriss A1, 3. Obergeschoss
Layout A1, 4th floor

N

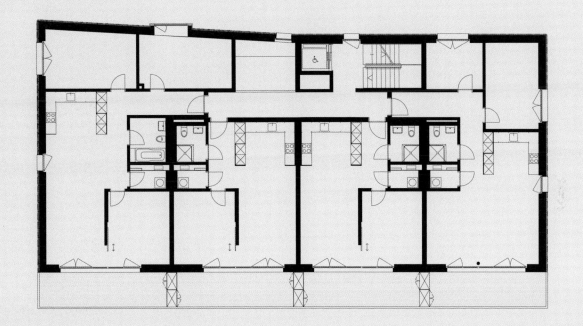

Grundriss A2, 3. Obergeschoss
Layout A2, 4th floor

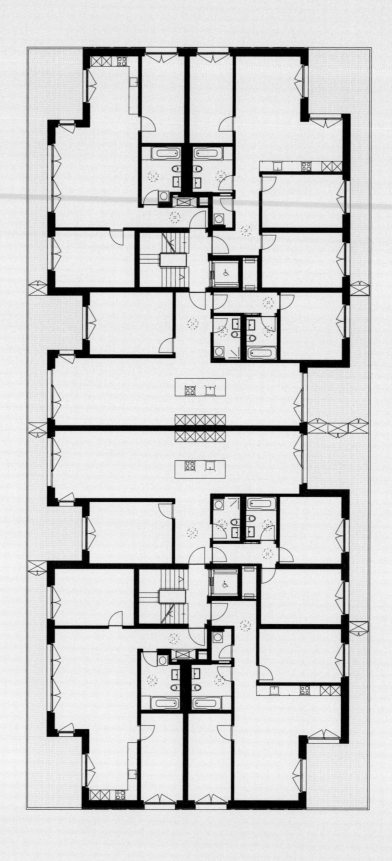

Grundriss B2, 3. Obergeschoss
Layout B2, 4th floor

N

Grundriss C6, Erdgeschoss
Layout C6, ground floor

Grundriss C6, Regelgeschoss
Layout C6, standard floor

N

Grundriss C6, Attikageschoss
Layout C6, attic floor

PRÄGNANTES STADTHAUS AM ZÜRICHBERG

PROMINENT TOWNHOUSE NEAR ZÜRICHBERG

PROJEKTNAME: «Reflect»
IMMOBILIE: Mehrfamilienhaus mit 13 Eigentumswohnungen
STANDORT: Gladbachstrasse 117, 8044 Zürich, Schweiz
AUFTRAGGEBER: Fundamenta Group AG, Zug, Schweiz
ARCHITEKTUR: Linearch GmbH, Zürich, Schweiz
VERMARKTUNG: 2014–2015

PROJECT NAME: "Reflect"
PROPERTY: Multi-party residential building with 13 condominiums
LOCATION: Gladbachstrasse 117, 8044 Zurich, Switzerland
CLIENT: Fundamenta Group AG, Zug, Switzerland
ARCHITECTURE: Linearch GmbH, Zurich, Switzerland
MARKETING PERIOD: 2014–2015

EINMALIGES WOHNGEFÜHL,
HOHER KOMFORT UND
ECHTES PRESTIGE IN EINEM
UNIQUE AMBIANCE, HIGH
COMFORT, AND GENUINE
PRESTIGE ALL IN ONE

DIE BASIS

Als Basis für das Immobilienmarketing dient ein Neubau am Zürichberg. Ein modernes, prägnantes Stadthaus an einer der exklusivsten Wohngegenden Zürichs. Die Eigentumswohnungen im diamantförmigen Gebäude werden den höchsten Ansprüchen gerecht und vermitteln ein einmaliges Wohngefühl, hohen Komfort und den Prestigefaktor eingeschlossen. Der Neubau liegt, eingebettet in eine parkähnliche Landschaft, nahe des Zentrums, mit Tram, Schulen und Einkaufsmöglichkeiten in Gehdistanz. Ein echter Mix aus städtischem Flair und grünen Erholungszonen.

DIE ESSENZ

Das Stadthaus steht wie ein Fels, der sich harmonisch in sein Umfeld einfügt, durch seine Erscheinung aber auch eigenständig wirkt. Hinter der rauen Fassade lebt eine vielbeschäftigte Zielgruppe, die sich gerne einmal zurückzieht und der Hektik des Alltags entfliehen möchte. Ohne dabei den Komfort der Standortqualität (Lage am Zürichberg, Verkehrsanbindungen, Einkaufsmöglichkeiten, Erholungsraum) und Lifestyle (Prestige, Wohngefühl) missen zu müssen.

Daraus leitet sich der Kerngedanke ab: Balanced Life. Ein Ausgleich zum hektischen Leben außerhalb der Mauern, Zeit für Reflektion, Raum für die wahren Werte des Lebens wie Freundschaft, Gemeinsamkeit, Geborgenheit oder Kreativität. Etwas Besonderes für besondere Menschen.

THE BASIS

The real estate marketing is based on a new building near Zürichberg. A modern, prominent townhouse in one of the most exclusive residential areas of Zurich. The condominiums in the diamond-shaped building meet the most discerning demands and convey a unique ambiance coupled with high comfort and prestige. The new building is nestled in a park-like landscape, near the center of town, with streetcar stops, schools, and shopping opportunities within walking distance. It offers a genuine mix of urban flair and green leisure zones.

THE ESSENCE

The townhouse rises like a rock that is nevertheless harmoniously embedded in its environment while its appearance makes it unique. The rough facade shelters a very busy target group whose members like to withdraw occasionally to escape the hustle and bustle of everyday life. Without having to forego the comfort of the location (near Zürichberg, public transportation connections, shopping opportunities, recreation areas) and lifestyle (prestige, ambiance).

This is what inspired the core concept: Balanced life. A contrast to the hectic life outside, time for reflection, room for what really matters in life such as friendship, togetherness, security, or creativity. Something special for special people.

DIE STANDORTFAKTOREN
THE LOCATION FACTORS

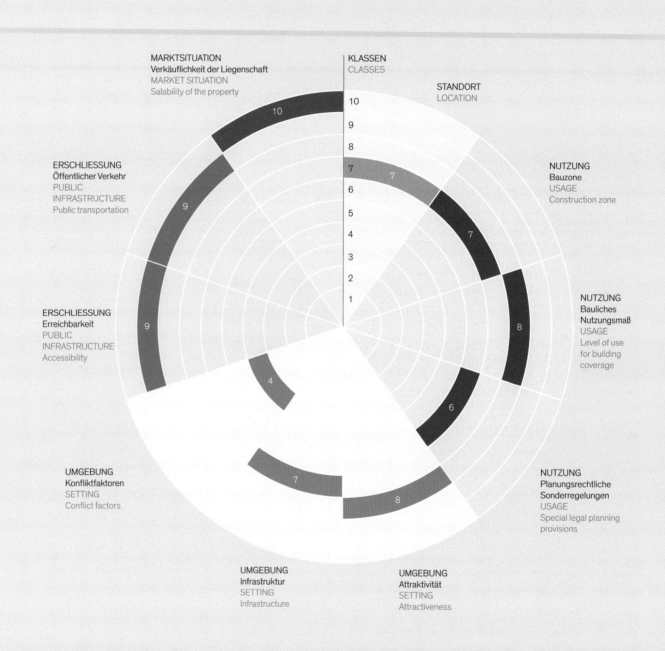

MARKTSITUATION
Verkäuflichkeit der Liegenschaft
MARKET SITUATION
Salability of the property

KLASSEN
CLASSES

STANDORT
LOCATION

ERSCHLIESSUNG
Öffentlicher Verkehr
PUBLIC
INFRASTRUCTURE
Public transportation

NUTZUNG
Bauzone
USAGE
Construction zone

NUTZUNG
Bauliches
Nutzungsmaß
USAGE
Level of use
for building
coverage

ERSCHLIESSUNG
Erreichbarkeit
PUBLIC
INFRASTRUCTURE
Accessibility

NUTZUNG
Planungsrechtliche
Sonderregelungen
USAGE
Special legal planning
provisions

UMGEBUNG
Konfliktfaktoren
SETTING
Conflict factors

UMGEBUNG
Infrastruktur
SETTING
Infrastructure

UMGEBUNG
Attraktivität
SETTING
Attractiveness

DIE STANDORTQUALITÄT VON «REFLECT»

+ Sehr gesuchte Wohnlage

+ Attraktiv mit Abendsonne

+ Naherholung und Einkaufen in direkter Nähe

+ Direkte Anschlüsse an den öffentlichen und privaten Verkehr

+ Hohe Ausnutzung möglich

– Starke Lärmbelastung

THE LOCATION QUALITY OF "REFLECT"

+ Highly coveted residential area

+ Attractive and exposed to the evening sun

+ Local recreation and shopping in the immediate vicinity

+ Direct connections to public and private transportation

+ High utilization possible

– Extensive noise pollution

DER MARKT

Das traditionsreiche und privilegierte Zürcher Wohnquartier Fluntern ist kein klassisches Neubauquartier. Die wenigen Projekte, die hier entstehen, sind gefragt. Ein exklusiver Markt, eine erstklassige Lage: für die Kommunikation eine spannende Aufgabe. Hinzu kommen für diesen Standort absolut konkurrenzfähige Quadratmeterpreise und einige unverwechselbare architektonische Highlights, die sich für die eng fokussierte Zielgruppe im Verkauf sehr gut einsetzen lassen.

DER AUFTRAG

In enger Zusammenarbeit mit der Bauherrschaft, dem Architekturbüro und dem Immobilienmakler entwickelt Felix Partner ein maßgeschneidertes Immobilienmarketing-Konzept und setzt dieses in allen Phasen der Vermarktung um. Klar, direkt und effektiv. Der Aspekt, dass hier etwas Besonderes für besondere Menschen gebaut wird, steht als Kommunikationsschwerpunkt im Vordergrund und wird gezielt hervorgehoben. Das Konzept beinhaltet die Namens- und Markenentwicklung, Positionierung und Claim sowie die gesamte Umsetzung im Corporate Design und den angestrebten Kommunikationsmaßnahmen.

DER ZIELRAUM

– Stadt Zürich

– Großraum Zürich

– Nahes Ausland (Deutschland)

THE MARKET

The highly traditional and privileged Zurich residential quarter of Fluntern is not a new residential area in the classical sense. The few projects that are created here are in great demand. An exclusive market in a top-notch location constitutes an exciting communication task. Added to this are competitive square meter prices given the location and a few unique architectural highlights that can be excellently utilized for selling to the precisely focused target group.

THE ASSIGNMENT

In close cooperation with the owners, the architectural firm, and the real estate agent, Felix Partner developed a customized real estate concept and implemented it in all phases of the marketing. Clear, direct, and effective. The communication focus was on the aspect that something special was being built for special people, which was specifically highlighted. The concept incorporates the name and brand development, positioning and the claim, as well as the entire implementation of the corporate design and planned communication measures.

THE TARGET AREA

– City of Zurich

– Zurich metropolitan area

– Nearby neighboring countries (Germany)

DIE ZIELGRUPPE

Die spezifische Markt- und Standortsituation lässt eine klare und enge Zielgruppendefinition für die Immobilie zu:

Quantitativ:
– Paare und Singles ohne Kinder (DINKs – double income no kids)
– Paare nach Familienphase

Qualitativ:
– Sie suchen die Vorteile der Stadt
– Sie legen Wert auf eine hervorragende Infrastruktur
– Sie wünschen sich viel Privatsphäre
– Sie lieben hohe Qualität
– Sie mögen das Understatement
– Sie geben Geld aus für Design und Materialien

Schlüsselargumente:
– Urbanität
– Gute Gesamtinfrastruktur (Verkehr, Einkaufen, Freizeit)
– Werterhaltung
– Erholung
– Hohe Lebensqualität
– Exklusive Lage
– Unikatcharakter

THE TARGET GROUP

The specific market and location situation allowed a clear and precise target definition for the property:

Quantitative:
– Couples and singles without children (DINKs – double income no kids)
– Couples after the family phase

Qualitative:
– They are seeking the advantages of the city
– They appreciate an excellent infrastructure
– They desire great privacy
– They love high quality
– They like understatements
– They spend money on design and materials

Key arguments:
– Urbanity
– Good general infrastructure (traffic, shopping, recreation)
– Conservation of value
– Relaxation
– High quality of life
– Exclusive location
– Unique character

DIE SINUS-ANALYSE DER ZIELGRUPPE FÜR «REFLECT»
THE SINUS ANALYSIS OF THE TARGET GROUP FOR "REFLECT"

SOZIALE LAGE UND GRUNDORIENTIERUNG
SOCIAL STATUS AND BASIC VALUES

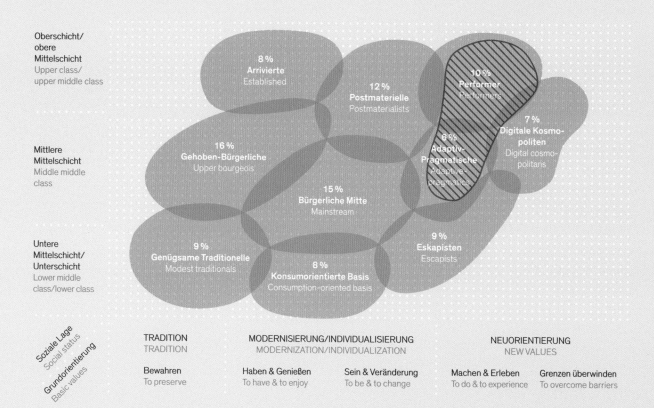

Oberschicht/
obere
Mittelschicht
Upper class/
upper middle class

8 % Arrivierte
Established

12 % Postmaterielle
Postmaterialists

10 % Performer
Performers

7 % Digitale Kosmo-
politen
Digital cosmo-
politans

Mittlere
Mittelschicht
Middle middle
class

16 % Gehoben-Bürgerliche
Upper bourgeois

6 % Adaptiv-
Pragmatische
Adaptive
pragmatics

15 % Bürgerliche Mitte
Mainstream

Untere
Mittelschicht/
Unterschicht
Lower middle
class/lower class

9 % Genügsame Traditionelle
Modest traditionals

8 % Konsumorientierte Basis
Consumption-oriented basis

9 % Eskapisten
Escapists

Soziale Lage
Social status
Grundorientierung
Basic values

TRADITION
TRADITION

MODERNISIERUNG/INDIVIDUALISIERUNG
MODERNIZATION/INDIVIDUALIZATION

NEUORIENTIERUNG
NEW VALUES

Bewahren
To preserve

Haben & Genießen
To have & to enjoy

Sein & Veränderung
To be & to change

Machen & Erleben
To do & to experience

Grenzen überwinden
To overcome barriers

Die Kombination aus urbaner Nähe und gehobenem Wohnquartier suchen vor allem Paare aus dem höheren Mittelstand, die den Sinus-Milieus der Performer und Adaptiv-Pragmatischen zuzurechnen sind.
The combination of urban vicinity and exclusive residential quarter appeals especially to higher middle class couples that are included in the Sinus milieus of performers and adaptive-pragmatics.

STATUSORIENTIERTE STADTMENSCHEN

«Das könnten wir sein.» «So will ich auch sein.» Das soll die angesprochene Zielgruppe denken. Aus diesem Grund werden persönliche Porträts möglicher Käufer und künftiger Bewohner erstellt und diese in den definierten Kommunikationsmedien platziert. Wiedererkennung senkt Entscheidungshürden und vermittelt das Gefühl, aufgehoben und am richtigen Ort zu sein.

Monika und Robert Fischer sind Menschen, die gerne leben und genießen. Beide sind Mitte 50 und sie haben gemeinsam eine der bedeutendsten privaten Galerien der Schweiz aufgebaut. Noch heute verkehren die Großen der Kunst- und der Finanzwelt Tag für Tag in ihren Ausstellungshallen und an einer Vernissage dabei zu sein, ist so etwas wie ein Ritterschlag der Queen. Da beide mittelfristig kürzertreten möchten, und auch privat der Aufwand ihres Stadthauses im Englischviertel auf Dauer zu viel wird, suchen sie eine exklusive Stadtwohnung am Zürichberg. Wichtig ist ihnen eine gute Anbindung hinunter zur Stadt und auch zum Flughafen. Ebenfalls sollte die Wohnung einen repräsentativen Eindruck hinterlassen und Prestige kommunizieren. Das Ehepaar wohnt gerne, zieht sich in seine Räume zurück und erholt sich in den eigenen vier Wänden. Komfort ist wichtig, ebenso schöne Materialien und höchste Qualität bis ins letzte Detail.

STATUS-ORIENTED CITY DWELLERS

"That could be us. I want to be like that too," is what the addressed target group is supposed to think. For this reason, the real estate marketers created personal profiles of potential buyers and future residents and placed them in the defined communication media. Recognition lowers the decision-making barriers and provides a feeling of security and of being in the right place.

Monika and Robert Fischer are people who enjoy life and its pleasures. Both are in their mid-50s and have jointly set up one of Switzerland's most prominent private galleries. To this day, the prominent members of the worlds of art and finance frequent their exhibition halls daily, and being part of one of their vernissages is like being knighted by the Queen. As both want to cut down their work in the medium term and the upkeep of their townhouse in the English quarter is getting too much, they are looking to buy an exclusive urban apartment near Zürichberg. To them a good connection down to the city and to the airport is key. The apartment should also be very presentable with a prestigious aura. The spouses enjoy being at home, like to retreat to their own space, and relax within their own four walls. Comfort is important to them, as are beautiful materials and the highest quality up to the minutest detail.

PRIVILEGIERT WOHNEN AM ZÜRICHBERG

PRIVILEGED LIVING NEAR ZÜRICHBERG

DIE POSITIONIERUNG

«Privilegiert wohnen am Zürichberg» – die Essenz aus dem Positionierungsbeschrieb bringt den Marketingfokus auf den Punkt. An der Gladbachstrasse 117, einer der exklusivsten Wohngegenden Zürichs, entsteht ein prägnantes Mehrfamilienhaus mit einzigartigem Grundriss. Die 13 Eigentumswohnungen zielen auf Käufer mit hohen Ansprüchen an Design und Materialwahl – ein einmaliges Wohngefühl, hohen Komfort und Prestigefaktor eingeschlossen.

DER ANALYSE-SCHWERPUNKT

Lage und Lifestyle verwenden Felix Partner als die zwei Analyse-Schwerpunkte, auf die es in der Kommunikation ankommt. Diese beiden überwiegen klar, obwohl auch in der Architektur unübersehbare und wirksame Verkaufsargumente vorhanden sind.

Die Analyse-Schwerpunkte Lage und Lifestyle:
- **Lage am Zürichberg in privilegiertem Wohnquartier**
- **Verkehrsanbindungen**
- **Nahe Einkaufsmöglichkeiten**
- **Prestige**
- **Wohngefühl**
- **Komfort**
- **Cocooning**

THE POSITIONING

"Privileged living near Zürichberg" – the essence of the positioning description brings the marketing focus to a point. At Gladbachstrasse 117, in one of Zurich's most exclusive residential areas, a prominent multi-party residential building with a unique floor plan is under construction. The 13 condominiums are targeted at buyers with high demands regarding design and the choice of materials – coupled with a unique ambiance, high comfort, and prestige.

THE FOCUS OF THE ANALYSIS

Felix Partner used the location and lifestyle as the two focal points of the analysis that are emphasized in the communication. Even though the architecture also offers quite obvious and effective sales arguments, the above factors are clearly predominant.

The location and lifestyle focus of the analysis:
- Location near Zürichberg in a privileged residential quarter
- Transportation connections
- Nearby shopping opportunities
- Prestige
- Ambiance
- Comfort
- Cocooning

DER NAME: «REFLECT»

Der Name vermittelt bereits die Kernaussage, die sich durch alle Kommunikationsmittel hindurchzieht. Sie richten sich an diejenigen, die zuerst in sich gehen, bevor sie entscheiden. Das Objekt ist nicht geeignet für jugendlich Übermütige oder Kurzentschlossene. Die Zielgruppe hat schon einiges erreicht im Leben, schon vieles gesehen – hier am Zürichberg reflektiert und konzentriert sich alles, was es für ein erfülltes und erfolgreiches Leben braucht.

DER CLAIM: «BALANCED LIFE»

Er setzt den Namen fort und emotionalisiert ihn, holt Harmoniesuchende ab, aber schließt aktive Performer nicht aus.

DIE FARBEN UND DIE TYPOGRAFIE

«Balanced Life», das spiegelt sich in den Farben und unterstützt den Claim visuell. Harmonie, Wohlbefinden, Ruhe, Tiefe: alles in Erdtönen. Ein tragender Hintergrund für starke Bilder. Die Typografie geht in die gleiche Richtung, ergänzend. Weichheit transportieren, Verletzlichkeit, runde Formen ohne Opulenz und Aufdringlichkeit.

DIE IDEE: HIER KANN ICH MICH VERWIRKLICHEN

Die Idee baut auf dem Bedürfnis der Selbstverwirklichung auf. Die vielbeschäftigte Zielgruppe schafft sich mit dem neuen Zuhause einen persönlichen Ruhepol beziehungsweise Ausgleich und damit Raum zum Entspannen und Nachdenken. Hier können die wahren Werte des Lebens wie Freundschaft, Geborgenheit, Kreativität gefunden und gelebt werden.

DAS WERBLICHE KONZEPT

Die Kommunikation zeichnet einen emotionalen Lifestyle mit stilvollen Räumen und erfolgreichen Menschen und kombiniert diesen mit zielgruppenadäquaten Headlines und Aussagen, die den Bauch treffen. Eigenständig und ästhetisch, dezent und Ruhe ausstrahlend.

THE NAME: "REFLECT"

The name already conveys the core statement that is repeated in all communication tools. They are addressed to individuals who first engage in soul-searching before making any decision. The building is not suitable for a youthful carefree attitude or spontaneous decisions. The target group has already accomplished things in life and seen much – here near Zürichberg everything they need for a fulfilled and successful life is reflected and conglomerated.

THE CLAIM: "BALANCED LIFE"

It enhances the name and adds emotions to it, addresses persons in search of harmony while not excluding active performers.

THE COLORS AND THE TYPOGRAPHY

"Balanced Life" is reflected in the colors and visually supports the claim. Harmony, comfort, tranquility, depth: all in earth colors. A strong background for powerful images. The complementary typography has the same effect. Conveying softness, vulnerability, round shapes without opulence or obtrusiveness.

THE IDEA: HERE I CAN REALIZE MY POTENTIALS

The idea is based on the desire for self-actualization. The very busy members of the target group create their own personal quiet zone in their new home as a balance that gives them room for relaxation and reflection. This is where they can find and live out what truly matters in life such as friendship, security, and creativity.

THE ADVERTISING CONCEPT

The communication evokes an emotional lifestyle with stylish rooms and successful people combined with target-group-specific headlines and statements that target the subconscious. Independent and esthetic, unobtrusive and emanating tranquility.

DAS CORPORATE DESIGN FÜR «REFLECT»
THE CORPORATE DESIGN FOR "REFLECT"

LOGO
LOGO

reflect
Zürichberg

TYPOGRAFIE
TYPOGRAPHY

Kelson Sans

Im Zürcher Quartier

Im Zürcher Quartier Fluntern steht ein prägnantes Stadthaus mit besonderem Grundriss und unverwechselbarem Markencharakter. Die 13 Eigentumswohnungen bieten ein einmaliges, emotionales Wohngefühl an exklusiver Lage am Zürichberg.

FARBEN
COLORS

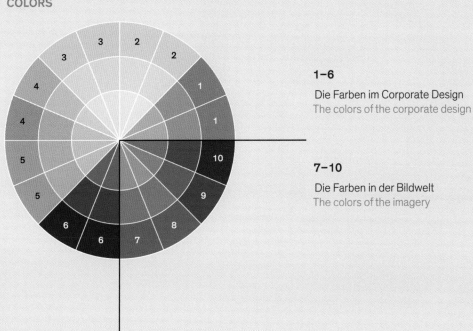

1–6

Die Farben im Corporate Design
The colors of the corporate design

7–10

Die Farben in der Bildwelt
The colors of the imagery

Balanced Life

Active, secure

Ausgefallen
Urban

Exceptional, urban

Zentral
Lebensqualität

Central, quality of life

DIE KOMMUNIKATIONSMITTEL

Presite und Website zum Projekt, Projektbroschüre für den Verkauf, Micro-Guide, Dokumentenmappe, Detailpläne im Maßstab 1:100, Baubeschrieb, Verkaufspreisliste, Bautafel, Außen- und Innen-Visualisierungen

THE COMMUNICATION MEDIA

Pre-site and website for the project, project sales brochure, micro-guide, document folder, detailed plans with a scale of 1:100, construction description, sales price list, construction site sign, external and internal images

Presite und Website zum Projekt
Pre-site and website for the project

Micro-Guide
Micro-guide document folder

Micro-Guide
Micro-guide document folder

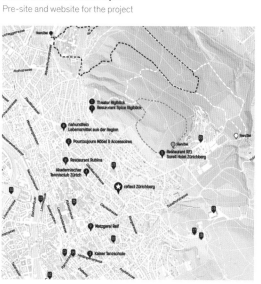

Micro-Guide
Micro-guide document folder

Micro-Guide
Micro-guide document folder

Bautafel
Construction site sign

Projektbroschüre für den Verkauf
Project sales brochure

Projektbroschüre für den Verkauf
Project sales brochure

Projektbroschüre für den Verkauf
Project sales brochure

Projektbroschüre für den Verkauf
Project sales brochure

Projektbroschüre für den Verkauf
Project sales brochure

EINZIGARTIGKEIT UND HARMONIE IM DIAMANTFÖRMIGEN GEWAND

UNIQUENESS AND HARMONY IN A DIAMOND SHAPE

DIE IMMOBILIE

Das prägnante, im Split Level konzipierte Stadthaus mit individuellen Eigentumswohnungen fügt sich trotz oder gerade wegen seines außergewöhnlichen Charakters harmonisch in die Umgebung ein. Der diamantförmige Baukörper verspricht Schutz, ist aber gleichzeitig in einer leichten, modernen und zeitlosen Handschrift gestaltet. «Reflect» am Zürichberg vereint Einzigartigkeit und Harmonie und bietet mit seinen weiten Räumen und Terrassen sowie der parkähnlichen Landschaft die perfekte Balance zwischen Aktivität und Rückzug, Reflexion und Ausblick.

THE PROPERTY

Despite, or maybe because, of its exceptional character, the distinctive townhouse with its split-level design and individual condominiums is harmoniously integrated into the setting. The diamond-shaped structure promises protection while at the same time featuring a light, modern, and timeless look. "Reflect" near Zürichberg combines uniqueness and harmony, while its expansive rooms and terraces plus park-style landscape offer the perfect balance between activity and retreat, reflection and outlook.

Ein Diamant im Park
A diamond in the park

Großzügige Verglasung bringt viel Licht
Generous glazing illuminates the rooms

Weite offene Räume für einen modernen Lebensstil
Wide, open rooms for a modern lifestyle

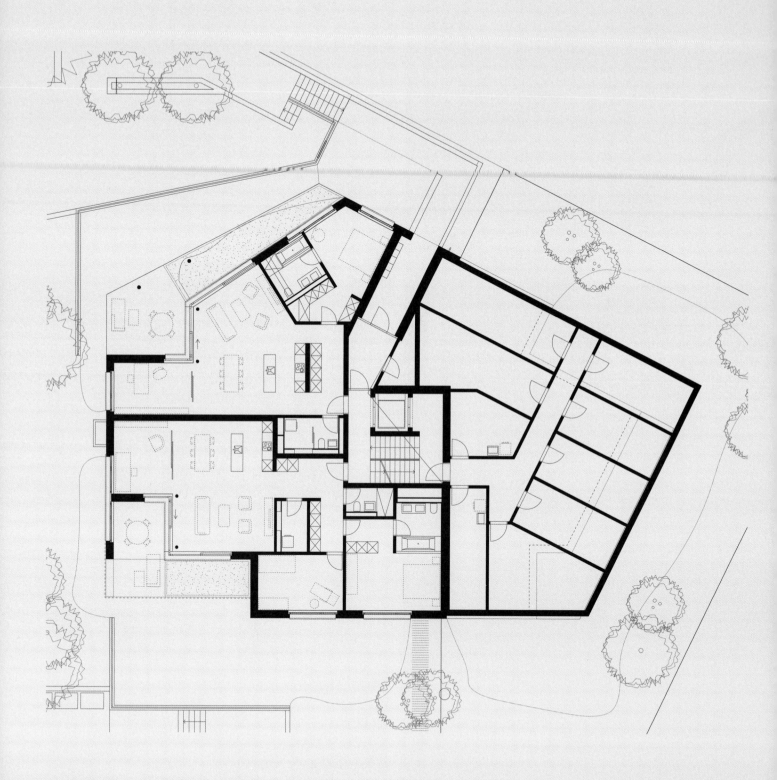

Grundriss Garten-/Eingangsgeschoss
Layout garden/entrance floor

Grundriss Erdgeschoss
Layout ground floor

KOMPAKTES MEHRFAMILIENHAUS IN ZÜRICHS GRÖSSTEM QUARTIER
COMPACT MULTI-PARTY RESIDENTIAL BUILDING IN ZURICH'S LARGEST QUARTER

PROJEKTNAME: «Spirgartenstrasse»
IMMOBILIE: Mehrfamilienhaus mit 10 Eigentumswohnungen
STANDORT: Spirgartenstrasse 13, 8048 Zürich, Schweiz
AUFTRAGGEBER: R. Fuchs AG, Zürich, Schweiz (Bauherrschaft),
Rhombus Partner Immobilien AG, Zürich, Schweiz (Beratung und Verkauf)
ARCHITEKTUR: R. Fuchs Partner AG, Zürich, Schweiz
VERMARKTUNG: 2015–2016

PROJECT NAME: "Spirgartenstrasse"
PROPERTY: Multi-party residential building with 10 condominiums
LOCATION: Spirgartenstrasse 13, 8048 Zurich, Switzerland
CLIENT: R. Fuchs AG, Zurich, Switzerland (owner); Rhombus Partner
Immobilien AG, Zurich, Switzerland (consulting and sales)
ARCHITECTURE: R. Fuchs Partner AG, Zurich, Switzerland
MARKETING PERIOD: 2015–2016

EIN ERZÄHLER MIT ZWEI RÄDERN
A NARRATOR ON TWO WHEELS

DIE BASIS

Die Basis für das Projekt bildet die sehr zentrale Lage des Neubaus mit seiner E-Mobilitäts-Ladestation in der Tiefgarage in Zürich Altstetten sowie die sehr gute Anbindung zu Fuß, mit dem Auto oder via öffentlichem Nahverkehr. Das Quartier, als flächenmäßig größter Teil der Stadt Zürich, ist voller Leben und hat seine eigene Dynamik. Der Standort zeichnet sich nebst der guten Anbindungen auch durch vieles anderes in mittelbarer Distanz aus: Naherholung, Einkaufen, Restaurants, Kultur und Sport, Schulen, Schwimmbad und mehr.

DIE ESSENZ

Das neue Mehrfamilienhaus an der Spirgartenstrasse 13 liegt schön gelegen zwischen zwei historischen Gebäuden. In einem Quartier, in dem es vieles zu entdecken gibt.

Daraus leitet sich der Kerngedanke ab: Luca. Luca führt uns an die verschiedensten Plätze, erkundet Neues und dient als ständiger, praktischer Begleiter. So wird eine Geschichte rund um das, was man mit Luca erleben kann, erzählt. Übrigens, Luca ist ein E-Bike, das nach dem Verkauf aller Wohnungen unter den neuen Eigentümern verlost wird.

THE BASIS

The project is based on the very centralized location of the new building with its e-mobility docking station in the underground garage in Zurich Altstetten, as well as the excellent connectivity by foot, car, or public transportation. The largest district of Zurich is vivacious and has its own dynamics. In addition to the good traffic connections, the location is also distinguished by its vicinity to many other facilities: local recreation, shopping, restaurants, culture and sports, schools, swimming pool, and much more.

THE ESSENCE

The new multi-party house at Spirgartenstrasse 13 is beautifully located between two historical buildings. In a quarter that has many things to discover.

This is what inspired the core concept: Luca. Luca takes us to a variety of locations, discovers many new things, and acts as a constant and useful companion. Thus, a tale emerges of everything one can experience with Luca. By the way, Luca is an electronic bicycle that will be raffled off among the new owners once all apartments are sold.

LAGE
LOCATION

DIE STANDORTFAKTOREN
THE LOCATION FACTORS

MARKTSITUATION
Verkäuflichkeit der Liegenschaft
MARKET SITUATION
Salability of the property

KLASSEN
CLASSES

STANDORT
LOCATION

ERSCHLIESSUNG
Öffentlicher Verkehr
PUBLIC
INFRASTRUCTURE
Public transportation

NUTZUNG
Bauzone
USAGE
Construction zone

ERSCHLIESSUNG
Erreichbarkeit
PUBLIC
INFRASTRUCTURE
Accessibility

NUTZUNG
Bauliches
Nutzungsmaß
USAGE
Level of use
for building
coverage

UMGEBUNG
Konfliktfaktoren
SETTING
Conflict factors

NUTZUNG
Planungsrechtliche
Sonderregelungen
USAGE
Special legal planning
provisions

UMGEBUNG
Infrastruktur
SETTING
Infrastructure

UMGEBUNG
Attraktivität
SETTING
Attractiveness

DIE STANDORTQUALITÄT VON «SPIRGARTENSTRASSE»

+ Nachgefragte Wohnlage
+ Attraktiv mit Abendsonne
+ Viele Angebote in direkter Nähe
+ Gute Anschlüsse an den öffentlichen und privaten Verkehr
+ Hohe Ausnutzung möglich
− Kirchenglockenläuten

THE LOCATION QUALITY OF "SPIRGARTENSTRASSE"

+ Popular residential location
+ Attractive and exposed to the evening sun
+ Many offers in the immediate vicinity
+ Good connections to public and private transportation
+ High utilization possible
− Church bells can be heard

DER MARKT

Die Nachfrage nach Neubau-Eigentum im zentralen, dörflichen und harmonisch gewachsenen Teil des Zürcher Quartiers Altstetten ist groß. Die klassische und harmonisch gehaltene Architektur des Mehrfamilienhauses trägt zusätzlich dazu bei, dass die Resonanz im Markt gut ist – umso mehr, als in der direkten Nachbarschaft keine vergleichbaren Konkurrenzprojekte geplant sind.

DER AUFTRAG

Felix Partner hat den Auftrag, ein auf den kleineren Umfang des Projekts angepasstes, gezieltes Immobilienmarketing zu entwickeln. Dies vor dem Hintergrund, dass im Rahmen des Neubaus zu wenig Parkplätze zur Verfügung gestellt werden. Mittelseitig soll dabei der Hauptfokus auf eine Objekt- und Verkaufsbroschüre inklusive Architekturpläne gelegt werden. Hinzu kommen Namensgebung, Zielgruppenrecherchen und -definitionen, Bildwelt sowie die gesamte Umsetzung der Maßnahmen.

DER ZIELRAUM

– Zürich Altstetten
– Stadt Schlieren
– Stadt Zürich
– Bezirk Dietikon

THE MARKET

The demand for newly constructed condominiums in the central rural and harmoniously grown section of the Altstetten quarter of Zurich is great. The individual and yet harmoniously-designed architecture of the multi-party house additionally contributes to its high resonance on the market – especially since there are no comparable competing projects planned for the neighborhood.

THE ASSIGNMENT

Felix Partner was commissioned to develop a limited real estate marketing campaign in line with the smaller size of the project, taking into consideration the limited number of parking spaces planned. The main focus is on the development of a project and sales brochure including the architectural plans. Added to this are the naming, target group research and definition, the imagery and implementation of all measures.

THE TARGET AREA

– Zurich Altstetten
– City of Schlieren
– City of Zurich
– District of Dietikon

DIE ZIELGRUPPE

Die Zielgruppe besteht aus einer heterogenen Mischung aus verschiedenen Alters- und Gesellschaftsgruppen – ein Spiegel der Bevölkerung des Quartiers:

Quantitativ:

– Jüngere Einzelpersonen 25 bis 35 Jahre
– Unverheiratete Paare und Ehepaare mit Kindern
  30 bis 45 Jahre
– Best Agers nach Familienphase 50 bis 60 Jahre
– Aktive ältere Paare und Alleinstehende
– Mittlere Einkommensschicht

Qualitativ:

– Schätzen das dörfliche Flair am Stadtrand
– Verkehrsanbindung (vor allem öffentlicher Verkehr)
  ist wichtig
– Schätzen die Vorzüge des Quartiers mit seiner Vielfalt
– Sind eher traditionell eingestellt

Schlüsselargumente:

– In der Stadt, aber mit dörflichem Flair
– Gute Gesamtinfrastruktur
– Vielfalt im Quartier
– Naherholung in Reichweite
– Gute Lebensqualität
– Modern wohnen

DIE SINUS-MILIEUS

Die heterogene Zielgruppe hat außer dem finanziellen Hintergrund wenig gemeinsam und platziert sich auf der ganzen Breite der mittleren Einkommen der Sinus-Milieus.

THE TARGET GROUP

The members of the target group are a heterogeneous mixture of various age and social groups – a reflection of the residents of the quarter:

Quantitative:

– Younger individuals (25 to 35 years old)
– Unmarried couples and couples with children,
  30 to 45 years old
– Best Agers after the family phase, aged 50 to 60
– Active older couples and singles
– Middle income strata

Qualitative:

– Appreciate the rural flair at the edge of the city
– Traffic connections (especially public) are important
– Appreciate the advantages of the diverse offers
  in the quarter
– Are rather traditional

Key arguments:

– In the city, but with a village character
– Good general infrastructure
– Diversity in the quarter
– Local recreation facilities within reach
– Good quality of life
– Modern living

THE SINUS MILIEUS

Members of the heterogeneous target group have little in common except for their financial background and are situated along the entire width of the middle income of the Sinus milieus.

**MITTLERE EINKOMMEN MIT
UNTERSCHIEDLICHEN BACKGROUNDS**

Die heterogene Zielgruppe erfordert sehr unterschiedliche Poträts möglicher Interessenten. Nachfolgend zwei Beispiele:

Monika Göldi ist 67 Jahre alt und hat Zeit ihres Lebens in Zürich Altstetten gelebt. Die dreifache Großmutter hat selbst zwei Töchter großgezogen und den Wandel weg von der Industrie hin zu mehr Büro und Wohnen im Zürcher Außenquartier hautnah miterlebt. Sie selbst betreibt seit 1984 einen florierenden Coiffeur-Salon und ist in der ganzen Umgebung gut bekannt. Nun ist die Zeit gekommen, etwas kürzerzutreten, umso mehr als das Gebäude mit ihrem Salon und der darüber liegenden Wohnung saniert oder gar ersetzt werden soll. Weg aus ihrem Quartier will die ältere, sehr rüstige Dame aber keinesfalls. Daher schaut sie sich nun laufend um und sucht nach einer Wohngelegenheit, die zu ihr passen könnte. Idealerweise nicht zu weit vom Zentrum, dem Lindenplatz, weg, und auch der Bahnhof sollte zu Fuß oder mit dem Fahrrad erreicht werden können. Denn gerade hat sie sich ein E-Bike aus Schweizer Produktion gekauft und freut sich jedes Mal, wenn sie schneller als die langsam fahrenden Autos vorankommt.

**MIDDLE INCOMES WITH
DIFFERENT BACKGROUNDS**

The heterogeneous target group required very diverse portraits of potential buyers. Following are two examples:

Monika Göldi is 67 years old and has lived her whole life in Zurich Altstetten. The grandmother of three has raised two daughters and experienced the quarter's evolution from industry to more offices and residences up close. She has been running a successful hairdresser business since 1984 and is well known in the entire area. Now the time has come for her to slow down a little, especially since the building in which her salon and apartment are located is scheduled for renovation or even replacement. However, the elderly, very fit woman does not want to leave her quarter by any means. This is why she is constantly on the lookout for a new home that matches her needs. Ideally not too far from the center, the Lindenplatz public square, and the railway station should also be accessible by foot or bicycle. As she has just bought a Swiss-made e-bike, she is happy every time she moves faster than the slow car traffic.

Christian Zimmerli ist im Limmattal aufgewachsen und seit zwölf Jahren als Sachbearbeiter beim Kantonalen Steueramt in Zürich Altstetten tätig. Der heute 34-Jährige ist ledig, arbeitet ehrenamtlich als Sekretär einer Lokalpartei und liebt es, in seiner Freizeit mit dem Fahrrad an der Limmat entlangzufahren und auf einer Bank ein Buch zu lesen oder dem Treiben des Flusses zuzuschauen. Er ist eher der ruhige Typ und schätzt es sehr, gebraucht zu werden. Um dem für ihn stressigen Pendeln aus dem Nachbarkanton nach Zürich Altstetten zu entgehen, sucht er im Umkreis seines Arbeitsortes ein neues Zuhause. Bei der Suche ist ihm das Angebot an der Spirgartenstrasse aufgefallen. Idealerweise liegt die Liegenschaft nur sieben Fahrradminuten weg von seiner Arbeitsstelle und bietet seinen E-Bike-Besitzern komplett eingerichtete Ladestationen in der Tiefgarage. Das und die ruhige, aber doch zentrale Lage für alles, was den Alltag angeht, macht das Angebot zu seinem Favoriten.

Christian Zimmerli grew up in the Limmat Valley and has been employed for twelve years as a clerk in the Canton tax office in Zurich Altstetten. The 34-year-old is unmarried, volunteers as the secretary of a local political party, and loves riding his bicycle along the Limmat river in his spare time to read a book on a bench or simply watch the river flow past. He is a quiet person who appreciates being needed. To avoid commuting between the neighboring canton and Zurich Altstetten, which he considers rather stressful, he is looking for a new home near his workplace. During his search, he came across the offer at Spirgartenstrasse. The building is ideally located only seven minutes by bicycle from his job and offers its e-bike owners fully equipped docking stations in the underground garage. This fact, coupled with the quiet, yet central location when it comes to the necessities of daily life, make this offer his favorite.

BLITZSCHNELL AM ZIEL
QUICK AS LIGHTNING EVERYWHERE

DIE POSITIONIERUNG

«Blitzschnell am Ziel» ist als Positionierungssatz die kleine, aber evidente Schnittmenge aus der heterogenen Zielgruppendefinition und der Markt- und Standortanalyse. Wer an der Spirgartenstrasse in Zürich Altstettens Arbeiterquartier seinen Lebensmittelpunkt hat, genießt es, kurze Wege und rundum alles vorhanden zu haben – ein kleiner Kosmos am Rande der Stadt für alle jene, die ohne große Distanzen ihr Leben leben wollen.

THE POSITIONING

"Quick as lightning everywhere" is the positioning statement for the small, but clear intersection of the heterogeneous target group definition and the market and location analysis. Residents of Spirgartenstrasse in the workers' district of Zurich Altstetten enjoy having short distances to everything they need for their daily life – a small microcosm at the edge of the city for people who want to live their lives without having to cross large distances.

DER ANALYSE-SCHWERPUNKT

Die Lage sticht beim Projekt «Spirgartenstrasse» als Hauptargument und Analyse-Schwerpunkt deutlich hervor. Architektur und Lifestyle sind in diesem Fall eher zweitrangig.

THE FOCUS OF THE ANALYSIS

For the "Spirgartenstrasse" project, the location clearly stands out as the main selling argument and focus of the analysis. Architecture and lifestyle are rather secondary in this case.

Der Analyse-Schwerpunkt Lage:
- **Eingebunden in angenehmes Quartier**
- **Historische Gebäude an der Seite**
- **Ruhiges Umfeld**
- **Gute Lebensqualität**
- **Attraktive Angebote für Einkaufen und Freizeit**
- **Sehr gute Verkehrsanbindung**

The location focus of the analysis:
- **Integrated into a pleasant quarter**
- **Surrounded by historic buildings**
- **Quiet environment**
- **Good quality of life**
- **Attractive shopping and leisure offers**
- **Excellent traffic connection**

DER NAME: «SPIRGARTENSTRASSE»

Den Straßennamen als Projektnamen zu verwenden, erscheint auf den ersten Blick simpel. Vor dem Hintergrund der Positionierung und der Zielgruppendefinition bringt der traditionelle Straßenname die Vorgaben aber genau auf den Punkt.

DIE FARBEN UND DIE TYPOGRAFIE

Eine satte, knallige Farbigkeit in Grün. Dynamik auf der einen Seite, Frische auf der anderen. Ganz wie der Standort dieses Stadthauses. Eingebettet zwischen Aktivität und Ruhe. Unbeschwertheit zeigen, aktiv sein oder ruhen, in jedem Moment die freie Entscheidung haben. In die gleiche Ecke stößt die Schrift. Sie ist eckig und kraftvoll, Stimmung transportierend.

DIE IDEE: KOMM, ICH ZEIG DIR ALLES

Mobilität im Nahverkehr, einer der wichtigsten Werte und Ansprüche der Zielgruppe, visualisiert und personalisiert Felix Partner in Form eines E-Bikes namens Luca. Es geht zusammen mit den potenziellen Käufern auf Erkundungstour durch das Quartier – die Quintessenz aus der Positionierung «Blitzschnell am Ziel».

DAS WERBLICHE KONZEPT

Da im fertigen Gebäude in der Tiefgarage Ladestationen für Elektromobile installiert werden, wird ein E-Bike zum Testimonial und führt, emotional visualisiert und vertextet, durch Zürich Altstetten und zu den Hotspots in der Umgebung.

THE NAME: "SPIRGARTENSTRASSE"

Using the street name as the project name seems simple at first glance. However, given the positioning and the target group definition, the traditional street name precisely reflects the requirements.

THE COLORS AND THE TYPOGRAPHY

A vivid and saturated green color. Dynamical on the one hand, fresh on the other. Just like the location of this townhouse. Nestled between action and tranquility. Appearing lighthearted, being active or at rest, with freedom of choice at any moment. The typeface portrays the same idea. It is angular and powerful, conveying a mood.

THE IDEA: COME, I WILL SHOW YOU EVERYTHING

Mobility in short-distance traffic, one of the most important values and demands of the target group, is visualized and personified by Felix Partner in the form of an e-bike called Luca. It takes potential buyers on a journey of discovery through the quarter – the quintessence of the positioning "Quick as lightning everywhere."

THE ADVERTISING CONCEPT

As the finished building will feature docking stations for electric vehicles in the underground garage, an e-bike serves as a testimonial that takes people on a tour through Zurich Altstetten and the hotspots of the area with emotional images and texts.

DAS CORPORATE DESIGN FÜR «SPIRGARTENSTRASSE»
THE CORPORATE DESIGN FOR "SPIRGARTENSTRASSE"

LOGO
LOGO

TYPOGRAFIE
TYPOGRAPHY

Conduit ITC

WOHNEIGENTUM
SPIRGARTENSTRASSE
ZÜRICH ALTSTETTEN

IN ZÜRICH ALTSTETTEN

In Zürich Altstetten entsteht ein modern interpretiertes Stadthaus. Die zehn Eigentumswohnungen mit 2,5 bis 5,5 Zimmern bieten ein angenehmes Wohngefühl an guter Lage, Fahrradabstellplätze mit Ladestation inklusive.

FARBEN
COLORS

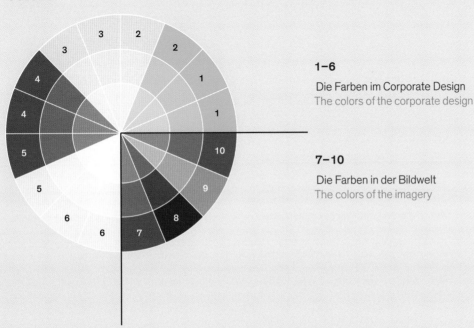

1–6

Die Farben im Corporate Design
The colors of the corporate design

7–10

Die Farben in der Bildwelt
The colors of the imagery

ICH BIN LUCA.

Ein E-Bike von Smart.

So eines wie mich gewinnen Sie mit etwas Glück

beim Kauf einer Wohnung im neuen Mehrfamilienhaus an der Spirgartenstrasse in Zürich Altstetten. Die Spirgartenstrasse ist ja für Elektrofahrräder wie mich absolut ideal gelegen und mein neues Zuhause bietet sogar Fahrradständer mit Stromanschluss. Vieles ist da in der Nähe anzusteuern, was natürlich auch zu Fuss ginge – allerdings viel weniger elegant. Und anstelle von vier Minuten haben Sie mit mir nur deren zwei, maximal. Und wenn Sie mal in Richtung Üetliberg hoch wollen, lernen Sie mich so richtig schätzen. Denn mit meinem kraftvollen E-Motor unterstütze ich Sie nicht nur beim Bergabfahren. Doch auch sonst bin ich der Hammer. Und habe in allen Tests mit gut bis sehr gut abgeschnitten. Was kein Wunder ist, wurde ich doch von Smart entwickelt und mit exklusiven Komponenten und Teilen von allerlei Spezialisten ausgestattet. Doch genug Werbung. Im Alltag bin ich einfach klasse und gut zu gebrauchen. Neulich hat mein Mensch ganz dringend seinen Zug im Hauptbahnhof Zürich erreichen müssen. Trotz bester Verbindungen ab Altstetten war das mit allen Verkehrsmitteln des ÖV oder mit dem Auto nicht zu schaffen. Und mit einem klassischen Fahrrad wäre er wohl heute noch unterwegs. Doch mit mir sind die rund sechs Kilometer ohne Schwitzen und wie im Fluge ein Kinderspiel gewesen. So geht das immer, mit meinem Menschen und mir. Egal, wo er hin will, wir sind meist blitzschnell am Ziel. Im Moment überlegt er gar, sich ein weiteres E-Bike wie mich zu kaufen. Für seine Partnerin, wie mein Mensch sagt. Damit auch sie die Vorzüge der tollen Lage an der Spirgartenstrasse noch mehr schätzen lernt. Und etwas für die Fitness tut. Wobei das ja nicht so viel ist, die Hauptarbeit liegt schliesslich bei mir und meinesgleichen. Überhaupt soll nicht die Gesundheit, sondern die Freude an den kurzen und schnellen Verkehrswegen im Vordergrund stehen. Allerdings habe ich auch meine Grenzen. So sind Freunde aus dem Ausland zu Besuch gekommen. Mit Sack und Pack. Da gabs dann nur Auto oder ÖV, denn wer würde mich schon wie einen Esel vollpacken!

I am Luca. An e-bike from Smart. With a bit of luck, you can win an e-bike like me when buying an apartment in the new multi-party residential building on Spirgartenstrasse in Zurich Altstetten. Spirgartenstrasse is perfectly located for e-bikes like me and my new home even offers bicycle stands with electrical connections. There are many places to visit nearby. Of course, this could be done on foot, but much less elegantly and instead of four minutes, it takes you no longer than two minutes with me. And should you head up Üetliberg hill at some time or another you will really come to appreciate me. Because with my powerful electrical engine I can support you uphill as well. In other respects, I am also something else. I passed all tests with good or excellent grades. This is not surprising as I was developed by Smart and equipped with exclusive components and parts by a number of specialists. But enough advertising. In everyday use, I am simply convenient and very useful. The other day, my owner had to urgently reach his train at Zurich central station. Despite the excellent connections from Altstetten, this was not feasible with any public transportation means, nor with the car. And with a standard bicycle, he would probably still be pedaling right now. But with me, he covered the roughly six kilometers in no time without breaking a sweat. This is how it always is with my owner and me. No matter where he wants to go, we usually reach our destination quick as lightning. He is even currently considering buying another e-bike like me. For his significant other, he says. So that she can also get to better appreciate the advantages of the great location on Spirgartenstrasse. And improve her fitness. Which will not amount to much actually, as the main work is done by me and my kind. At any rate, the main aim is not health improvement but to enjoy the short and quick journeys. However, I also have my limitations. For example, when some friends came to visit from abroad. With everything but the kitchen sink. They had to take the car or public transportation because you cannot load me like a mule!

DAS KOMMUNIKATIONSMITTEL
THE COMMUNICATION MEDIA

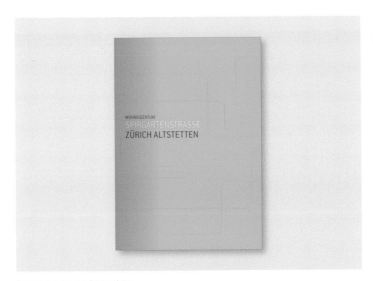

Objekt- und Verkaufsbroschüre
Project and sales brochure

Objekt- und Verkaufsbroschüre
Project and sales brochure

Objekt- und Verkaufsbroschüre
Project and sales brochure

Objekt- und Verkaufsbroschüre
Project and sales brochure

HISTORISCHES NEU UND MODERN INTERPRETIERT

A NEW AND MODERN
INTERPRETATION OF
HISTORICAL ELEMENTS

DIE IMMOBILIE

Das Mehrfamilienhaus an der Spirgartenstrasse reiht sich zwischen zwei historischen Gebäuden ein und interpretiert die vorhandene Architektur in einer neuen, modernen Art. Der Neubau setzt sich aus zwei höhenversetzten Gebäudeteilen zusammen, die durch unterschiedliche Größen und Farben als eigenständige Körper in Erscheinung treten. Die auf der Südostseite in das Gebäude eingezogenen Balkone unterstützen die klare Form und haben den Charakter einer privaten Loggia. Für die Wohnungen im Erdgeschoss sind die Außenräume großzügig gehalten und sorgen für ein flexibles Zusammenleben.

THE PROPERTY

Situated between two historic buildings, the multi-party residential building on Spirgartenstrasse offers a new and contemporary interpretation of the existing architecture. The new building consists of two vertically offset sections that appear as independent structures due to their different sizes and colors. The balconies situated on the southeastern side of the building underline the clear shape and have the characteristics of private loggias. The outdoor areas of the ground floor apartments are generously proportioned and ensure flexible social interactions.

Loggias statt Balkone ergeben einen klaren Baukörper
Loggias instead of balconies give the building a clearly structured look

Einblick in die Attikawohnung
View of the attic apartment

Einblick in eine 4,5-Zimmer-Wohnung
View of a 4.5-room apartment

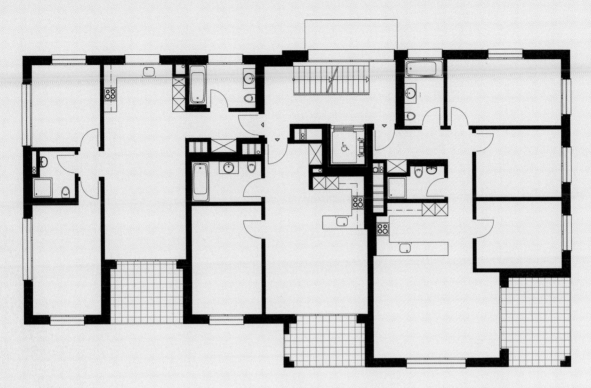

Grundriss Erdgeschoss, 1. und 2. Obergeschoss
Layout ground floor, 2nd and 3rd floor

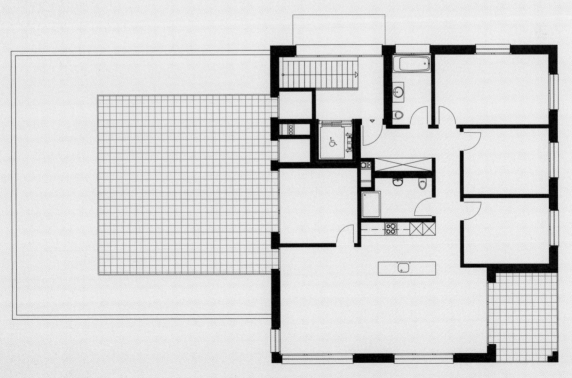

Grundriss Attikageschoss
Layout attic floor

EIN GEBÄUDEENSEMBLE
WEIT ÜBER DER STADT
A BUILDING ENSEMBLE
HIGH ABOVE THE CITY

PROJEKTNAME: «Grandeur Zurich»
IMMOBILIE: Mehrfamilienhaus mit 8 exklusiven Eigentumswohnungen
STANDORT: Drusbergstrasse 62, 8053 Zürich, Schweiz
AUFTRAGGEBER: Felix Partner Invest Drei AG, Zürich, Schweiz
ARCHITEKTUR: Felix Partner Architektur AG, Zürich, Schweiz
VERMARKTUNG: 2015–2017
AUSZEICHNUNGEN: Iconic Awards 2016, Architecture Winner und
German Design Award Special 2017

PROJECT NAME: "Grandeur Zurich"
PROPERTY: Multi-party residential building with 8 exclusive condominiums
LOCATION: Drusbergstrasse 62, 8053 Zurich, Switzerland
CLIENT: Felix Partner Invest Drei AG, Zurich, Switzerland
ARCHITECTURE: Felix Partner Architektur AG, Zurich, Switzerland
MARKETING PERIOD: 2015–2017
RECOGNITIONS: Iconic Awards 2016, Architecture Winner and German
Design Award Special 2017

GRÖSSE UND GROSSARTIGKEIT ZUM SAVOIR-VIVRE GEMACHT
GRANDEUR AND MAGNIFICENCE TURNED INTO SAVOIR-VIVRE

DIE BASIS

Wohnen in der Stadt Zürich mit einzigartiger Lebensqualität hoch über der City, das bietet hier die Grundlage für das Immobilienmarketing. Eine gute, unverbaubare Lage an der Drusbergstrasse in Zürich Witikon, ein stimmiges, zeitloses und perfekt in die Natur eingepasstes Gebäudeensemble von drei Mehrfamilienhäusern und einem Einfamilienhaus, alles in moderner, innovativer und anspruchsvoller Art umgesetzt.

DIE ESSENZ

Die Immobilie hält ein Stück gehobene Lebensqualität bereit. Mit wirklicher Größe und gefühlter Großzügigkeit, mit einer unverbaubaren Lage, Sicherheit, Naherholung, Dorfcharakter und einer hervorragenden Infrastruktur, die alles für den Alltag bietet. Wohlgemerkt, in direkter Nähe zur City und zum Stadtgebiet.

Daraus leitet sich der Kerngedanke ab: großzügig und großartig Leben. Lebensart, Lebenslust und Lebenskunst verbunden im Savoir-vivre.

THE BASIS

The basis for the real estate marketing was residing in the city of Zurich with a unique quality of life high above the city. A good location closed to further development at Drusbergstrasse in Zurich Witikon, a building ensemble of three multi-party residential buildings and a single-family home that is harmonious, timeless, and perfectly embedded in nature with everything implemented in a modern, innovative, and demanding way.

THE ESSENCE

The property offers high quality of life on an elevated level. With genuine grandeur and tangible generosity, with an unobstructed location closed to further development, safety, local recreation, rural character, and an excellent infrastructure covering all necessities of daily life. All this in the direct vicinity of the city and the cosmopolitan area.

This is what inspired the core concept: Living generously and grandly. Lifestyle, love of life and joyful living all combined into savoir-vivre.

LAGE
LOCATION

DIE STANDORTFAKTOREN
THE LOCATION FACTORS

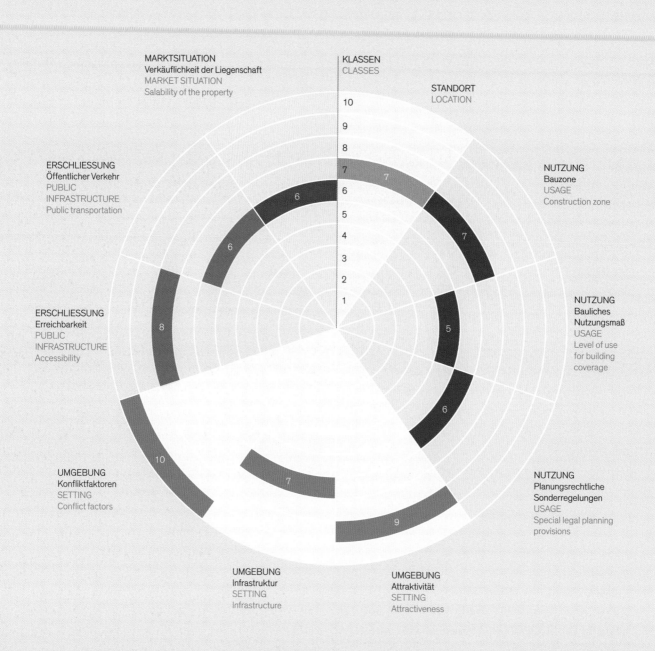

MARKTSITUATION
Verkäuflichkeit der Liegenschaft
MARKET SITUATION
Salability of the property

KLASSEN
CLASSES

STANDORT
LOCATION

ERSCHLIESSUNG
Öffentlicher Verkehr
PUBLIC
INFRASTRUCTURE
Public transportation

NUTZUNG
Bauzone
USAGE
Construction zone

ERSCHLIESSUNG
Erreichbarkeit
PUBLIC
INFRASTRUCTURE
Accessibility

NUTZUNG
Bauliches
Nutzungsmaß
USAGE
Level of use
for building
coverage

UMGEBUNG
Konfliktfaktoren
SETTING
Conflict factors

NUTZUNG
Planungsrechtliche
Sonderregelungen
USAGE
Special legal planning
provisions

UMGEBUNG
Infrastruktur
SETTING
Infrastructure

UMGEBUNG
Attraktivität
SETTING
Attractiveness

DIE STANDORTQUALITÄT VON «GRANDEUR ZURICH»

+ Beste Wohnlage

+ Sehr sonnig

+ Ruhige Lage

+ Naherholung vor der Haustür

+ Privatverkehr gut erschlossen

+ Mittlere Anbindung an den öffentlichen Verkehr

− Geringe Ausnutzung möglich

THE LOCATION QUALITY OF "GRANDEUR ZURICH"

+ Best residential area

+ Very sunny

+ Quiet location

+ Local recreation at the doorstep

+ Good private traffic infrastructure

+ Mediocre public transportation connection

− Limited utilization possible

DER MARKT

Das Marktumfeld für Neubauwohnungen im Stockwerkeigentum und zur Miete im oberen Preissegment ist in der Schweiz auch nach der Finanz- und Bankenkrise 2008 sehr attraktiv, wenn auch zunehmend umkämpft. Für erfolgreiche Projekte in diesem Segment muss von der Makro- und Mikrolage über die Grundrisse bis zur Detailmaterialisierung bei der Käufer- und Mieterschaft alles stimmen.

Großzügigkeit und Privatsphäre zeichnen die Eigentumswohnungen aus. Die Grundrisse sind speziell auf diese Ansprüche ausgerichtet und klassisch geschnitten. Auch die Außenräume weisen eine sehr überdurchschnittliche Weitläufigkeit auf. Durch die hohe Quadratmeterzahl der Wohnungen liegen die einzelnen Angebote trotz guter und moderater Quadratmeterpreise auf einem hohen Preisniveau. Dem ist in der Kommunikation wie auch in der Planung Rechnung zu tragen.

THE MARKET

After the financial and banking crisis of 2008, the market for newly constructed apartments as condominiums or for rent in the upper price segment remains very attractive in Switzerland, albeit increasingly competitive. For projects to succeed in this sector, everything has to be perfectly coordinated for the buyers and tenant, from the macro- and micro-location via the layouts up to the materialization of details.

The condominiums are distinguished by their generous proportions and privacy. The floor plans are specifically designed for these demands and classically laid out. The outdoor areas are also much more spacious than standard. Despite the good and moderate square meter prices, the condominiums are very highly priced due to their large square meter size. This should be taken into account in the communication and the planning.

DER UMWEG

Das erste Konzept für die Überbauung entstand bereits 2010, ausgerichtet auf die zu diesem Zeitpunkt aktuelle Marktlage und Kundenbedürfnisse. Die Bautätigkeit wurde anschließend jedoch zwei Jahre lang durch Einsprüche blockiert und die ersten Wohnungen erst im Dezember 2015 bezugsbereit. Für die Vermarktung wurde bis Ende 2014 mit zwei verschiedenen Immobilienmaklern gearbeitet. Die Maßnahmen wurden dabei einmal auf die gesamte Überbauung mit Vermietung und Verkauf und einmal nur auf den Verkauf ausgerichtet. Da sich der Immobilienmarkt zwischen 2010 und 2015 jedoch ein Stück weit gewandelt hatte und Objekte im oberen, aber noch nicht im Luxussegment, wie die Käuferliegenschaft Drusbergstrasse 62, nun mit einem konkreten Überangebot zu kämpfen hatten, wurde 2015 ein radikaler Schnitt gemacht und das ganze Projekt komplett neu aufgestellt. Name, Positionierung, Werte und viele Details wurden nochmals erarbeitet und neu implementiert und die vermeintliche Schwäche, die Größe und daher der hohe Preis der Wohnungen, zum Vorteil gedreht. Das hat den gewünschten Umschwung und somit auch den Erfolg gebracht.

THE DETOUR

The first concept for the construction was already developed in 2010 based on the current market situation and customer needs of the time. However, construction was blocked for two years due to objections. The first apartments were only ready for occupation in December 2015. Until late 2014, the marketing was handled by two different real estate agents. One of them handled the entire estate including apartment rental and sales, while the other handled only the sales. However, as the real estate market changed to some degree between 2010 and 2015, buildings in the upper, but not the luxury sector, such as the property at Drusbergstrasse 62, had to struggle with evident oversupply. In 2015, a radical cut was made and the entire project restructured. The name, positioning, values, and many details were revised and newly implemented and the presumed weakness, the size and the associated high price of the condominiums, was turned into an advantage. This brought the desired turn-around and success.

DER AUFTRAG

Investment, Projektentwicklung, Architektur, Planung und Marketing entstehen aus einem Guss. Die interdisziplinären Stärken von Felix Partner machen auch bei diesem Projekt den Unterschied. Der Einbezug der Gestalter in die Architektur kommt bereits in einer frühen Planungsphase mit harmonischen Farbkonzepten zum Tragen. Das angestrebte Immobilienmarketing wird maßgeschneidert und adaquat auf das Projekt umgesetzt, emotional, nutzen- und nutzerorientiert. Das Konzept beinhaltet die Namens- und Markenentwicklung, Positionierung und Claim sowie die gesamte Umsetzung im Corporate Design und den Kommunikationsmaßnahmen.

DER ZIELRAUM

– Stadt Zürich

– Nähere Agglomeration Zürich

– Kanton Zürich

– Kantone Basel und Bern

– Schweiz

– Schweiz angrenzender, deutschsprachiger Raum

THE ASSIGNMENT

The investment, project development, architecture, planning, and marketing are all matched. The interdisciplinary strengths of Felix Partner also made a difference in this project. The involvement of the designers with the architecture already came to play in an early planning phase with harmonious color schemes. The desired real estate marketing was customized and adequately applied to the project in an emotional manner focused on the use and users. The concept incorporates the name and brand development, positioning and the claim, as well as the entire implementation of the corporate design and communication measures.

THE TARGET AREA

– City of Zurich

– Nearby Zurich vicinity

– Canton Zurich

– Cantons Basel und Bern

– Switzerland

– German-speaking areas bordering Switzerland

DIE ZIELGRUPPE

Status, aber kein Prunk, traditionsverbunden, aber nicht verstaubt, das Bedürfnis nach Privat- und Freiraum: Werte, die der definierten Zielgruppe wichtig sind und in der Kommunikation direkt oder indirekt über Formen und Farben wieder aufgenommen werden.

Quantitativ:
– Einzelpersonen oder Paare ab 35 Jahren mit
   Schenkung, Erbvorbezug, Erbe
– Unverheiratete Paare und Ehepaare ohne Kinder
   oder nach Familienphase
– Hausverkäufer (eher älter, Wohnung an
   schöner Lage anstelle Haus)
– Zugezogene aus dem Ausland
– Hohe Einkommensschicht, Doppelverdiener

Qualitativ:
– Sind stadtorientiert, schätzen aber ein eher
   ruhiges Quartier mit Dorfcharakter
– Sind zum Großteil konservativ eingestellt: Sicherheit,
   Tradition, Werteerhaltung
– Wissen um den Wert einer guten Immobilienlage
– Wollen schön und großzügig wohnen und lassen sich das
   etwas kosten

Schlüsselargumente:
– In der Stadt, aber mit Dorfcharakter
– Gute Gesamtinfrastruktur (Verkehr, Einkaufen, Freizeit)
– Gute Schulen
– Werterhaltung und Unverbaubarkeit
– Erholung
– Hohe Lebensqualität
– Großes und großzügiges Wohneigentum

THE TARGET GROUP

Status-conscious but not pompous, committed to traditions but not old-fashioned, with a desire for privacy and free space – these values describe the defined target group and are directly or indirectly expressed in the communication via colors and shapes.

Quantitative:
– Individuals or couples aged 35+ who received a
   bestowal, advancement on inheritance, or an inheritance
– Unmarried couples and married couples without children
   or after the family phase
– Home sellers (rather older, replacing a house
   by a condominium in a beautiful location)
– Expatriates
– High income strata, double incomes

Qualitative:
– Are city-oriented, yet appreciate a rather quiet
   quarter with a rural character
– Have mostly conservative attitudes: security, tradition,
   value conservation
– Recognize the value of a good real estate location
– Want to have a beautiful and spacious home and are
   willing to pay for it

Key arguments:
– In the city, but with a village character
– Good general infrastructure (traffic, shopping, recreation)
– Good schools
– Value conservation and no future construction around it
– Relaxation
– High quality of life
– Large and spacious residential property

DIE SINUS-ANALYSE DER ZIELGRUPPE FÜR «GRANDEUR ZURICH»
THE SINUS ANALYSIS OF THE TARGET GROUP FOR "GRANDEUR ZURICH"

SOZIALE LAGE UND GRUNDORIENTIERUNG
SOCIAL STATUS AND BASIC VALUES

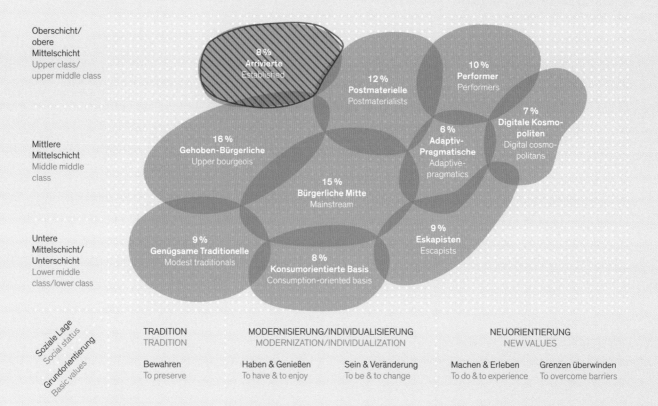

Oberschicht/
obere
Mittelschicht
Upper class/
upper middle class

8 %
Arrivierte
Established

12 %
Postmaterielle
Postmaterialists

10 %
Performer
Performers

7 %
**Digitale Kosmo-
politen**
Digital cosmo-
politans

Mittlere
Mittelschicht
Middle middle
class

16 %
Gehoben-Bürgerliche
Upper bourgeois

6 %
**Adaptiv-
Pragmatische**
Adaptive-
pragmatics

15 %
Bürgerliche Mitte
Mainstream

Untere
Mittelschicht/
Unterschicht
Lower middle
class/lower class

9 %
Genügsame Traditionelle
Modest traditionals

8 %
Konsumorientierte Basis
Consumption-oriented basis

9 %
Eskapisten
Escapists

Soziale Lage
Social status
Grundorientierung
Basic values

TRADITION
TRADITION

MODERNISIERUNG/INDIVIDUALISIERUNG
MODERNIZATION/INDIVIDUALIZATION

NEUORIENTIERUNG
NEW VALUES

Bewahren
To preserve

Haben & Genießen
To have & to enjoy

Sein & Veränderung
To be & to change

Machen & Erleben
To do & to experience

Grenzen überwinden
To overcome barriers

Statusorientierte, traditions- wie stilbewusste Paare oder Einzelpersonen: Die Zielgruppe
von «Grandeur Zurich» deckt sich sehr gut mit dem Sinus-Milieu der Arrivierten.
Status-oriented, traditional, and stylish couples or individuals: the target group of "Grandeur Zurich"
coincides to a large degree with the Sinus milieu of the established.

TRADITION MIT STIL

Von der Zielgruppenanalyse ausgehend werden Paare aus der definierten Zielgruppe porträtiert, um über Identifikation Emotionen potenzieller Käufer zu wecken .

Jolanda Steiner und Thomas Arbenz sind 38 beziehungsweise 46 Jahre alt und arbeiten in der Finanzbranche. Sie ist erfolgreiche Analystin mit einer guten Nase für nachhaltige Anlagen und Thomas führt ein Team von Juristen in der Rechtsabteilung. Das Arbeitspensum der beiden ist enorm und die Luxus-Mietwohnung im Herzen von Zürich dient fast nur als Schlafstätte. Da bisher auch kaum Gelegenheiten zum Geldausgeben vorhanden waren, ist das Vermögen des Paares laufend angewachsen. Nachdem sie sich verschiedenste Wohneigentums-Angebote in Zürich angeschaut haben, ist etwas Ernüchterung eingetreten. Denn ganz so viele Objekte, die den beiden zusagen, haben sie nicht gefunden. Allerdings sind ihre Ansprüche auch nicht ohne: Viel Wohnfläche, modernster Ausbau, harmonische Farben, Weitblick und idealerweise Anschluss an eine Grünzone, das wären die wichtigsten Parameter. Und natürlich nicht irgendwo im Umland, sondern in der Stadt. Oder über der Stadt! Ein bisschen weniger arbeiten steht auf dem Lebensplan, mehr Zeit für sich, für das eigene Wohlbefinden, das steht in nächster Zukunft an. Mal raus können und wandern, das Wetter und das Leben spüren. Innerhalb und außerhalb der eigenen vier Wände.

STYLISH TRADITION

Based on the target group analysis, couples of the defined target group are portrayed to appeal to the emotions of potential buyers via identification.

Jolanda Steiner and Thomas Arbenz are 38 and 46 years old and work in the financial sector. She is a successful analyst with a good instinct for sustainable investments while Thomas heads a team of lawyers in the law department. Both have very heavy workloads and their luxury rental apartment in the heart of Zurich almost only serves them as a place to sleep. As so far they have not had many opportunities for spending money, the assets of the couple have increased steadily. After they have looked at various condominium offers in Zurich they have become rather disenchanted because they did not find many buildings that appealed to them. At the same time, their demands are also not simple: extensive floor space, latest finishing, harmonious colors, a view, and ideally direct connection to a green zone are the most important diameters. And of course not somewhere in the countryside but in the city. Or above the city! Their plan for the near future includes working a bit less, and taking more time for themselves and their well-being. To head outdoors and go for hikes to enjoy the weather and life. Inside and outside their own four walls.

GROSSZÜGIGES WOHNEN IN DER
STADT ZÜRICH MIT EINZIGARTIGER
LEBENSQUALITÄT HOCH ÜBER DER CITY
GENFROUS DWELLING IN THE CITY
OF ZURICH WITH A UNIQUE QUALITY
OF LIFE HIGH ABOVE THE CITY

DIE POSITIONIERUNG

Aus dem Positionierungsbeschrieb reduziert sich der Positionierungssatz: «Großzügiges Wohnen in der Stadt Zürich mit einzigartiger Lebensqualität hoch über der City». Viel Grünfläche, Freiraum, unverbaubar, der erhabene Blick über die Stadt – aber noch etwas Dorfcharakter und Rückzugsort, alles gepaart mit viel Sonne, Ruhe und Sicherheit: So positioniert sich das Projekt wirkungsvoll in den gewählten Kommunikationsmitteln, die sich an Menschen mit hohem Anspruch an Lebensqualität richten, denen eine Work-Life-Balance und eine gute Einbindung in eine funktionierende Infrastruktur – vom Verkehr über das Einkaufen bis hin zum breiten Ausbildungs- und Freizeitangebot – wichtig sind.

DER ANALYSE-SCHWERPUNKT

Von den drei Analyse-Schwerpunkten Lage, Lifestyle und Architektur sticht beim Projekt die Architektur mit ihrem ausgesprochen großzügigen Raumangebot hervor. Die Zielgruppe schätzt die Großzügigkeit im Wohnen und ist daher vermutlich auch bereit, einen in der Gesamtsumme höheren Preis zu bezahlen.

Die Schwerpunkt-Argumente der Architektur:
- **Wohnungen mit echtem Unique Selling Point (Größe)**
- **Großzügige Lebensräume innen und außen**
- **Eigenständig und doch zeitlos gestaltet**
- **Unverbaubare Wohnlage**

THE POSITIONING

The following positioning sentence was derived from the positioning description: "Generous dwelling in the city of Zurich with a unique quality of life high above the city." Much nature, free space, not open for development, with an elevated view across the city, at the same time with a bit of a village character coupled with plenty of sun, quiet and safety – this is how the project is effectively presented in the selected communication media. They address persons with high demands regarding their quality of life, who care about work-life balance and a functioning infrastructure from traffic via shopping to extensive educational and leisure offers.

THE FOCUS OF THE ANALYSIS

Among the three focal analysis areas of location, lifestyle and architecture, the architecture with its extremely generous proportions is outstanding for this project. The target group appreciates the generous living space and is therefore probably ready to pay an overall higher price.

The architecture focus of the analysis:
- **Apartments with a genuine unique selling point (size)**
- **Generous indoor and outdoor living spaces**
- **Independent and yet timeless**
- **Location closed to further development**

DER NAME: «GRANDEUR ZURICH»

«Grandeur» steht für Größe und Großartigkeit. Der Zusatz des internationalen Stadtnamens «Zurich» verstärkt diesen Eindruck und unterstreicht die Vorzüge der Architektur und der Lage. «Grandeur» steht aber auch für einen stilbewussten und genießerischen Lebensstil. Der französische Ursprung des Wortes verleiht dem Projekt zusätzlich Eleganz und Exklusivität.

DER CLAIM: «ZUHAUSE IN ALLEN DIMENSIONEN»

Der Claim soll Menschen ansprechen, die immer etwas mehr erwarten, von sich, vom Leben, von ihrem Zuhause. Er fügt dem Namen wortwörtlich eine weitere Dimension hinzu: die Bestätigung an die potenziellen Käufer, hier ihre großen Erwartungen erfüllt zu wissen.

DIE FARBEN UND DIE TYPOGRAFIE

Weite spüren lassen, die Großzügigkeit der hellen Gebäude unterstützen, die großen Fenster spiegeln. Mit hellen Farbtönen und viel Weiß. Dazu im Kontext das Erdige des Außenraums, sich wohl und sicher fühlen. Eine edle Kombination, die auch in den Schriften aufgenommen wird. Eleganz und Luftigkeit verbunden mit Tradition und Bodenständigkeit.

DIE IDEE: GRÖSSE ERLEBBAR MACHEN

Das Gefühl von Raum und Weite – die Lust wecken, darin einzutauchen. Die Idee, das beschriebene Lebensgefühl und die damit verbundenen Emotionen auf verschiedenen Kommunikationsebenen zu manifestieren, entsteht wie die ganze Projektplanung in disziplinenübergreifender Zusammenarbeit zwischen Marketern, Investoren, Bauherren und Architekten.

DAS WERBLICHE KONZEPT

Kein Pomp, sondern moderne Eleganz und Exklusivität. Die Idee findet sich wieder in hellen, lichtstarken Bildern, die eine emotionale Sogwirkung erzeugen und in Headlines, die Gefühle vermitteln. Abgerundet werden die Kommunikationsmittel durch Texte, die sowohl informieren als auch berühren. Dazu ein passender Mediamix, der exakt auf die potenzielle Käuferschaft zugeschnitten ist.

THE NAME: "GRANDEUR ZURICH"

"Grandeur" expresses grandness and magnificence. Adding the international city name of "Zurich" reinforces this impression while highlighting the advantages of the architecture and the location. At the same time, "Grandeur" also stands for a style conscious way of life and indulging savoir-vivre. The French origin of the word gives the project a little extra elegance and exclusivity.

THE CLAIM: "AT HOME IN ALL DIMENSIONS"

The claim is addressed at people who always expect a bit more from themselves, from life, and from their homes. It literally adds another dimension to the name – the confirmation to potential buyers that their great expectations will be fulfilled here.

THE COLORS AND THE TYPOGRAPHY

Convey a sense of space, underline the generous proportions of the light-colored buildings, and reflect the large windows. With light colors and plenty of white. Combined with the earth colors of the outdoors for a sense of well-being and safety. A noble combination that is also repeated in the typefaces. Elegance and weightlessness combined with tradition and pragmatism.

THE IDEA: MAKE GREATNESS PALPABLE

Evoke and provide positive feelings of space and expanse – awakening the desire to indulge in it. In line with the entire project planning process, the manifestation of the idea, the described lifestyle and the associated emotions at various communication levels resulted from the cross-discipline cooperation among marketers, investors, owners, and architects.

THE ADVERTISING CONCEPT

Nothing pompous, but modern elegance and exclusivity. The idea is reflected in light-colored bright pictures that trigger emotions and in headlines that convey feelings. The communication tools are completed by texts that inform and electrify the recipients. Furthermore, a suitable media mix was created precisely tailored to the potential buyers.

DAS CORPORATE DESIGN FÜR «GRANDEUR ZURICH»
THE CORPORATE DESIGN FOR "GRANDEUR ZURICH"

LOGO
LOGO

TYPOGRAFIE
TYPOGRAPHY

Brandon Grotesque
Baskerville

GRANDEUR
ZURICH

ZU HAUSE SEIN AUF

Zu Hause sein auf einem idyllischen Plateau, an einer Berg-schulter mit Blick auf die Stadt. Einzigartig gut aufgehoben in einer von acht großzügigen und großartigen Eigentums-wohnungen. Mit unschlagbarer Lebensqualität, mit Ruhe, Erholung und Sicherheit.

FARBEN
COLORS

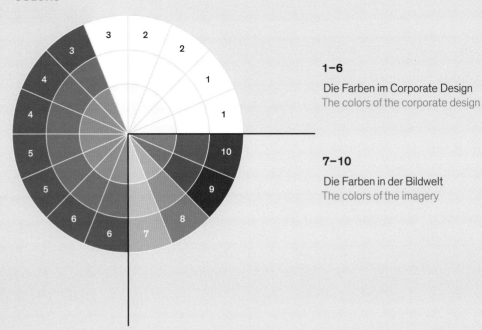

1–6

Die Farben im Corporate Design
The colors of the corporate design

7–10

Die Farben in der Bildwelt
The colors of the imagery

Living beauty, beyond one's own self. Delight, try every detail of new things, lean back

GRANDEUR
ZURICH

SCHÖNHEIT LEBEN,

ÜBER SICH SELBST HINAUS.

ENTZÜCKEN, NEUES

MIT ALLEN FACETTEN

AUSPROBIEREN,

ZURÜCKLEHNEN.

GRANDEUR

ZURICH

ELEGANZ VERMITTELN,

SCHLICHT UND PERSÖNLICH.

ZELEBRIEREN, DIE EIGENE

LEBENSLUST MIT ALLEN SINNEN

WAHRNEHMEN, STRAHLEN.

Convey elegance, simply and personally. Celebrate, enjoy life with all senses, and glow

DIE KOMMUNIKATIONSMITTEL

Website Teaserphase, Website Vollversion, Broschüre, Anzeigen, Online-Angebotsanzeigen, zielgruppenspezifisches Mailing, ausführliche Grundrisspläne mit einem Maßstab von 1:100, Fassadenpläne und Gebäudeschnitt, Situation und Umgebung, Verkaufspreisliste, Kurzbaubeschrieb, Zahlungskonditionen und rechtliche Hinweise, Bautafel, Ordner mit allen zum Objekt gehörenden Informationen und Unterlagen wie Verträge, Minergie-Zertifikate, Baubeschriebe etc.

THE COMMUNICATION MEDIA

Website teaser phase, website full version, brochure, advertisements, online advertising, target-group-specific mailing, detailed ground plans with a scale of 1:100, facade plans and building layout, situation and setting, sales price list, brief construction description, payment conditions and legal notifications, construction site sign, folder containing all project information and documents such as contracts, Minergie certificates, construction descriptions, etc.

Bautafel
Construction site sign

Website Teaserphase und Vollversion
Website teaser phase and website full version

Anzeige Teaserphase
Advertisement teaser phase

Anzeigen
Advertisements

Zielgruppenspezifisches Mailing
Target-group-specific mailing

Broschüre
Brochure

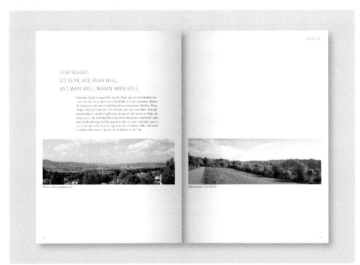

Broschüre
Brochure

Broschüre
Brochure

Broschüre
Brochure

Broschüre
Brochure

ENSEMBLE IN ZEITLOSER
HANDSCHRIFT, VON GROSSZÜGIGEM
GRÜNRAUM UMGEBEN
ENSEMBLE WITH A TIMELESS
STYLE, SURROUNDED BY EXTENSIVE
GREEN OUTDOOR AREAS

DIE IMMOBILIE

Ein- und Mehrfamilienhäuser prägen mit ihren Vorgärten und Vorplätzen den städtebaulichen Charakter und bilden den für das Quartier typischen, begrünten Straßenraum. Gegen Süden säumen steil abfallende Buchenwälder den Parzellenrand, wodurch sich immer wieder spektakuläre Sichtbezüge zum Zürichsee, den Bergen und in das Stadtzentrum öffnen. Das Wohnhaus Drusbergstrasse 62 ist Teil einer Überbauung, welche aus vier Einzelbauten besteht. Das Ensemble schließt die Baulücke entlang der Drusbergstrasse und fügt sich sowohl in seiner Anordnung als auch in seiner volumetrischen Ausbildung in das städtebauliche Gewebe ein. Durch die klare Setzung der Gebäude entlang der Straße bleibt zum Wald hin ein großer zusammenhängender Grünraum erhalten, der einen sanften und respektvollen Übergang zur Natur ermöglicht. Das Mehrfamilienhaus mit dem Wohneigentum wird durch vor- und zurückspringende Elemente plastisch moduliert. Die Gestaltung der Fassade geht auf die unterschiedlichen Gegebenheiten der Umgebung, die Topografie und die individuellen Grundrisse ein. Insgesamt enthält das Gebäude über vier Geschosse acht unterschiedliche Wohnungen. Der Bezug zum Außenraum, zum Wald, zum See und zur Stadt stand bei der Ausbildung der Grundrisse im Fokus. Alle Wohnungen verfügen über einen differenzierten Tages- und Nachtbereich mit präzis formulierten Übergängen. Anders bei der Attikawohnung: Hier können anhand mobiler Trennelemente der Raumfluss und die Art zu Wohnen flexibel gesteuert werden.

THE PROPERTY

The front gardens and front yards of the single- and multi-family homes define the urban character and constitute the greened street space typical of the quarter. Towards the south, steeply sloping beech forests line the edge of the plot, which results in various spectacular views of Lake Zurich, the mountains, and the city center. The residential building Drusbergstrasse 62 was created as part of a complex consisting of four individual buildings. The ensemble closes off the space among the buildings along Drusbergstrasse and its arrangement and volumetric design integrate it into the urban fabric. The deliberate positioning of the buildings along the street maintains a large cohesive green zone towards the forest that provides a gentle and respectful connection to nature. The multi-party condominium building is three-dimensionally shaped by receding and protruding elements. The facade design reflects the different features of the setting, the topography, and the individual layouts. Overall, the building contains eight different apartments on four floors. The design of the layouts focused on the interrelation with the outdoors, the forest, the lake, and the city. All apartments have different daytime and nighttime areas with precisely defined transitions. Except for the attic apartment in which mobile partition elements can be used to flexibly control the sequence of spaces and the desired lifestyle.

Gesamtansicht Ensemble vom Waldrand
General view of the ensemble from the edge of the forest

Wohnraum mit Aussicht auf den Zürichsee
Living area with view of Lake Zurich

Offene Küche mit Essbereich
Open kitchen with dining area

Badezimmer mit Fenster
Bathroom with window

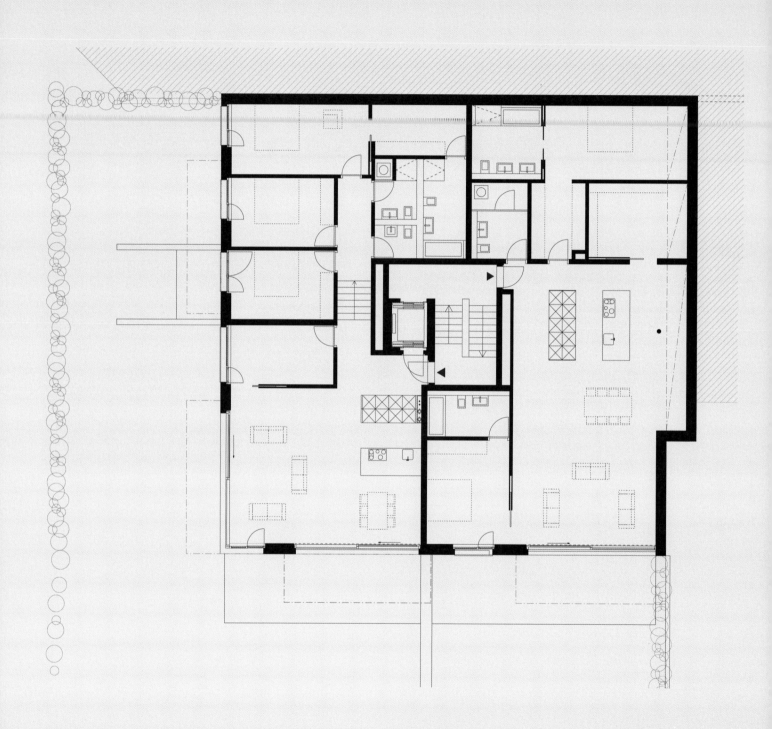

Grundriss Gartengeschoss
Layout garden floor

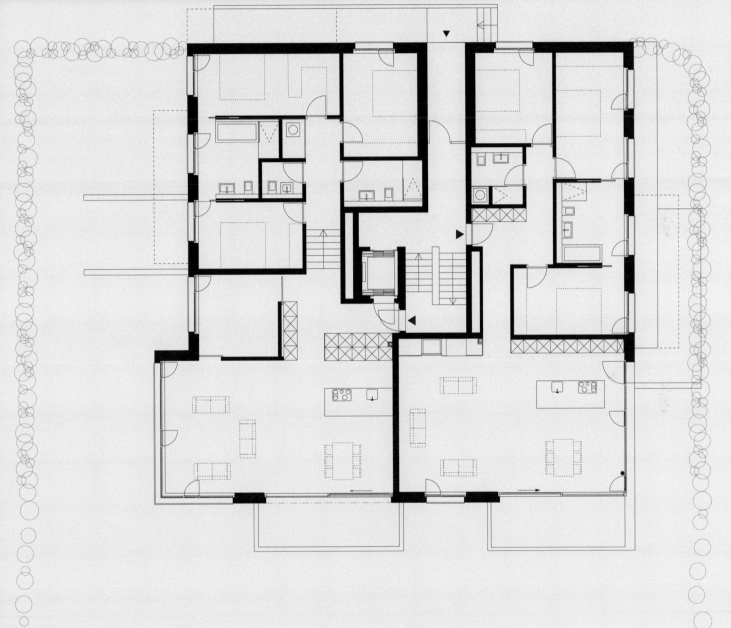

Grundriss Erdgeschoss/Eingangsgeschoss
Layout ground floor/entrance floor

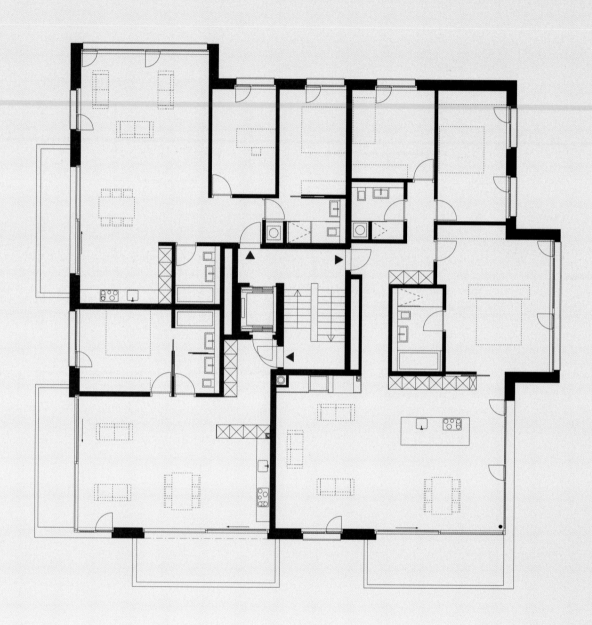

Grundriss 1. Obergeschoss
Layout 2nd floor

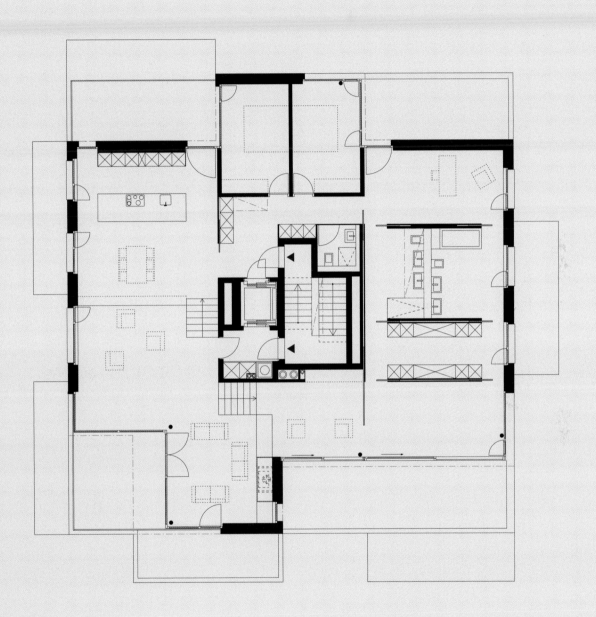

Grundriss Attikageschoss
Layout attic floor

ALS ENSEMBLE GESTALTETE MEHRFAMILIENHÄUSER NAHE ZÜRICHSEE

MULTI-PARTY RESIDENTIAL BUILDINGS DESIGNED AS AN ENSEMBLE NEAR LAKE ZURICH

PROJEKTNAME: «Divercity»
IMMOBILIE: Zwei Mehrfamilienhäuser mit 20 Eigentumswohnungen
STANDORT: Etzelstrasse 35/37, 8038 Zürich Wollishofen, Schweiz
AUFTRAGGEBER: Fundamenta Group AG, Zug, Schweiz
ARCHITEKTUR: Roefs Architekten AG, Zug/Zürich, Schweiz
VERMARKTUNG: geplant 2017

PROJECT NAME: "Divercity"
PROPERTY: Multi-party residential property consisting of two volumes and 20 condominiums
LOCATION: Etzelstrasse 35/37, 8038 Zurich Wollishofen, Switzerland
CLIENT: Fundamenta Group AG, Zug, Switzerland
ARCHITECTURE: Roefs Architekten AG, Zug/Zürich, Switzerland
MARKETING PERIOD: planned 2017

EIN ZUHAUSE MIT ALLEM, WAS MAN LIEBT, DRINNEN UND RUNDHERUM

A HOME OFFERING EVERYTHING THE HEART DESIRES INSIDE AND ALL-AROUND

DIE BASIS

Als Ausgangslage dienen zwei zu einem Ensemble zusammengebaute Mehrfamilienhäuser in Zürich Wollishofen, einem der ältesten und traditionellsten Stadtquartiere. Der Standort Etzelstrasse bietet ein Umfeld, das in seiner vielfältigen Art einmalig ist. Für Spiel und Erholung bieten sich die schönen Badeplätze am Zürichsee sowie die gepflegten Grünanlagen an. Zahlreiche Gewerbetreibende, Detailhändler und Vereine pflegen das Zusammensein und fördern das Quartierleben. Und divergente Vorstellungen von Kultur und Lebensformen, wie die Rote Fabrik und der Musikverein Harmonie oder das Altersheim und der Jugendtreff, verschmelzen hier zu einem Ganzen.

DIE ESSENZ

Seinen Lebensmittelpunkt an der Etzelstrasse zu haben, heißt an einer bevorzugten und optimal strukturierten Wohnlage daheim zu sein. Da, wo das Leben in seiner ganzen Vielfalt eins wird. Nur wenige Fahrminuten von der City entfernt, mit eigenem Bahnhof, dem See, vielen Grünanlagen und einem aktiven Quartierleben.

Daraus leitet sich der Kerngedanke ab: Vielfalt gehört zum Leben. Zu Hause oder unterwegs, Entspannung oder Hektik, Trubel oder Ruhe, Essen im stilvollen Ambiente oder in den eigenen vier Wänden, Privatsphäre oder Begegnungen noch und noch.

THE BASIS

The project was based on an ensemble of two multi-party residential buildings in Zurich Wollishofen, one of the city's oldest and most traditional quarters. The property is located on Etzelstrasse, a street offering a uniquely diverse setting. The beautiful swimming beaches on Lake Zurich and the area's carefully kept parks are available for many forms of leisure and recreation. A multifaceted range of small businesses, retailers, and local clubs foster interaction and enrich life in the quarter. Divergent cultural approaches and lifestyles such as the Rote Fabrik (Red Factory cultural center) and the Harmonie music club, or the retirement home and the youth center, merge to create a harmonious local community.

THE ESSENCE

Living on Etzelstrasse means calling a privileged and optimally structured residential area home. Where life can be enjoyed in all its diversity. Only a few minutes away from the downtown area, it boasts its own railroad station, access to the lake, many parks, and a lively community.

This is what inspired the core concept: Diversity is part of life. Whether at home or on the go, this includes relaxation as well as activity, hustle and bustle as well as tranquility, dinner in a stylish setting or at home, a great amount of privacy as well as plenty of interaction with others.

DIE STANDORTFAKTOREN
THE LOCATION FACTORS

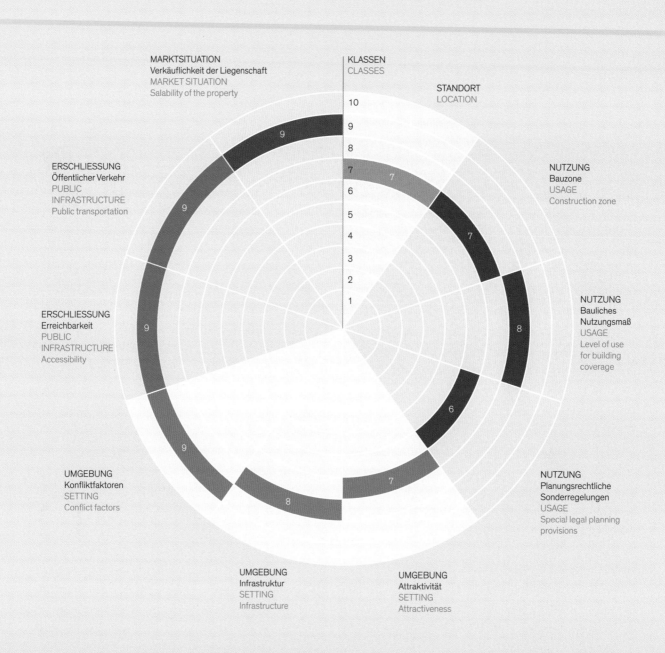

MARKTSITUATION
Verkäuflichkeit der Liegenschaft
MARKET SITUATION
Salability of the property

KLASSEN
CLASSES

STANDORT
LOCATION

NUTZUNG
Bauzone
USAGE
Construction zone

ERSCHLIESSUNG
Öffentlicher Verkehr
PUBLIC
INFRASTRUCTURE
Public transportation

NUTZUNG
Bauliches
Nutzungsmaß
USAGE
Level of use
for building
coverage

ERSCHLIESSUNG
Erreichbarkeit
PUBLIC
INFRASTRUCTURE
Accessibility

NUTZUNG
Planungsrechtliche
Sonderregelungen
USAGE
Special legal planning
provisions

UMGEBUNG
Konfliktfaktoren
SETTING
Conflict factors

UMGEBUNG
Infrastruktur
SETTING
Infrastructure

UMGEBUNG
Attraktivität
SETTING
Attractiveness

DIE STANDORTQUALITÄT VON «DIVERCITY»

+ Sehr gesuchte Wohnlage

+ Attraktiv mit Morgensonne

+ Ruhige Lage

+ Viele Angebote in direkter Nähe

+ Direkte Anschlüsse an den öffentlichen und privaten Verkehr

+ Hohe Ausnutzung möglich

− Eingeschränkte Aussicht

THE LOCATION QUALITY OF "DIVERCITY"

+ Highly coveted residential area

+ Attractive and exposed to the morning sun

+ Quiet location

+ Many offers in the immediate vicinity

+ Direct connections to public and private transportation

+ High utilization possible

− Limited view

DER MARKT

In Zürich Wollishofen bewegt sich der Immobilienmarkt sehr träge und Neubauten im Eigentum entstehen im Vergleich zu den umliegenden Quartieren nur wenige. Die Lage ist somit ein marktrelevanter Faktor. Nachteilig dürfte sich höchstens die zu niedrige Anzahl an Parkplätzen auswirken. Alles in allem dürfen die Entwickler jedoch davon ausgehen, dass die Wohnungen gut im Markt aufgenommen und rasch absorbiert werden.

DER AUFTRAG

Der klar umrissene Auftrag an die Kommunikationsspezialisten von Felix Partner beinhaltet ein engmaschiges und effektives Marketingkonzept einschließlich dessen Umsetzung in allen Phasen des Vermarktungsprozesses. Gemeinsam mit den Investoren, Maklern und Architekten erarbeitet Felix Partner ein schlankes, aber wirkungsstarkes Immobilienmarketing mit Namens- und Markenentwicklung, Positionierung und Claim sowie die gesamte Umsetzung im Corporate Design und den angestrebten Werbemitteln.

DER ZIELRAUM

– Stadt Zürich
– Nähere Agglomeration Zürich (Zürichseegemeinden)
– Kanton Zürich

THE MARKET

The real estate market of Zurich Wollishofen is very sluggish and compared to the surrounding districts only few new privately owned buildings are constructed. Therefore, the location is a market-relevant factor. The only drawback may be the limited number of parking spaces. Overall, however, the planners can expect the apartments to be well received and quickly absorbed by the market.

THE ASSIGNMENT

The clearly stated assignment of the communication specialists of Felix Partner consisted of a closely-knit and effective marketing concept including its implementation during all phases of the marketing process. In cooperation with the investors, realtors and architects, Felix Partner developed a streamlined yet powerful real estate marketing concept involving name and brand development, positioning and claim, as well as the entire implementation of the corporate design and planned advertising measures.

THE TARGET AREA

– City of Zurich
– Nearby Zurich vicinity (Lake Zurich communities)
– Canton Zurich

DIE ZIELGRUPPE

Die Lagevorteile und Lifestyle-Argumente führen in Einklang mit den Vorgaben und Analysen zu folgender Zielgruppe:

Quantitativ:

– Einzelpersonen 30+

– Unverheiratete Paare und Ehepaare ohne Kinder

– Unverheiratete Paare und Ehepaare mit Kindern 12+

– Unverheiratete Paare und Ehepaare nach Familienphase

– Aktive ältere Paare und Alleinstehende

– Höhere Einkommensschicht

Qualitativ:

– Schätzen ein schönes, am See liegendes, ruhiges Quartier

– Sind stadtorientiert

– Verkehrsanbindung (privater und öffentlicher Verkehr) ist wichtig

– Schätzen das vielfältige Angebot des Quartiers

– Bevorzugen schnelle, kurze Wege für einkaufen, arbeiten, Freizeit

– Schätzen die Möglichkeit des Rückzugs auf Stadtgebiet

Schlüsselargumente:

– Schönes, gepflegtes Quartier

– Nähe zum See

– Wollen alles um sich herum haben

– Agieren nach dem Lustprinzip

– Schätzen gute Verkehrsinfrastruktur

THE TARGET GROUP

The location advantages and lifestyle aspects in combination with the prerequisites and analyses resulted in the following target group:

Quantitative:

– Individuals aged 30+

– Unmarried couples and couples without children

– Unmarried couples and couples with children aged 12+

– Unmarried couples and couples after the family phase

– Active older couples and singles

– Higher income strata

Qualitative:

– Appreciate a beautiful quiet quarter located near the lake

– City-oriented

– Traffic connections (private and public) are important

– Appreciate the diverse offers in the quarter

– Prefer quick, short paths for shopping, working, leisure

– Appreciate the accessibility of the city

Key arguments:

– Beautiful, well-tended quarter

– Vicinity of the lake

– Want to have everything close by

– Follow the pleasure principle

– Appreciate good traffic infrastructure

DIE SINUS-ANALYSE DER ZIELGRUPPE FÜR «DIVERCITY»
THE SINUS ANALYSIS OF THE TARGET GROUP FOR "DIVERCITY"

SOZIALE LAGE UND GRUNDORIENTIERUNG
SOCIAL STATUS AND BASIC VALUES

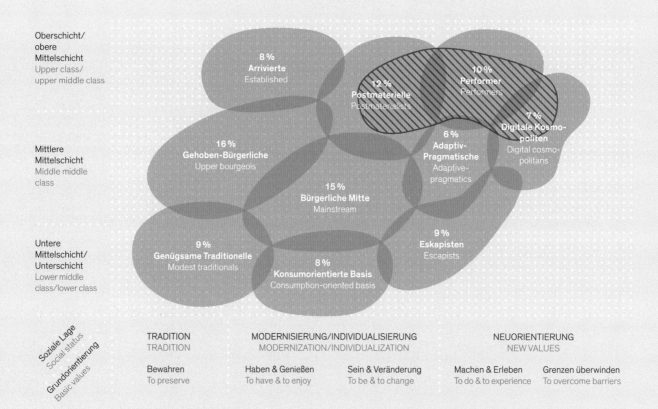

Oberschicht/
obere
Mittelschicht
Upper class/
upper middle class

8 %
Arrivierte
Established

12 %
Postmaterielle
Postmaterialists

10 %
Performer
Performers

7 %
**Digitale Kosmo-
politen**
Digital cosmo-
politans

Mittlere
Mittelschicht
Middle middle
class

16 %
Gehoben-Bürgerliche
Upper bourgeois

6 %
**Adaptiv-
Pragmatische**
Adaptive-
pragmatics

15 %
Bürgerliche Mitte
Mainstream

Untere
Mittelschicht/
Unterschicht
Lower middle
class/lower class

9 %
Genügsame Traditionelle
Modest traditionals

8 %
Konsumorientierte Basis
Consumption-oriented basis

9 %
Eskapisten
Escapists

Soziale Lage
Social status

Grundorientierung
Basic values

TRADITION	MODERNISIERUNG/INDIVIDUALISIERUNG		NEUORIENTIERUNG	
TRADITION	MODERNIZATION/INDIVIDUALIZATION		NEW VALUES	
Bewahren	Haben & Genießen	Sein & Veränderung	Machen & Erleben	Grenzen überwinden
To preserve	To have & to enjoy	To be & to change	To do & to experience	To overcome barriers

Individualisten mit hohen, wechselnden Ansprüchen an ihr Lebensumfeld – interessiert, aktiv, zukunftsorientiert:
Das entspricht den Sinus-Milieus der digitalen Kosmopoliten, Postmateriellen und Performer.
Individualists with high, changing demands regarding their surroundings –interested, active, and future-oriented:
this corresponds to the Sinus milieus of digital cosmopolitans, postmaterialists, and performers.

DER MODERNE PERFORMER MIT ETWAS STATUSBEWUSSTSEIN

Der Standort, der Lifestyle, der Preis: Wer sich eine Wohnung in «Divercity» kauft, macht ein Statement: Ich will alles – heute so, aber morgen vielleicht anders. Rudolf Hasler könnte so einer sein – das Porträt, welches für die Vermarktung eingesetzt wird:

Rudolf Hasler ist erfolgreicher Jurist und Partner in einer Anwaltskanzlei. Der großgewachsene, hagere Endvierziger ist geschieden, genießt sein Singleleben und auch den wiederkehrenden Besuch seines 17 Jahre alten Sohnes alle zwei Wochenenden. Da sich die Zinslage auf Vermögensseite laufend verschlechtert und er von seiner Mietwohnung ein bisschen genug hat, sucht er ein zu seinen Bedürfnissen passendes Wohneigentum. In der Stadt soll es sein, mit ein wenig Grün im Umfeld und nicht zu weit weg vom Zürichsee. Aber nicht im Trubel. Und doch gut angebunden und mit allem, was man braucht in der Nähe. Bei schönem Wetter fährt er mit dem Fahrrad zur Kanzlei am Central, sonst nutzt er den öffentlichen Verkehr. Seinen Sportwagen fährt er nur selten oder wenn er in das familieneigene Ferienhaus in die Berge möchte.

THE MODERN PERFORMER WITH SOME STATUS CONSCIOUSNESS

The location, the lifestyle, the price – people who buy an apartment in "Divercity" are making a statement: I want it all – today it is this, but tomorrow it may be something very different. Rudolf Hasler could be such an individual – following is the portrait that is used for the marketing campaign:

Rudolf Hasler is a successful lawyer and partner of a law firm. Tall, slim and in his late forties, he is divorced and enjoys the single life as well as the regular weekend visits of his 17-year-old son twice a month. As the returns on assets are getting progressively worse and he has had rather enough of his rented apartment, he is looking to purchase a residential property that suits his personal needs. He would like it to be in the city, surrounded by a bit of nature and not too far from Lake Zurich. But not at the center of the hustle and bustle. At the same time, it should be well connected and in close vicinity to the necessities of daily life. When the weather is fine, he rides his bicycle to his office near the Central public square in Zurich. When it is not, he takes the public transportation. He uses his sports car only infrequently or for trips to the family cabin in the mountains.

DA ZU HAUSE, WO DAS LEBEN IN
SEINER GANZEN VIELFALT EINS WIRD
BE AT HOME WHERE YOU CAN
ENJOY LIFE IN ALL ITS DIVERSITY

DIE POSITIONIERUNG

Die Positionierung ist das Kernversprechen, das sich aus den einzigartigen Lagevorteilen des beliebten Wohnquartiers Wollishofen ergibt: «Da zu Hause, wo das Leben in seiner ganzen Vielfalt eins wird». Die Vielfalt und die Abwechslung prägen das Umfeld, aber auch die flexiblen Grundrisse der Wohnungen und die Formsprache der Architektur. Entspannung am See und Kulturtrubel, Gourmet-Hotspots und gemütliche Abendessen zu Hause, spannende Begegnungen und Privatsphäre. Der treibende Rhythmus der Stadt und die ruhige Stube mit Sicht auf den Zürichsee, Opulenz und Nüchternheit, Lebensfreude und Lebensqualität, drinnen wie draußen.

THE POSITIONING

The positioning is the core promise derived from the unique location advantages of the popular Wollishofen residential quarter: "Be at home where you can enjoy life in all its diversity." Diversity and change characterize not only the setting, but also the flexible layouts of the apartments and the architectural design vocabulary. Relaxation near the lake, coupled with varied cultural events, gourmet hot spots and comfortable dinners at home, exciting interactions, and a great amount of privacy. The pulsating rhythm of the city and the quiet chamber with a view of the lake, opulence and sobriety, joy of life and a high-quality lifestyle inside and outside the home.

DER ANALYSE-SCHWERPUNKT

Hervorstechende Themen sind hier vor allem beim Schwerpunkt Lifestyle zu finden. Denn in Wollishofen kommen alle auf ihre Kosten. Exklusive Badeplätze am Zürichsee und gepflegte Grünanlagen. Ein aktives Quartierleben mit vielen Vereinen und Treffpunkten, heterogene Kultur- und Lebensformen wie die alternative Rote Fabrik neben dem Musikverein Harmonie Wollishofen oder das Altersheim neben dem Jugendtreff verschmelzen hier zu einem vielfältigen Ganzen.

THE FOCUS OF THE ANALYSIS

Prominent themes are primarily found in the lifestyle area. This is because in Wollishofen everyone can get what they are looking for. It offers exclusive swimming beaches on Lake Zurich and well-kept parks, an active local community with many clubs and meeting places, heterogeneous culture and lifestyle outlets such as the alternative Rote Fabrik (Red Factory cultural center) and the Harmonie music club, or the retirement home and the youth center, merge to create a harmoniously diverse local community

Die Analyse-Schwerpunkte Lage und Lifestyle:
- **Mittendrin mit etwas Distanz**
- **Moderne Lebensräume**
- **Vielfalt in jeder Lebenslage**
- **Potenzial Wertentwicklung**
- **Von Zusammensein bis Rückzug**
- **Attraktives Umfeld mit viel Grün und See**

The location and lifestyle focus of the analysis:
- **At the heart of things with a little distance**
- **Modern living environments**
- **Diversity in all walks of life**
- **Value development potential**
- **From togetherness to withdrawal**
- **Attractive setting with plenty of nature and the lake**

DER NAME: «DIVERCITY»

Die städtische Vielfalt. Diversität im Einklang mit der Stadt. Das englische Wortspiel beschreibt das Lebensgefühl und den Lifestyle, die das Projekt und dessen Ausstrahlung prägen.

DER CLAIM: «VIELFALT GEHÖRT ZUM LEBEN»

Der Claim verdeutlicht den Projektnamen und drückt Mut zum anders sein aus, einen Aufbruch in ein abwechslungsreiches Leben in einem lebendigen Quartier in engster Nähe zur Innenstadt und zum See.

DIE FARBEN UND DIE TYPOGRAFIE

Die Farben leiten sich hier fast ausschließlich aus der Architektur und dem Gebäude heraus ab. So wird den unterschiedlichen und speziellen Materialisierungen Rechnung getragen. Von der Fassade über die Brüstungen der Außenräume bis zu den Fensterrahmen. Dasselbe gilt für die Schrift. Zeitlos modern, klar, technisch geprägt und Ordnung schaffend.

DIE IDEE: SO ODER SO: ICH BIN ANDERS

Passend zum Claim und zum Lifestyle soll auch die Kommunikation der Marke unkonventionell sein und die Vielfalt im Leben und in der Stadt dokumentieren. Alltägliches in seiner Einzigartigkeit drückt das Leben in seiner abwechslungsreichsten Art aus.

DAS WERBLICHE KONZEPT

Alltagsgegenstände in urbanem, stilvollem Design visualisieren im Zusammenspiel mit Situationsbildern aus Wollishofen die Kommunikationsidee – ohne große Worte, überraschend, anders, frisch und direkt. Die Kompositionen erzählen eine Geschichte und spiegeln die Vielfalt des Lebens in Wollishofen wider, umgesetzt in allen relevanten Kommunikationsmitteln, mit starkem Wiedererkennungswert.

THE NAME: "DIVERCITY"

Urban diversity. Diversity in harmony with the city. The wordplay describes the enjoyment of life and the lifestyle that distinguishes the project and its image.

THE CLAIM: "DIVERSITY IS PART OF LIFE"

The claim expresses the courage to be different and to embark on a diversified lifestyle in a lively quarter in close vicinity to the downtown area and the lake. The claim illustrates the project name and is at the same time a call for an open and exciting life.

THE COLORS AND THE TYPOGRAPHY

The colors are almost exclusively derived from the architecture and the building. This way, the different and special materials are taken into account. From the facade, via the railings of the outdoor areas up to the window frames. The same applies to the typeface. Timeless modern, clear, technically oriented, and orderly.

THE IDEA: ANY WHICH WAY, I AM DIFFERENT

In line with the claim and the lifestyle, the brand communication should also be unconventional and document the diversity of life and the city. The unique nature of objects of everyday life reflects the most diverse nature of life.

THE ADVERTISING CONCEPT

Objects of everyday life with an urban stylish design in combination with situational images of Wollishofen visualize the communication concept – without many words, surprising, different, fresh, and direct. The compositions tell a story and reflect the diversity of life in Wollishofen, implemented across all relevant communication media with a strong recognition value.

DAS CORPORATE DESIGN FÜR «DIVERCITY»
THE CORPORATE DESIGN FOR "DIVERCITY"

LOGO
LOGO

TYPOGRAFIE
TYPOGRAPHY

Din Next Pro
Baskerville

DIVERCITY

VIELFALT
GEHÖRT
ZUM LEBEN.

SEINEN LEBENSMITTELPUNKT IN

Seinen Lebensmittelpunkt in einer der neuen Eigentumswohnungen in Zürich Wollishofen zu haben, bringt ein großes Maß an Möglichkeiten mit sich: Denn Ihr neues Zuhause ist so vielfältig, wie die Objekte, die Sie lieben. Und Wollishofen ist so vielfältig wie Ihr Zuhause.

FARBEN
COLORS

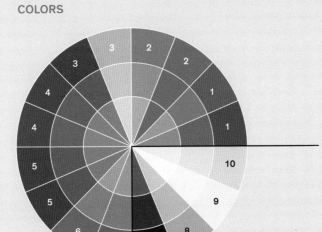

1–6

Die Farben im Corporate Design
The colors of the corporate design

7–10

Die Farben in der Bildwelt
The colors of the imagery

Ihr neues Zuhause ist so vielfältig wie die Objekte, die Sie lieben: Ihre mundgeblasene, handgeschliffene Karaffe aus edlem Bleikristall für alten Single Malt.

UND WOLLISHOFEN IST SO VIELFÄLTIG WIE IHR ZUHAUSE.

Your new home is as diverse as the objects you love – Your noble lead crystal mouth-blown hand-sanded decanter for aged single malt. And Wollishofen is as diverse as your home.

Ihr neues Zuhause ist so vielfältig wie die Objekte, die Sie lieben: Ihre von Meister-hand in der Schweiz gefertigten Brogues im Derby-Stil für höchsten Tragekomfort.

UND WOLLISHOFEN IST SO VIELFÄLTIG WIE IHR ZUHAUSE.

Your new home is as diverse as the objects you love – Your masterfully handmade Derby-style brogues for the highest wear comfort. And Wollishofen is as diverse as your home.

Ihr neues Zuhause ist so vielfältig wie die Objekte, die Sie lieben: Ihr individuell für Sie zusammengestelltes, praktisches Fahrrad fürs Cruisen in der Stadt.

UND WOLLISHOFEN IST SO VIELFÄLTIG WIE IHR ZUHAUSE.

Your new home is as diverse as the objects you love – Your individually configured convenient bicycle for cruising in the city. And Wollishofen is as diverse as your home.

Ihr neues Zuhause ist so vielfältig wie die Objekte, die Sie lieben: Ihr High-End-Kopfhörer für ein grossartiges Klangerlebnis und zum Geniessen magischer Momente.

UND WOLLISHOFEN IST SO VIELFÄLTIG WIE IHR ZUHAUSE.

Your new home is as diverse as the objects you love – Your high-end headphones for a great listening experience and enjoyment of magical moments. And Wollishofen is as diverse as your home.

DIE KOMMUNIKATIONSMITTEL

Website zum Projekt, Projektbroschüre für den Verkauf, Fächer als Give-away mit Infos und vielen Tipps zu Wollishofen, Planbroschüre mit Detailplänen, Baubeschrieb, Verkaufspreisliste

THE COMMUNICATION MEDIA

Project website, project sales brochure, giveaway fan-shaped brochure containing information and many tips for Wollishofen, plan brochure with detailed plans, construction description, sales price lisl

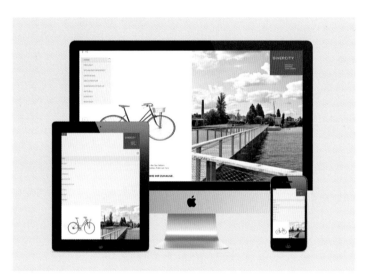

Website
Website

Fächer (Give-away)
Giveaway fan-shaped brochure

Fächer (Give-away)
Giveaway fan-shaped brochure

Fächer (Give-away)
Giveaway fan-shaped brochure

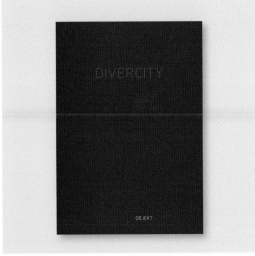

Projektbroschüre
Project sales brochure

Projektbroschüre
Project sales brochure

Projektbroschüre
Project sales brochure

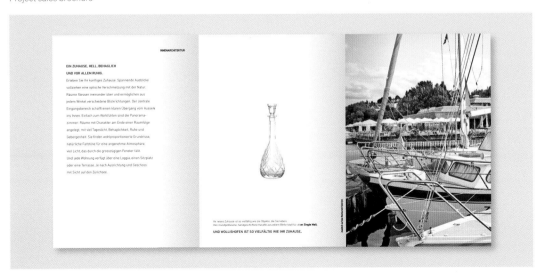

Projektbroschüre
Project sales brochure

ZWEI VERSETZTE VOLUMEN
VERSCHMELZEN ZU EINEM KÖRPER
TWO OFFSET VOLUMES BLEND
INTO A SINGLE BODY

DIE IMMOBILIE

Die Etzelstrasse befindet sich im durchgrünten Stadtkörper im Stadtteil Wollishofen. Der Baukörper des Mehrfamilienhauses verankert sich durch seine Verformung auf dem Grundstück. Die additive Situation von zwei versetzten Volumen, die zu einem Körper verschmelzen, fügt sich in ihrer Körnigkeit in den Kontext des Quartiers ein. Die Setzung der Volumen nimmt Rücksicht auf den bestehenden Baumbestand. Der architektonische Ausdruck des Gebäudes ist geprägt von der muralen Erscheinung der umliegenden Gebäude.

THE PROPERTY

Etzelstrasse is located in the greened urban development area of the Wollishofen quarter. The body of the multi-party residential building is anchored to the plot by its distorted shape. The granularity of the additive situation of two offset volumes that blend into a single body fits into the context of the quarter. The placement of the volumes takes the existing trees into account. The architectural design of the building is influenced by the mural style of the surrounding buildings.

Attraktive Wohnlage im Quartier Zürich Wollishofen
Attractive residential area in the Zurich Wollishofen quarter

Die Setzung der Volumen nimmt Rücksicht auf den alten Baumbestand
Placement of the volumes takes the old existing trees into account

Attikawohnung mit Blick auf den See
Attic apartment with view of the lake

Harmonische Farben und hochwertige Materialien prägen die Wohnungen
Harmonious colors and high-quality materials characterize the apartments

Wohlproportionierte Grundrisse für einen vielfältigen Lebensstil
Well-proportioned layout for a diversified lifestyle

Grundriss Eingangsgeschoss
Layout entrance floor

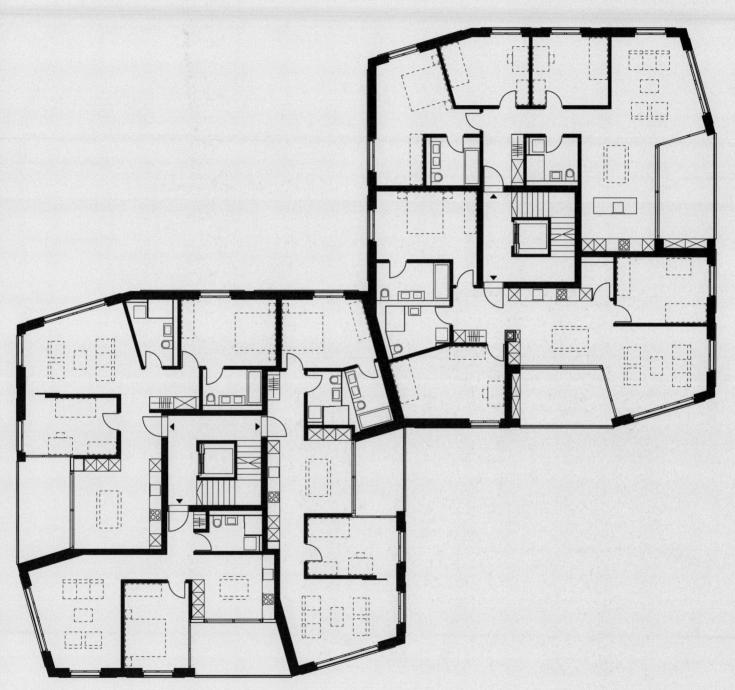

Grundriss Regelgeschoss
Layout standard floor

Grundriss Ober-/Attikageschoss
Layout top/attic floor

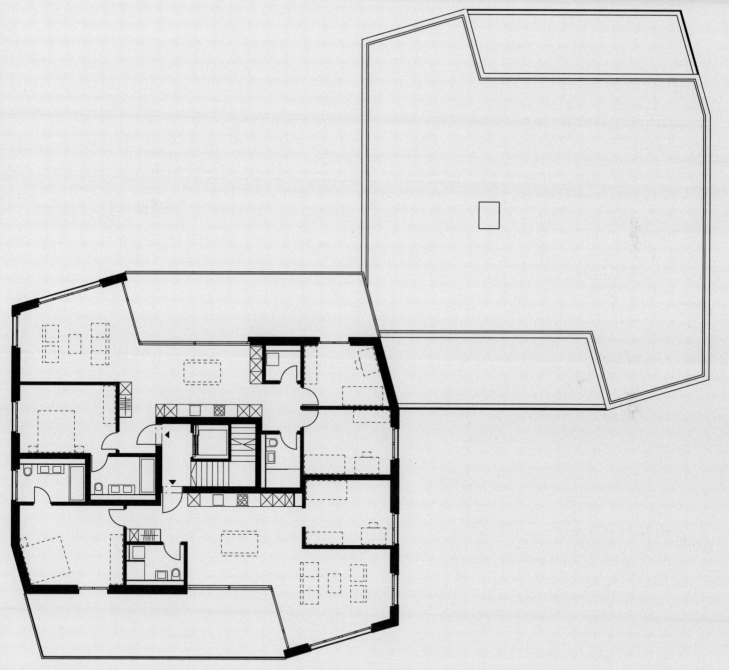

Grundriss Attikageschoss
Layout attic floor

NEUBAU MIT EIGENEM LICHTHOF IM BOOMQUARTIER ZÜRICH WEST

NEW CONSTRUCTION WITH ITS OWN ATRIUM IN THE BOOMING QUARTER OF ZURICH WEST

PROJEKTNAME: «Atrium West»
IMMOBILIE: Mehrfamilienhaus mit 47 Eigentumswohnungen
STANDORT: Förrlibuckstrasse 183/185, 8005 Zürich, Schweiz
AUFTRAGGEBER: Swiss Life AG, Zürich, Schweiz
ARCHITEKTUR: Felix Partner Architektur AG, Zürich, Schweiz
VERMARKTUNG: 2015–2016
AUSZEICHNUNGEN: Real Estate Award 2016 Schweiz,
Nomination in der Kategorie Vermarktung, 2. Platz durch
Publikumswahl und Iconic Awards 2016, Architecture Winner

PROJECT NAME: "Atrium West"
PROPERTY: Multi-party residential building with 47 condominiums
LOCATION: Förrlibuckstrasse 183/185, 8005 Zurich, Switzerland
CLIENT: Swiss Life AG, Zurich, Switzerland
ARCHITECTURE: Felix Partner Architektur AG, Zurich, Switzerland
MARKETING PERIOD: 2015–2016
RECOGNITIONS: Real Estate Award 2016 Switzerland,
nominated in the category marketing, 2nd place by audience vote,
and Iconic Awards 2016, Architecture Winner

MITTENDRIN SEIN, DEN PULS
FÜHLEN UND ALLES ERLEBEN
BE AT THE HEART OF THINGS,
FEEL THE PULSE OF THE CITY,
AND DON'T MISS A THING

DIE BASIS

Die Grundlage für das Immobilienmarketing bildet ein Neubau in Zürichs Kreis 5, genauer gesagt im Herzen des boomenden Quartierteils Zürich West. Einem Quartier, das sich in Zürich am rasantesten verändert und sich von der Industriebrache zum angesagten Lebensraum entwickelt. In der Nachbarschaft des Projekts befinden sich prominente Neubauten wie der Mobimo Tower, das Viadukt, die Escher Terrassen oder auch das Löwenbräu-Areal. Der Standort an der Förrlibuckstrasse zeichnet sich durch gute Anbindungen an den öffentlichen und privaten Verkehr aus und alles, was man im Leben braucht oder Spaß macht, liegt vor der Haustür.

DIE ESSENZ

Das Umfeld bietet für Schweizer Verhältnisse ein riesiges Angebot verschiedenster Themen, die das Leben bereichern. Essen in allen Variationen und Preisen, Sport von Aerobic bis Zumba, Musik- und Theaterangebote, Ausgehmöglichkeiten für jeden Anlass, Genuss für allerlei Geschmack, Spaß mit Freunden drinnen und draußen und ein Zuhause, in dem man ganz nah dran ist.

Daraus leitet sich der Kerngedanke ab: So leben, wie man ist, dort sein, wo man will, nach seinen eigenen, individuellen Regeln handeln. Immer mit seinem Zuhause als Ruheoase, als Rückzugsort, als zentrale Lebensbasis. Oder kompakt verpackt: Mitten im Leben erleben.

THE BASIS

The basis for the real estate marketing is a new building in Zurich's district 5, more precisely at the heart of the booming Zurich West quarter. A quarter that is undergoing the most rapid change in Zurich and evolving from an industrial fallow into a trendy living environment. The neighborhood of the project features prominent new buildings such as the Mobimo Tower, the Viadukt, the Escher Terraces, or the Löwenbräu premises. The location at Förrlibuckstrasse is distinguished by excellent public and private traffic connections, while everything needed for daily life or for having fun is at the doorstep.

THE ESSENCE

In Swiss terms, the setting offers a gigantic variety of various elements that enrich life. Food in all variations and at all prices, sports ranging from Aerobics to Zumba, music and theater offers, various options for going-out, treats to suit every taste, fun with friends and family indoors and outdoors, and a home that is close to everything.

This is what inspired the core concept: Live the way you are, be where you want to be, and act according to your own individual rules. Always with your home as an oasis of calm, as a retreat, the central basis of your life. Or more concisely stated: Experience things where life is happening.

LAGE
LOCATION

DIE STANDORTFAKTOREN
THE LOCATION FACTORS

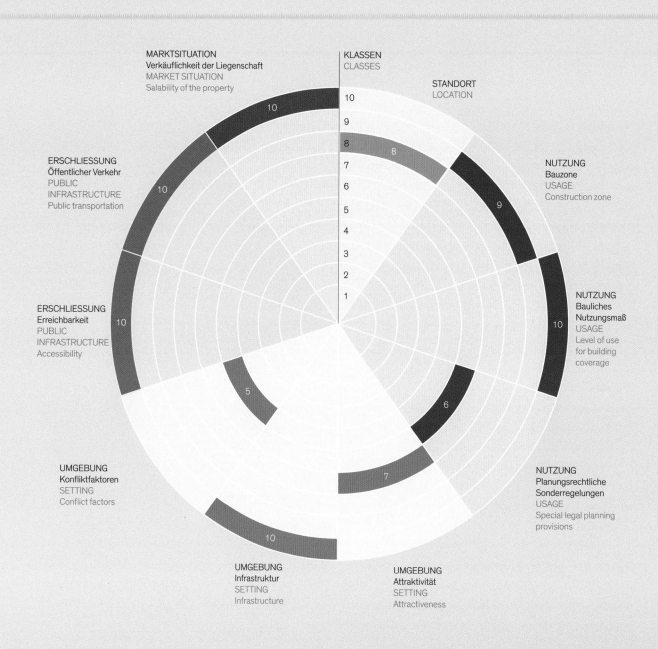

MARKTSITUATION
Verkäuflichkeit der Liegenschaft
MARKET SITUATION
Salability of the property

ERSCHLIESSUNG
Öffentlicher Verkehr
PUBLIC
INFRASTRUCTURE
Public transportation

ERSCHLIESSUNG
Erreichbarkeit
PUBLIC
INFRASTRUCTURE
Accessibility

UMGEBUNG
Konfliktfaktoren
SETTING
Conflict factors

UMGEBUNG
Infrastruktur
SETTING
Infrastructure

KLASSEN
CLASSES

STANDORT
LOCATION

NUTZUNG
Bauzone
USAGE
Construction zone

NUTZUNG
Bauliches
Nutzungsmaß
USAGE
Level of use
for building
coverage

NUTZUNG
Planungsrechtliche
Sonderregelungen
USAGE
Special legal planning
provisions

UMGEBUNG
Attraktivität
SETTING
Attractiveness

DIE STANDORTQUALITÄT VON «ATRIUM WEST»

+ Sehr gesuchte Wohnlage

+ Viele Angebote in direkter Nähe

+ Beste Anschlüsse an den öffentlichen und privaten Verkehr

+ Sehr hohe Ausnutzung möglich

+ Wertsteigernde Wohnzone

− Eingeschränkte Aussicht

− Starke Lärmbelastung

THE LOCATION QUALITY OF "ATRIUM WEST"

+ Highly coveted residential area

+ Many offers in the immediate vicinity

+ Best connections to public and private transportation

+ Very high utilization possible

+ Increasing value residential zone

− Limited view

− Extensive noise pollution

DER MARKT

Die Nachfrage nach Wohneigentum mit moderater Preisstruktur an bevorzugter Lage im Boomquartier Zürich West ist bei der definierten Zielgruppe potenziell groß. Der Markt ist übersichtlich, muss jedoch in einem sehr schnell wachsenden Quartier als volatil bezeichnet werden. Trotz Konkurrenzprojekten im direkten Umfeld kann sich die Immobilie mit seiner konsequenten Zielgruppenausrichtung und der eigenständigen Architektur mit dem einladenden und auffälligen Lichthof gut am Markt behaupten und erreicht die angestrebten Marketingziele frühzeitig.

DER AUFTRAG

Bereits zu Beginn des Projekts arbeiten die Entwickler, Architekten und Marketer von Felix Partner Seite an Seite. Gemeinsam entwickeln sie auf der Grundlage einer detaillierten Marktanalyse eine fundierte und verlässliche Zielgruppendefinition, die wiederum als Basis für die Bestimmung des Wohnungsmix, der architektonischen Schwerpunkte, des Materials und der Farbspektren sowie für die Ausgestaltung der Marketingmaßnahmen und des Mediamix dient. Es ist eine der ausgewiesenen Stärken von Felix Partner, dass Immobilienprojekte auch in dieser Größenordnung mit interdisziplinären Synergien geplant und umgesetzt werden. Das Beispiel zeigt, welche Vorteile und Möglichkeiten sich aus dieser Konstellation ergeben können. Das Immobilienmarketing beinhaltet Namens- und Markenentwicklung, Positionierung und Claim sowie die gesamte Umsetzung im Corporate Design und den Werbemaßnahmen.

DER ZIELRAUM

– Kreis 5
– Stadt Zürich
– Gemeinden der Westumfahrung
– Kanton Aargau und das Mittelland
– Kanton Zürich

THE MARKET

The demand for residential property with a moderate price structure in a favorable location in the booming quarter of Zurich West is potentially rather large among members of the defined target group. The market is clearly laid out, but should be described as volatile in a very quickly growing quarter. Despite competing projects in the direct vicinity, the property with its consistent target group focus and unique architecture with the inviting and striking atrium can hold its own on the market and accomplish its marketing goals at an early stage.

THE ASSIGNMENT

Right from the start, the developers, architects, and marketers of Felix Partner worked hand in hand. Based on a detailed market analysis they developed a substantiated and reliable target group definition. This was used in turn as the basis for determining the mix of apartments, the architectural focus, the material and color ranges, as well as the design of marketing measures and mix of media. One of the key strengths of Felix Partner is that even real estate projects of this size can be planned and implemented with interdisciplinary synergies. The example illustrates the advantages and possibilities that can be derived from this constellation. The real estate marketing incorporates the name and brand development, positioning and the claim, as well as the entire implementation of corporate design and the advertising measures.

THE TARGET AREA

– District 5
– City of Zurich
– Communities located on the west highway bypass
– Canton Aargau and Swiss Plateau
– Canton Zurich

DIE ZIELGRUPPE

Die Markt- und Standortanalysen führen im Zusammenspiel mit den strategischen Marketingzielen zu folgender Zielgruppendefinition:

Quantitativ:
– Einzelpersonen 25 bis 35 Jahre
– Unverheiratete Paare und Ehepaare ohne Kinder 30 bis 40 Jahre
– Best Agers nach Familienphase 50 bis 60 Jahre
– Aktive ältere Paare und Alleinstehende 60+
– Mittlere Einkommensschicht

Qualitativ:
– Schätzen Urbanität und Industriecharme
– Wollen alles um sich herum haben
– Verkehrsanbindung (privater und öffentlicher Verkehr) ist wichtig
– Schätzen die Vorzüge des Quartiers mit seiner enormen Vielfalt
– Sind aufgeschlossen gegenüber Neuem

Schlüsselargumente:
– Urbanität
– Quartier, das sich neu entwickelt
– Alles um mich herum haben
– Wenn ich will, läuft immer etwas
– Gute Verkehrsinfrastruktur

THE TARGET GROUP

The market and location analyses in combination with the strategic marketing goals resulted in the following target group definition:

Quantitative:
– Individuals, aged 25 to 35
– Unmarried couples and couples without children, aged 30 to 40
– Best Agers after the family phase, aged 50 to 60
– Active older couples and singles, aged 60+
– Middle income strata

Qualitative:
– Appreciate urbanity and industrial charm
– Want to have everything close by
– Traffic connections (private and public) are important
– Appreciate the advantages of the vastly diverse offers in the quarter
– Are open to new experiences

Key arguments:
– Urbanity
– Newly developing quarter
– Having everything close by
– Whenever I want, things are happening
– Good traffic infrastructure

DIE SINUS-ANALYSE DER ZIELGRUPPE FÜR «ATRIUM WEST»
THE SINUS ANALYSIS OF THE TARGET GROUP FOR "ATRIUM WEST"

SOZIALE LAGE UND GRUNDORIENTIERUNG
SOCIAL STATUS AND BASIC VALUES

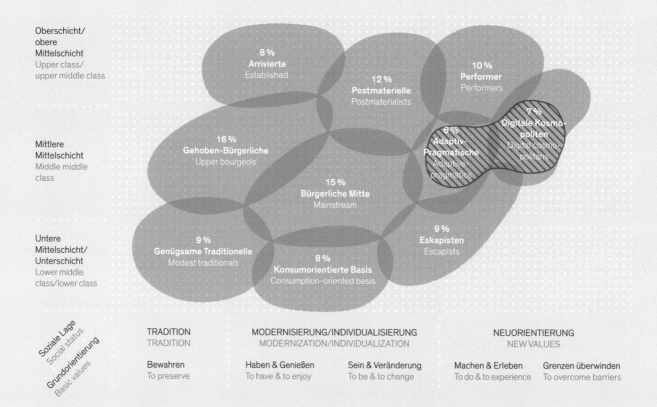

Oberschicht/
obere
Mittelschicht
Upper class/
upper middle class

Mittlere
Mittelschicht
Middle middle
class

Untere
Mittelschicht/
Unterschicht
Lower middle
class/lower class

8 %
Arrivierte
Established

12 %
Postmaterielle
Postmaterialists

10 %
Performer
Performers

7 %
Digitale Kosmo-
politen
Digital cosmo-
politans

6 %
Adaptiv-
Pragmatische
Adaptive-
pragmatics

16 %
Gehoben-Bürgerliche
Upper bourgeois

15 %
Bürgerliche Mitte
Mainstream

9 %
Genügsame Traditionelle
Modest traditionals

8 %
Konsumorientierte Basis
Consumption-oriented basis

9 %
Eskapisten
Escapists

Soziale Lage
Social status
Grundorientierung
Basic values

TRADITION	MODERNISIERUNG/INDIVIDUALISIERUNG		NEUORIENTIERUNG	
TRADITION	MODERNIZATION/INDIVIDUALIZATION		NEW VALUES	
Bewahren	Haben & Genießen	Sein & Veränderung	Machen & Erleben	Grenzen überwinden
To preserve	To have & to enjoy	To be & to change	To do & to experience	To overcome barriers

Urbanes Lebensgefühl, Entwicklung, Abwechslung: Werte, die genau auf die Sinus-Milieus
der Adaptiv-Pragmatischen und der digitalen Kosmopoliten zutreffen.
Urban lifestyle, development, variety – these values precisely match the Sinus milieus of the
adaptive-pragmatics and digital cosmopolitans.

DER POSTMODERNE, EXPERIMENTIERFREUDIGE KOSMOPOLIT

Von der Sinus-Milieu-Analyse ausgehend werden verschiedene Porträts potenzieller Käufer als weiteres Mittel innerhalb der Marketingkommunikation verwendet. Sie machen die Zielgruppendefinition für das Publikum in allen Medien als Storytelling-Element erlebbar.

Hubert Jahn ist 36 Jahre alt und arbeitet seit drei Jahren als führender Koch in einem der angesagten Szenelokale in Zürich West. Der aus Frankfurt stammende Gourmet-Kreateur liebt die kurzen Wege im Kreis 5 und dass es hier alles zu finden gibt, was das Herz begehrt und man fast alles tun kann, wozu man Lust hat. Kurz: Er fühlt sich wohl hier. Daher hat er sich auch umgeschaut, was es an Eigentumswohnungen auf dem Markt gibt, die seinen Bedürfnissen entsprechen: gute Verkehrsanbindung, nahe an der Arbeit, kurze Wege für die Freizeitgestaltung und das einkaufen von Alltagsdingen und Sonstigem, kein Altbau, sondern etwas modernes, frisches, großzügiges und zu alledem auch noch bezahlbar. Da der schlaksige, blonde Mann immer wieder seine siebenjährige Tochter zu Besuch hat und auch zu Hause gerne an neuen Rezepten tüftelt, wäre eine 3,5-Zimmer-Wohnung für ihn ideal. Sein Daheim ist ihm wichtig, dient als Rückzugsort ebenso wie als Lebensmittelpunkt und schafft für ihn Sicherheit für die Zukunft.

THE POST-MODERN ADVENTUROUS COSMOPOLITAN

Based on the Sinus milieu analysis, different portraits of potential buyers are used as an additional means of marketing communication. They allow the audience to experience the target group definition as a stoytelling element in all applied media.

Hubert Jahn is 36 years old and has been working as head chef of one of the trendy hot spots in Zurich West for the past three years. A native of Frankfurt, the gourmet cook loves the short distances in district 5 and the fact that it offers everything he needs and allows him to do almost anything he feels like doing. In short: he is very comfortable here. This is why he has been recently looking at offers of condominiums on the market that meet his demands: good traffic connections, close to his work, short distances to leisure and recreation facilities, as well as shopping and other amenities, not in an old building, but something new, fresh, generously sized and affordable to boost. As the lanky blond man is often visited by his seven-year-old daughter and loves experimenting with new recipes at home, a 3.5-room apartment would be perfect for him. His home is important to him, as it is his retreat and the center of his life, as well as an asset for the future.

MITTEN IM LEBEN ERLEBEN
EXPERIENCE THINGS WHERE
LIFE IS HAPPENING

DIE POSITIONIERUNG

«Mitten im Leben erleben» – so lässt sich der Positionierungsbeschrieb der Immobilie auf einen Satz reduzieren. Die
Essenz aus den Vorzügen der Lage (aufstrebendes Quartier,
Urbanität), der eigenwilligen Architektur (Lichthof) und der
moderaten Preise bei gleichzeitig hochwertigen Materialien macht das Projekt attraktiv für Menschen, die von allem
etwas mehr erwarten, am gleichen Ort zur gleichen Zeit mehr
erleben wollen – nah an allem, egal ob Ruhe, Kultur, Arbeit,
Einkaufen oder Mobilität. Ein ruhiger Pol im pulsierenden
Quartier, die Heterogenität, das Nonkonforme sind die Posi-
tionierungsmerkmale und Signale, die nach außen wirksam
kommuniziert werden.

DER ANALYSE-SCHWERPUNKT

Von den drei Analyse-Schwerpunkten Lage, Lifestyle und
Architektur setzt Felix Partner auf die Architektur als zentralen
Kommunikationskern – ergänzt und unterstützt von den eben-
falls wichtigen Vorzügen des Lifestyles.

Die Schwerpunkt-Argumente der Architektur:
- **Gebäude mit echtem Unique Selling Point: Lichthof**
- **Zielgruppengerechte Grundrisse**
- **Großzügige Wohnräume**
- **Potenzial Wertentwicklung**
- **Zentraler Standort**
- **Attraktives Umfeld**

THE POSITIONING

"Experience things where life is happening" – this is how the
positioning description can be summarized in one sentence.
The essence derived from the advantages of the location (up
and coming quarter, urbanity), the unique architecture (atrium)
and moderate prices in combination with high-quality materials makes the project attractive for people that expect a bit
more of everything, who want to experience more at the same
time and the same place – close to everything whether leisure,
culture, work, shopping, or mobility. A quiet zone in the vibrant
quarter, heterogeneity, and non-conformity are the positioning
characteristics and signals that are effectively communicated
to the audience.

THE FOCUS OF THE ANALYSIS

Felix Partner selected architecture as the central communication core among the three analysis focal points of location, lifestyle, and architecture – complemented and enhanced by the
equally important lifestyle advantages.

The architecture focus of the analysis:
- Building with unique selling point: atrium
- Target-group oriented layouts
- Generous living spaces
- Value development potential
- Central location
- Attractive setting

DER NAME: «ATRIUM WEST»

In der römischen Architektur war das Atrium als zentraler Raum eines Gebäudes weit verbreitet. Meist rechteckig und von allen Seiten zugänglich, diente er als Aufenthaltsraum und Treffpunkt für die ganze Familie. Als Lichthof nach oben offen, aber nach außen geschlossen und geschützt, wird das Atrium zum Sinnbild der Überbauung – in Verbindung mit dem ebenso offenen, aber in sich geschlossenen Mikrokosmos Zürich West: «Atrium West».

DER CLAIM: «MEINE ART ZÜRICH»

Aus der Positionierung «Mitten im Leben erleben», der Zielgruppe «Digitale Kosmopoliten/Adaptiv-Pragmatische», der Lage «heterogenes, urbanes Quartier» und der offenen und gleichzeitig abschirmenden Architektur reduziert sich wirksam der Claim «Meine Art Zürich». Unterschiedliche Lebensentwürfe, individuelle Lebensarten, wechselnde Lebensansprüche – sie finden hier auf kleinem Raum, zur selben Zeit, mit- und nebeneinander ihre Verwirklichung. Meine Art neben deiner Art, vielleicht dasselbe, aber auf eine andere Art.

DIE FARBEN UND DIE TYPOGRAFIE

Ein Gebäude voller visueller Kontraste. Die dunklen Fensterrahmen heben sich auf der hellen Fassade ab und schaffen im Licht eine Vielfalt an Schattierungen. Das strahlt Ruhe aus und gibt Geborgenheit. Ein Bollwerk, eine Oase inmitten eines hektischen, lauten und sehr lebhaften Umfelds, das im Gegensatz dazu durch satte, bunte Farbtöne lebt. Die Schrift wie gemacht dazu. Kantig und rau.

THE NAME: "ATRIUM WEST"

In Roman architecture, the atrium was a popular feature at the center of a building. Usually rectangular and accessible from all sides, it served as the common room and meeting place for the entire family. As a light shaft that is open to the top but closed off and secured from the outside, the atrium becomes the symbol of the construction – in combination with the equally open yet enclosed microcosm of Zurich West: "Atrium West."

THE CLAIM: "ZURICH MY WAY"

The positioning "Experience things where life is happening," the target group "digital cosmopolitans/adaptive-pragmatics," the location "heterogeneous urban quarter," and the open and at the same time shielding architecture, are effectively condensed into the claim "Zurich my way." Different life scripts, individual lifestyles, changing life outlooks – all take place in a limited place at the same time, with and next to each other. My way next to your way, maybe even the same, but in a different way.

THE COLORS AND THE TYPOGRAPHY

A building full of visual contrasts. The dark window frames are offset from the light-colored facade and create a variety of shades in the light. This emanates peacefulness and a sense of security. A bastion, an oasis in the middle of hectic, loud, and very active surroundings that presents a contrast of very saturated and bright colors. The typeface is perfectly matched. Edgy and rough.

DIE IDEE: HIER BIN ICH ICH

So sein, wie man ist, dort sein, wo man will, nach seinen eigenen, individuellen Regeln leben – das ehemalige Zürcher Industriequartier und im Besonderen die Überbauung «Atrium West» sollen dazu die Grundlage bieten. Eine bunte Interessens- und Themenvielfalt bildet den Kern des zu kommunizierenden Lebensgefühls: Spaß haben, Träume verwirklichen, Karriere machen, Freunde treffen, erholen, bewegen, entspannen. Dynamisierte Gegensätze wie Offenheit/Geschlossenheit, Individualität/Gemeinsamkeit, Ruhe/pulsierende Kultur werden reduziert in Einklang gebracht, personalisiert erlebbar gemacht und für die verschiedenen Medien übersetzt und heruntergebrochen.

DAS WERBLICHE KONZEPT

Ein fiktiver Erzähler bringt Orte im Quartier mit persönlichen Aussagen zusammen. Darauf basiert das Textkonzept, das zu verschiedenen Themen Informationen vermittelt: Meine Art Zukunft, Meine Art Bewegung, Meine Art Spielplatz, Meine Art Geldanlage etc. Die Bildwelt passt zum pulsierenden Umfeld und orientiert sich mit ihren dunklen, kontrastreichen und starken Farbtönen an der Gebäudefassade mit ihren dunklen Fensterrahmen und der hellen Mauerfarbe des Mehrfamilienhauses. Passend zur heterogenen Zielgruppe wird ein nachhaltiger Wiedererkennungseffekt sichergestellt. Alle Kommunikationsmaßnahmen zielen darauf ab, den Abverkauf der Wohnungen zu steigern und bis zur Fertigstellung des Neubaus sicherzustellen. Ergänzend zur Basiskommunikation entsteht eine konzepttreue Abverkaufskampagne mit einem Mix aus klassischen sowie Ambient-Media-Maßnahmen, welche kurzfristig zusätzliche Akzente setzen können und im Herzen der Zielgruppe wirken.

THE IDEA: HERE I CAN BE MYSELF

To allow people to be just the way they are, to be where they want to be and to live according to their own rules – the former industrial quarter of Zurich and in particular the construction "Atrium West" are intended to provide the basis for this. At the core of the communicated lifestyle is a colorful mix of interests and topics: having fun, living out dreams, having a career, meeting friends, relaxing, moving, unwinding. Dynamic contrasts such as open/close, individual/community, quiet/vibrating culture are narrowed down and harmonized, made available for experience on a personal level and translated and broken down for use in different media.

THE ADVERTISING CONCEPT

A fictitious narrator connects different places in the quarter to personal statements. The text concept is based on this, conveying information about a variety of topics – Future my way, Movement my way, Playground my way, Investment my way, etc. The images match the vibrant setting and their dark, contrasting and strong colors reflect the facade of the multi-party residential building with its dark window frames and light colored walls. In line with the heterogeneous target group, a sustained recognition effect is ensured. All communication measures are aimed at increasing the sales of the condominiums and to ensure all are sold by the time the building is finished. In addition to the basic communication, a matching sales campaign with a mix of classical and ambient media measures is being conceived, which could add additional accents in the short run and address the emotions of the target group.

DAS CORPORATE DESIGN FÜR «ATRIUM WEST»
THE CORPORATE DESIGN FOR "ATRIUM WEST"

LOGO
LOGO

TYPOGRAFIE
TYPOGRAPHY

Geogrotesque

ATRIUM
WEST
MEINE ART ZÜRICH

IM KREIS 5 IN ZÜRICH

Im Kreis 5 in Zürich entsteht ein Mehrfamilienhaus mit 47 Eigentumswohnungen. Moderne, zeitlose Architektur, ästhetisch, klar und reduziert in der Formsprache. Ganz im Gegensatz zum lebendigen, aufstrebenden Quartierteil Zürich West, der vor Urbanität strotzt.

FARBEN
COLORS

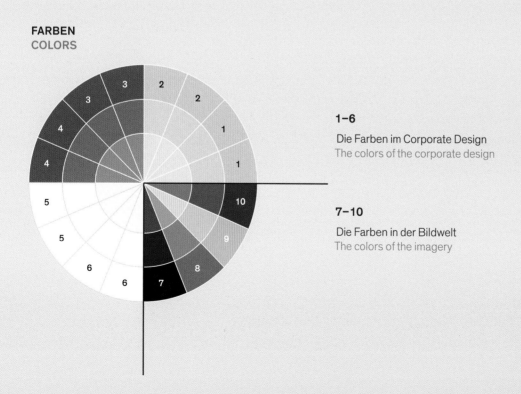

1–6

Die Farben im Corporate Design
The colors of the corporate design

7–10

Die Farben in der Bildwelt
The colors of the imagery

MEINE ART
ZÜRICH

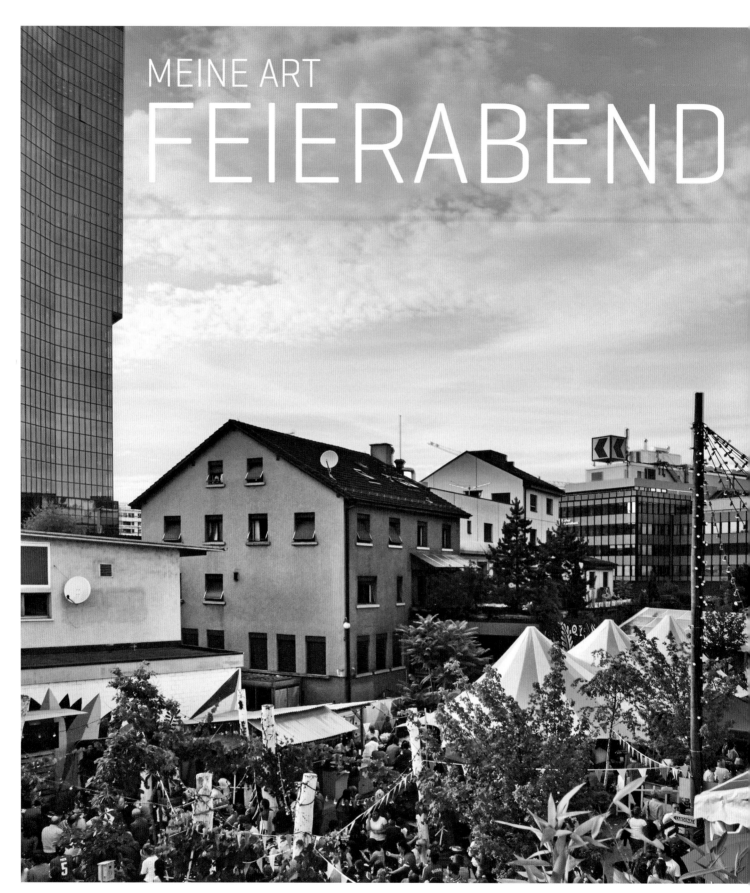

MEINE ART
FEIERABEND

After work my way

Mobility my way

Movement my way

Future my way

DIE KOMMUNIKATIONSMITTEL

Website (Presite und Vollversion), Imagebroschüre, Anzeigen, Straßenplakate F12 und F200, Fenstertransparente im öffentlichen Verkehr, Google Ads, Ambient-Media mit Indoorplakaten A3 und A2 sowie Clean-Wire-Anhängern, Verkaufsdokumentation, Angebotsflyer, Baureklametafel vor Ort, ausführliche Grundrisspläne mit einem Maßstab von 1:100, Fassadenpläne und Gebäudeschnitt, Situations- und Umgebungsplan, Verkaufspreisliste und Kurzbaubeschrieb

THE COMMUNICATION MEDIA

Website (pre-site and full version), image brochure, advertisements, F12 and Γ200 street posters, window banners in public transportation vehicles, Google ads, ambient media including A3 and A2 indoor posters as well as "Clean Wire" clothes hanger advertising, sales documentation, offer flyer, construction site banner, detailed ground plans with a scale of 1:100, facade plans and building layout, location and setting plan, sales price list and brief construction description

Website (Presite und Vollversion)
Website (pre-site and full version)

Clean-Wire-Anhänger
"Clean Wire" clothes hanger advertising

Straßenplakat F200
F200 street poster

Fenstertransparent im öffentlichen Verkehr
Window banner in public transportation vehicles

Anzeigen
Advertisements

Imagebroschüre
Image brochure

Imagebroschüre
Image brochure

Imagebroschüre
Image brochure

Imagebroschüre
Image brochure

Imagebroschüre
Image brochure

NEUBAU MIT LICHTHOF, GRÜN UND HOCHWERTIG GESTALTET

NEW CONSTRUCTION WITH AN ATRIUM, GREEN AND HIGH QUALITY DESIGN

DIE IMMOBILIE

Das Umfeld des Projekts präsentiert sich sehr heterogen. Stadteinwärts erstrecken sich bis zum Escher-Wyss-Gebiet größere, ungenutzte Geschäfts- und Industriebauten. Gegen Westen füllen neuere Wohnresidenzen verlassene Industriebrachen mit Leben. So eingebettet, positioniert sich das «Atrium West» als Wohnoase und Rückzugsort im hektischen Alltag. Das Gebäude ist als Hoftyp konzipiert. Insgesamt ordnen sich 47 Wohnungen über sechs Geschosse in sehr kompakter Bauweise. Die effiziente Volumennutzung leitet sich aus den engen städtischen Verhältnissen ab. Nach außen präsentiert sich der Bau als geordnete Stadtarchitektur. Die Fassaden sind umlaufend ausgeglichen gestaltet, mit wohlproportionierten Fenstern, die in einem harmonischen Verhältnis zur Fassadenfläche stehen. Mit der Einführung des Hochparterres grenzen sich die bodennahen Wohnungen vom gewerblich geprägten Umfeld ab und können so die notwendige Intimität gewährleisten. Im Innern profitieren die Wohnungen von einem ruhigen Lichthof, der einen Kontrast zum hektischen Stadtleben bildet und für eine angenehme Belichtung der Küchen, Essräume und Treppenhäuser sorgt. Über dieses Atrium können die Bewohner die vielfältige Ausprägung des Zusammenlebens erfahren und das Zugehörigkeitsgefühl für einen Ort teilen.

THE PROPERTY

The setting of the project is very heterogeneous. Towards the city up to the Escher-Wyss area, there are rather large unused business and industrial buildings. Towards the west, newer residential concepts fill abandoned industrial fallow areas with new life. In these surroundings, the "Atrium West" presents itself as a residential oasis and retreat from the hustle and bustle of everyday life. The building is designed in the courtyard style. A total of 47 apartments are divided among six floors in a very compact manner. The efficient use of the space is derived from the crowded urban situation. On the outside, the building presents a neatly arranged urban architecture. The facades are balanced on all sides, with well-proportioned windows that are in harmonious relation to the facade surface. The introduction of a mezzanine level creates a border between the ground floor apartments and their commercial surroundings, which ensures the required privacy. On the inside, the apartments benefit from a quiet atrium that offers a contrast to the hectic city life, while pleasantly illuminating the kitchens, dining rooms, and staircases. This atrium allows the residents to experience various forms of social interaction and share a sense of belonging to a single place.

Außenansicht
External view

Lichthof
Atrium

Eingangsbereich
Entrance area

4,5-Zimmer-Eckwohnung
4.5-room corner apartment

3,5-Zimmer-Wohnung zum Innenhof
3.5-room apartment facing the atrium

2,5-Zimmer-Eckwohnung
2.5-room corner apartment

Blick vom Treppenhaus zum Lichthof
View from the staircase to the atrium

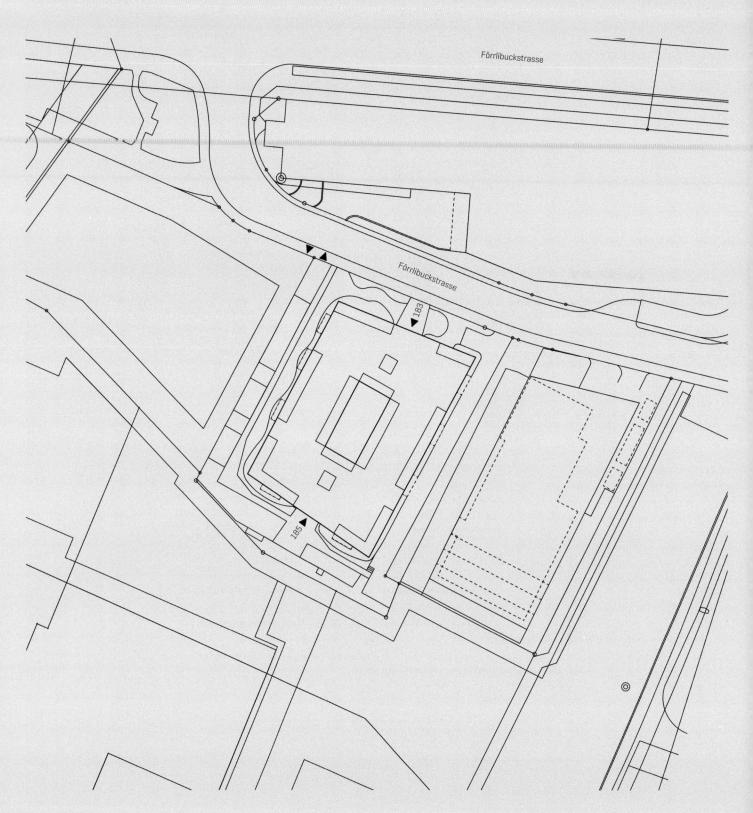

Förrlibuckstrasse

Förrlibuckstrasse

183

185

Situationsplan
Situation plan

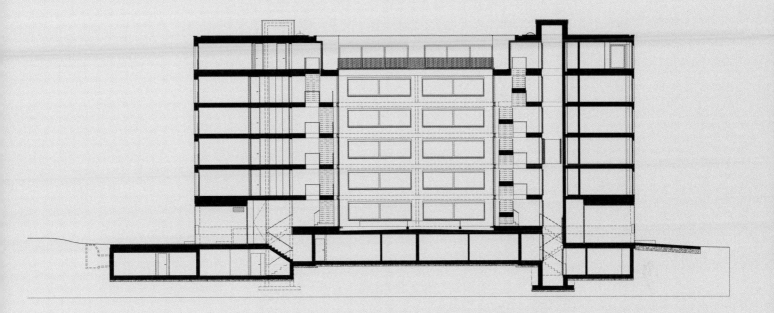

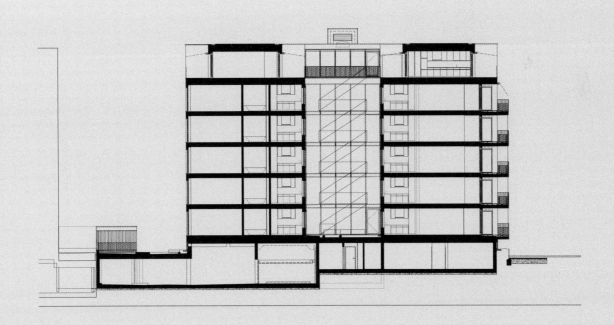

Längs- und Querschnitt
Vertical and horizontal sections

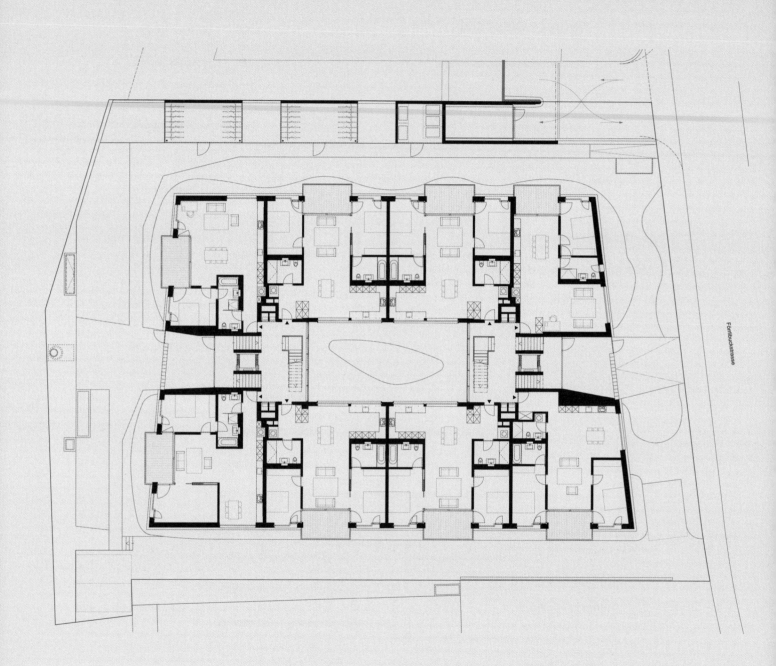

Grundriss Eingangsgeschoss/Hochparterre
Layout entrance floor/mezzanine

Förrlibuckstrasse

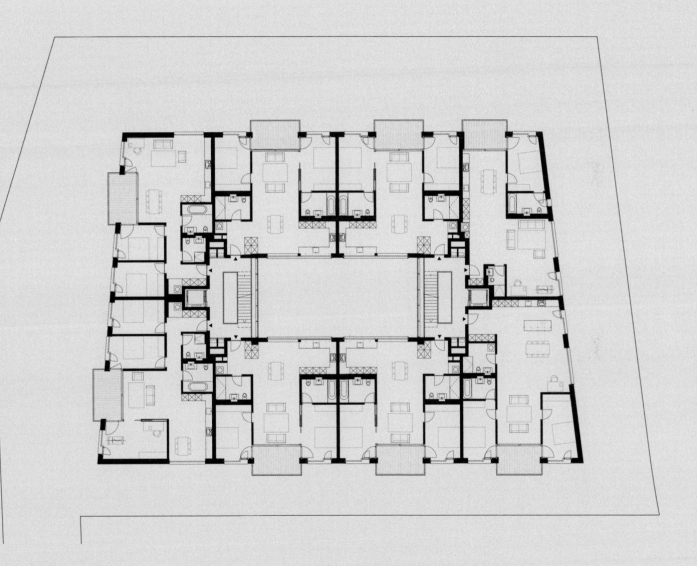

Grundriss Regelgeschoss
Layout standard floor

ANHANG
APPENDIX

DAS TEAM FELIX PARTNER

Als interdisziplinäres Team von Projektentwicklern, Architekten, Designern, Markenstrategen und Kommunikationsprofis geht Felix Partner Aufgabenstellungen mit möglichst großer Weitsicht an. Die Vielfalt der Blickwinkel, dessen bewährte Arbeitsprozesse sowie die konstruktive Teamkultur erlauben ein schnelles Fokussieren auf die tragfähigste, ästhetisch und wirtschaftlich beste Lösung auf lange Sicht. Es sind Teamplayer, die ihre Gesprächspartner ernst nehmen und sich in ihr Denken, ihre Mentalität und ihr Handeln einfühlen. Das Team ist schweizerisch multikulturell und agiert lokal und national.

Peter Felix, Geschäftsführer, Architekt; Rahel M. Felix, Geschäftsführerin, Creative Director; Ralph von Fellenberg, Konzepter, Texter; Suzette Fischer, Assistenz der Geschäftsleitung; Mark Furrer, Leitung Beratung und Markenführung; Giovanni Mammone, Architekt, Assoz. Partner; Veruschka Müller Suter, Planerin Marketingkommunikation/Desktop Publishing; Patrick Sprecher, Architekt; Furio Sordini, Architekt; Ron Stelzig, Assoz. Projektarchitekt; Dieter Stocker, Visueller Gestalter; Ruben Szabo, Techniker Innenarchitektur; Marc Urban, Assoz. Projektarchitekt; Balduin, Hund.

THE FELIX PARTNER TEAM

An interdisciplinary team of project developers, architects, designers, marketing experts and communication professionals, Felix Partner approaches any task with the greatest possible vision. The diversity of perspectives and its reliable work processes as well as the constructive team culture allow Felix Partner to focus quickly on the most sustainable, esthetic and economical solution in the long term. They are all team players who take their business partners seriously and empathically relate to their line of thought, their mentality, and their actions. The team is Swiss multi-cultural and operates locally and nationally.

Peter Felix, Managing Director, Architect; Rahel M. Felix, Managing Director, Creative Director; Ralph von Fellenberg, Concept Developer and Copywriter; Suzette Fischer, Executive Assistant; Mark Furrer, Management, Consulting and Branding; Giovanni Mammone, Architect, Assoc. Partner; Veruschka Müller Suter, Marketing Communication Planner/Desktop Publishing; Patrick Sprecher, Architect; Furio Sordini, Architect; Ron Stelzig, Assoc. Project Architect; Dieter Stocker, Visual Designer; Ruben Szabo, Architectural draftsman specialized in structural engineering; Marc Urban, Assoc. Project Architect; Balduin, dog.

Team von Projektentwicklern, Architekten, Designern, Markenstrategen und Kommunikationsprofis
The team of project developers, architects, designers, marketing experts, and communication professionals

DIE INTERDISZIPLINARITÄT VON FELIX PARTNER AUF EINEN BLICK
THE INTERDISCIPLINARY APPROACH OF FELIX PARTNER AT A SINGLE GLANCE

DAS UNTERNEHMEN FELIX PARTNER

Felix Partner ist eine Unternehmensgruppe, die in den Bereichen Projektentwicklung, Architektur und Innenarchitektur, Investment sowie Immobilienmarketing und Markendesign seit 1997 interdisziplinär tätig ist. Unter einem Markendach fungieren vier unabhängige Unternehmen: Die beiden Hauptfirmen sind Felix Partner Architektur AG und Felix Partner Design AG. Das Spannende daran: Felix Partner kann mit ihren Leistungen die gesamte Wertschöpfungskette eines Bauvorhabens oder auch nur als Partnerunternehmen einen Teilbereich abdecken. Zum Beispiel Markendesign und Marketingkommunikation oder auch Projektentwicklung und Architektur. Immer mit einer disziplinübergreifenden Gruppe von Menschen, die ihre langjährige Erfahrung in allen Bereichen einbringen können und diese ständig erweitern.

FELIX PARTNER, THE COMPANY

Felix Partner is a group of companies that has been interdisciplinary active in the areas of project development, architecture and interior design, investment as well as real estate marketing and brand design since 1997. Four independent companies are active under a single umbrella brand — the two main companies are Felix Partner Architektur AG and Felix Partner Design AG. The exciting thing about this constellation is the fact that it allows Felix Partner to provide all services of the entire value-added chain of a construction project or only in one area as a partner company. For example, brand design and marketing communication or project development and architecture. Always relying on a powerful cross-discipline group of people who can contribute their extensive expertise in all areas while constantly enhancing it.

DIE GASTAUTOREN

Oona Horx-Strathern kommt aus London. Seit über 20 Jahren ist sie Journalistin, Trendforscherin, Beraterin, Rednerin und Autorin. 1999 gründete sie zusammen mit ihrem Mann Matthias Horx das renommierte zukunftsInstitut, ein Prognose-Think-Tank, der zahlreiche europäische Unternehmen in allen Wirtschaftsbereichen berät. Sie schrieb Bücher über die Geschichte der Futurologie, die Architektur der Zukunft und arbeitete an zahlreichen Studien des zukunftsInstituts mit. Als Trendberaterin war sie für internationale Firmen wie Unilever, Beiersdorf und Deutsche Bank tätig. Das Spektrum ihrer Auftritte reicht von Architektenkonferenzen über Universitäten bis zur Bauindustrie und Designbranche. Sie teilt ihr Leben zwischen Deutschland, England und dem «Future Evolution House», das sie mit ihrem Mann in Wien baute. Ihre Lieblingsthemen: Architektur als Lebensstil, Stadtentwicklung und soziodemografischer Wandel sowie das Verhältnis von Emotionen und Technologie.

Martin A. Meier hat an der ETH Zürich Architektur studiert und ist Gründer und CEO der Raumgleiter AG, Zürich, einer Agentur für sämtliche 3D-Themen im Immobilienbereich, Virtual Reality, Drohnenaufnahmen und Digitalisierung. Er ist ebenfalls Mitgründer und Mitglied des Verwaltungsrats der Firma Kugelmeiers AG, einem Spin-off des Universitätsspitals Zürich. Gemeinsam verfolgen sie die Vision, die durch Diabetes Typ 1 bedingte Pankreastransplantation durch eine modifizierte Form der Inselzelltransplantationen zu ersetzten und damit sowohl die hohen gesundheitlichen Risiken des Eingriffs als auch die Kosten massiv zu reduzieren. Im Jahre 2015 hat er sein Executive MBA an der HSG abgeschlossen mit einem mittlerweile bewilligten BFE-Projekt zum Bau von vier elektrisch angetriebenen Kehrichtfahrzeugen für den Schweizer Markt. Seit 2016 ist er Stiftungsrat von Greenpeace Schweiz.

THE GUEST AUTHORS

Oona Horx-Strathern is a native of London. For more than 20 years, she has been active as a journalist, trend consultant, consultant, speaker, and author. In 1999, she established together with her husband Matthias Horx, the renowned zukunftsInstitut, a predictive outlook think-tank that advises many European companies across all business sectors. She has published books on the history of futurology and the architecture of the future, and contributed to many studies of the zukunftsInstitut. She has worked as a trend consultant for international companies such as Unilever, Beiersdorf, and Deutsche Bank. Her speech customers range from architectural conferences via universities, up to the building industry and the design sector. She divides her time between Germany, London, and the Future Evolution House in Vienna, which she built with her husband. Her favorite topics include architecture as a lifestyle, urban development and socio-demographic change as well as the relationship between emotions and technology.

Martin A. Meier studied architecture at ETH Zurich and is the founder and CEO of Raumgleiter AG, an agency for all 3D topics in the real estate sector, virtual reality, drone recordings, and digitalization. He is also co-founder and member of the administrative board of Kugelmeiers AG, a spin-off of the Zurich university hospital. Together they are pursuing the aim of replacing transplantation of the pancreas caused by diabetes type 1 by a modified form of islet cell transplantation to considerably reduce the high health risks of the operation as well as its costs. In the year 2015, he received his Executive MBA from HSG with a BFE project, which has been approved in the meantime, involving the construction of four electrically operated road-sweeping vehicles for the Swiss market. In 2016, he joined on the board of trustees of Greenpeace Switzerland.

Sven Ruoss arbeitet seit über fünf Jahren im Business Development bei verschiedenen Medienunternehmen wie Ringier, Tamedia und AZ Medien und setzt sich für die digitale Transformation in der Medienbranche ein. Nebenamtlich ist Ruoss als Studienleiter des CAS Social Media Management und als Dozent am Center for Digital Business der HWZ Hochschule für Wirtschaft Zürich engagiert. Für ihn gilt: «Digital knowledge is the new oil.» In seiner Freizeit schreibt er auf seinem Blog www.svenruoss.ch über den digitalen Wandel und dessen Herausforderungen. Mindestens einmal im Jahr macht Sven Ruoss eine digitale Diät und besteigt Berge – ohne Smartphone, Internet, Facebook und Snapchat.

Prof. Dr. Cary Steinmann ist Professor für Marketing und Markenführung an der Zürcher Hochschule für Angewandte Wissenschaften ZHAW in Winterthur. Er studierte an der Universität Bern VWL und BWL und promovierte an der Universität Freiburg bei Herrn Prof. Dr. Richard Kühn zum Thema «Ansätze zur wirkungsbezogenen Gewichtung der Instrumente im Marketingmix». 1987 stieg er als erster Strategischer Planner der Schweiz bei der Werbeagentur Lintas in Zürich ein und wechselte 1988 als Planning Director zu ASGS/BBDO, Zürich. 1992–99 war er Executive Planning Director bei Scholz & Friends in Hamburg. 2000 kehrte er in die Schweiz zurück, um bei Wirz die Strategie zu leiten. Es folgten drei Jahre als Geschäftsführer Strategie bei TBWA Switzerland, um dann die Aufgabe an der ZHAW zu übernehmen. Cary Steinmann ist Ende 2013 aus dem Art Directors Club Schweiz ausgetreten.

Sven Ruoss has been working for more than five years in business development for various media companies such as Ringier, Tamedia, and AZ Medien and is dedicated to digital transformation in the media sector. In addition, Ruoss is active as a director of studies of CAS Social Media and as a lecturer at the Center for Digital Business of the Hochschule für Wirtschaft Zürich (HWZ – University of Applied Sciences Zurich). His motto is "Digital knowledge is the new oil." In his spare time he works on his blog www.svenruoss.ch focusing on digital transformation and its challenges. At least once a year, Sven Ruoss goes on a digital diet and climbs mountains – without his smartphone, Internet, Facebook and Snapchat.

Prof. Cary Steinmann, is a professor of marketing and brand management at the Zürcher Hochschule für Angewandte Wissenschaften (ZHAW – Zurich University of Applied Sciences) in Winterthur. He studied business and economics at the University of Bern and received his doctorate from the University of Freiburg under Prof. Richard Kühn with a dissertation entitled "Approaches to the effect-related weighting of tools in the marketing mix." In 1987, he was Switzerland's first strategic planner to join the Lintas advertising agency in Zurich and in 1988, he assumed the post of Planning Director at ASGS/BBDO, Zurich. From 1992–99 he was Executive Planning Director at Scholz & Friends in Hamburg. In 2000, he returned to Switzerland to head the strategy department at Wirz. For the next three years, he held the post of Strategic Managing Director at TBWA Switzerland before assuming his post at ZHAW. Cary Steinmann left the Art Directors Club Switzerland at the end of 2013.

DIE HERAUSGEBER

Hinter Felix Partner in Zürich stehen das Ehepaar Rahel M. und Peter Felix – sie Designerin und Planerin Marketingkommunikation, er Architekt – sowie ein eingespieltes, interdisziplinäres Team von Spezialisten.

Rahel M. Felix ist diplomierte Planerin Marketingkommunikation sowie Grafikdesignerin mit Diplomabschluss der Hochschule der Künste Bern. Am Central Saint Martins College of Art and Design (London) bildete sie sich im Bereich Kommunikationsdesign weiter. Arbeitserfahrung sammelte Rahel M. Felix in diversen Werbeagenturen, Designbüros und IT-Unternehmen in der ganzen Schweiz. 1997 gründete sie ihre Einzelfirma für visuelle Kommunikation. Als diplomierte Ausbildnerin und ausgebildete Fachhochschuldozentin unterrichtete sie zudem an mehreren Institutionen, unter anderem der Zürcher Hochschule der Künste (ZHdK) und der Hochschule der Künste Bern (HKB).

Peter Felix studierte nach einer Lehre zum Hochbauzeichner Architektur am Technikum Winterthur. Später schloss er einen Master of Architecture an der renommierten Columbia University in New York ab. Internationale Berufserfahrung sammelte er durch diverse Projekte mit Büros wie Richard Meier & Partners (New York) und Theo Hotz (Zürich). Seine eigenen Unternehmungen baute er ab 1997 kontinuierlich auf. An der ETH Zürich sowie der Accademia di architettura, Università della Svizzera italiana in Mendrisio war er als wissenschaftlicher Mitarbeiter beschäftigt, in Mendrisio unter Prof. Kenneth Frampton (New York).

THE EDITORS

The people behind Felix Partner in Zurich are the spouses Rahel M. and Peter Felix – she is a designer and marketing communication planner and he is an architect – along with an orchestrated interdisciplinary team of specialists.

Rahel M. Felix is a graduate planner for marketing communication and a graduate graphic designer of the Bern University of the Arts. She received further training in Communication Design at Central Saint Martins College of Art and Design, London. She gained her work experience at various agencies, design agencies and IT companies across Switzerland. In 1997, she established her own company for visual communication. As a graduate instructor and graduate lecturer at universities of applied sciences she also taught at several institutions such as the ZHdK and the HKB.

Peter Felix completed his vocational training as an architectural drafter specialized in structural engineering and then studied Architecture at the Technikum Winterthur. He later received a Master of Architecture from the renowned Columbia University in New York. He gained international professional expertise by working on various projects for companies such as Richard Meier & Partners (New York) and Theo Hotz (Zurich). He has been continuously expanding his own group of companies since 1997. He held academic posts at ETH Zurich and under Prof. Kenneth Frampton (New York) at the Accademia di architettura, Università della Svizzera italiana, Mendrisio.

UNSER DANK

Seinen Dank spricht man üblicherweise gegenüber Personen aus. Was wir auch von Herzen gerne tun. Denn die letzten 20 Jahre unserer Unternehmertätigkeit wären ohne großartige Menschen nicht möglich gewesen: unseren Familien Keller-Veraguth und Felix sowie unseren immer wieder inspirierenden Kindern Laurin und Fadraina und deren Nanny Elisabeth Huber, ohne die wir oft verzweifelt gewesen wären. Den engen Freunden Corinne Wälchli, Thomas Aus der Au und Mirjam Lauber, die uns mit Rat und Tag zur Seite standen. Aber auch Mitarbeiter wie Giovanni Mammone und Marc Urban, die uns in stürmischen wie ruhigen Zeiten die Stange gehalten haben. Wie Geschäftspartner, die zu Freunden wurden und Investoren, die an uns geglaubt haben.

Und ohne große Unterstützung, Hingabe, Geduld und viel Herzblut wäre auch dieses Buch nicht entstanden. Ein großes Danke an dieser Stelle an unsere Gastautoren Oona Horx-Strathern, Martin A. Meier, Sven Ruoss und Prof. Dr. Cary Steinmann. Und ein mindestens ebenso großes Danke an unser sich immer wieder neu motivierendes Team Ralph von Fellenberg (Konzeption und Text), Veruschka Müller Suter (Koordination und Layout/Desktop Publishing), Dieter Stocker (Visuelle Gestaltung) und Jörg Suter (Text).

Rückblickend möchten wir uns aber nicht nur bei Menschen bedanken, sondern auch bei Ereignissen und Projekten. Denn diese haben mit dazu beigetragen, dass wir unsere Erfahrungen machen konnten, lernen durften und es beim nächsten Mal noch besser machen konnten. Durch diese Prägungen sind wir das geworden, was wir heute sind. Und wir entwickeln uns weiter. Auch durch dieses Buch.

OUR GRATITUDE

One usually expresses gratitude towards certain persons. Which we will gladly do. This is because the past 20 years of our business would not have been possible without the help of some terrific people: our families Keller-Veraguth and Felix and our ever-inspiring children Laurin and Fadraina and their nanny Elisabeth Huber without whom we would have often been driven to despair. Our close friends Corinne Wälchli, Thomas Aus der Au and Mirjam Lauber who always helped us with words and deeds. And also our colleagues such as Giovanni Mammone and Marc Urban who were at our side in rugged and in quiet times. In addition to various business partners who became friends and investors who believed in us.

Similarly, this book would not have been created without a great amount of support, dedication, patience and much lifeblood. Within this context, we would like to sincerely thank our guest authors Oona Horx-Strathern, Martin A. Meier, Sven Ruoss, and Prof. Dr. Cary Steinmann. And an at least equally special thank you goes out to our constantly self-motivated team Ralph von Fellenberg (concept developer and copywriter), Veruschka Müller Suter (coordination and layout/desktop publishing), Dieter Stocker (visual design), and Jörg Suter (text).

In retrospect, we would like to not only thank people but also events and projects. Because they have also contributed to our experiences and allowed us to learn to make things even better next time. These influences made us into what we are today. As we continue to develop. Also through this book.

IMPRESSUM
IMPRINT

Gesamtkonzept, Creative Direction
General Concept, Creative Direction
Felix Partner; Rahel M. Felix

Grafik, Layout, Desktop Publishing
Graphic Design, Layout, Desktop Publishing
Felix Partner; Veruschka Müller Suter, Dieter Stocker

Textredaktion
Editing
Felix Partner; Ralph von Fellenberg, Jörg Suter

Lektorat/Korrektorat
Copyediting/Proofreading
Braun Publishing; Sophie Steybe

Übersetzung
Translation
Cosima Talhouni

Lithografie
Reproduction
Bild1Druck GmbH, Berlin

Printed in the EU

The Deutsche Nationalbibliothek lists this publication in the Deutsche
Nationalbibliografie; detailed bibliographic data are available in the Internet
at http://dnb.dnb.de

ISBN 978-3-03768-221-0
© 2017 by Braun Publishing AG, Salenstein, Switzerland,
www.braun-publishing.ch, and Felix Partner, Zurich, Switzerland,
www.felixpartner.com

BILDNACHWEIS
PICTURE CREDITS

FOTOGRAFIE
PHOTOGRAPHY

Heinz Unger, Zurich-Schlieren
6, 93, 102, 108–109, 164 –167, 181, 205, 225, 281, 291–293, 309

Klaus Vyhnalek Fotografie, Vienna
12

Amandine Alexandra for The Collective Old Oak, London
20

Property Research Partners LLC, propertyshark.com
26

Bilddatenbanken
Photo Databases
47–48, 70, 73, 97, 125, 139, 153, 185, 190–191, 209, 231, 236–239, 259, 264–265, 285

Niklaus M. Wächter, Adligenswil
121

Fotostudio Bühler, Romanshorn
121

Thomas Aus der Au, Winterthur
244–245, 298–301

Susanne Völlm, Zurich
255, 264–265

GRAFIKEN
DIAGRAMS

Felix Partner, Zurich
13, 15, 17, 51–52, 56, 69, 79–85, 92, 101–103, 120, 129, 143, 157, 189, 204, 213, 224, 235, 254, 263, 280, 290, 310

SINUS-Institut
96, 124, 138, 152, 184, 230, 258, 284

VISUALISIERUNGEN
VISUALIZATIONS

Raumgleiter GmbH, Zurich
30–32, 37, 40, 109–111, 196–197, 218, 270–271

Swiss Interactive AG, Aarau-Rohr
130–131, 158–159